The New Ethnic Mobs

THE CHANGING FACE OF
ORGANIZED CRIME IN AMERICA

WILLIAM KLEINKNECHT

FP THE FREE PRESS

New York London Toronto Sydney Tokyo Singapore

THE FREE PRESS
A Division of Simon & Schuster Inc.
1230 Avenue of the Americas
New York, NY 10020

THE FREE PRESS and colophon are trademarks
of Simon & Schuster Inc.

Designed by Carla Bolte

Manufactured in the United States of America

10 9 8 7 6 5 4 3 2 1

Library of Congress Cataloging-in-Publication Data

Kleinknecht, William, 1960–
    The new ethnic mobs: the changing face of organized crime in
    America / William Kleinknecht.
        p.   cm.
    Includes bibliographical references (p.   ) and index.
    ISBN 0-684-82294-6
    1. Organized crime—United States. 2. Ethnic groups—United
States.   I. Title.
    HV6446.K54   1996
    364.1'08'0973—dc20   95-53201
                                                           CIP

ISBN 0-684-82294-6

To

GEORGE AND LOIS KLEINKNECHT,

whose gifts of love and intellect made this
book possible

Contents

Preface

This book is about criminals. Although I have attempted to place them in the context of their immigrant or ethnic communities, the reader should bear in mind that they make up a tiny percentage of those communities. The vast majority of immigrants and ethnic minorities in this country are law-abiding citizens who are as outraged by underworld violence as anyone else. Indeed, they are often more outraged, since it is their communities being pillaged by organized crime.

I would also ask the reader not to mistake this work for an argument against immigration. My views are quite to the contrary. I see the last two decades of immigration as having been a windfall for urban America, breathing new life into neighborhoods that others had left behind. Most new immigrants came here to work and start businesses, not collect welfare.

This book is the product of more than 100 interviews with law enforcement officials, community leaders, social workers and street sources, most of whom are named in quotations or in the end notes. Despite their generous assistance, they bear no responsibility for the contents of the book, especially since some of the gangsters identified in the text have never been convicted of serious crimes. These sources are too numerous to thank individually, but I owe something to each of them. The Federal Bureau of Investigation, the U.S. Drug Enforcement Administration, and the Bureau of Alcohol, Tobacco and Firearms were particularly generous in giving me access to agents around the country.

I would like to extend special thanks to Sgt. Dan Foley of the San Francisco Police Department's Asian gang task force, who put up with three lengthy interviews. And special thanks should also go to four police investigators who allowed me to ride with their units and see the action firsthand: Sgt. Williams Nevins of the Asian gang squad in Queens; Lt. John Gallo of the Philadelphia police narcotics unit; Lt. Michael Molchan, commander of the detective squad in Lawrence, Mass.; and Detective Mark Nye, a gang investigator in Westminster, Calif.

This book would also not have been possible without enormous help from my agent, Donald Cutler of the Bookmark literary agency in Salem, Mass.; my editor Beth Anderson; Randy Lund, who helped collect newspaper articles from around the country; Hassan Yazdi, who supplied the computer equipment on generous terms; Karl Johnson, who supplied hundreds of articles and years of moral support; and the late editor and publisher of The Free Press, Erwin Glikes, who gave this book a chance.

Finally, I would like to thank three people who sacrificed more than anyone else for this project: my wife Margarita and our children, Christopher and Danica.

1: The Criminal Mosaic

On September 4, 1977, two black automobiles pulled up in front of the Golden Dragon restaurant in San Francisco's Chinatown. It was 2:40 A.M. on a dreary Sunday morning. The morning mist had already settled over the city's hills, and a cool breeze blew the promise of autumn through the streets. But the Golden Dragon's dining room was warm and inviting. The luminous mirrored walls, the crystal chandeliers, the gilt-and-bronze dragons twined fiendishly around the columns all shone brightly through the front windows. The five young men—boys really—who sat in these cars could hear laughter and conversation wafting from the crowded restaurant. They could see the gaiety of the young people, Chinese and whites, as they fiddled with chopsticks and lifted strings of rice noodles to their mouths. But they chose to see none of this. They chose to see only the face of the man they had come to kill.

Slowly and methodically, three of the five men pulled masks over their heads, picked up weapons, and stepped to the sidewalk. They yanked on the mezzanine door and found it locked. They walked the few feet to the main door and entered. Many of the patrons didn't even notice them walk in. Some would say later they thought the initial burst of gunfire was firecrackers. But the assault had begun. The smallest gunman stood just inside the door and swept the dining room with warning bursts from a .45-caliber machine gun. Some of the bullets shattered a mirror and clipped off sections of a chandelier. Others ripped through tablecloths, splintering glasses and plates. Still others found a home in human flesh. Fong Wong, a 48-year-old waiter with six children waiting for him in his cramped Chinatown apartment, was shot in the chest and mortally wounded. Carolina Sanchez, a young aspiring actress, fled across the room using a chair as shield. One of the heavy .45-caliber slugs tore through the chair and shattered her jaw.

The gunman then spotted his target: a stocky young Asian man in a black jacket who was sitting at a table in the center of the room with three women. He charged the table and resumed his fire. Bullets tore into the victim's head and torso and he crashed to the floor. The woman next to him threw her body on top of him as a shield, but the gunman was relentless. He stood over them and sprayed their bodies with lead. (A pathologist would later testify that he found rows of .45-caliber slugs pinned into the floor.) The gunman stitched another woman at the table from head to toe with bullets, leaving her paralyzed. The fourth he blasted in the face, disfiguring her for life.

Meanwhile, another gunman had walked to the mezzanine and found his own targets. He zeroed in on a table of Chinese teenagers, also wearing black jackets popular with the neighborhood's gang members. He let fly with the thunder of a 12-gauge shotgun. The shells were loaded with buckshot, designed to take down deer and other big game. The bulky pellets swept plates off the teenagers' table and smashed into their heads and faces. One of them, Calvin Fong, 18, was killed instantly. Robert Yuen, also 18, lingered in a hospital bed for a few days before dying.

The rampage took only 90 seconds, but by the time the gunmen fled, the Golden Dragon looked like a slaughterhouse. Pools of blood glistened on carpets littered with broken dishes and overturned tables. The moans of the injured and dying mingled with the horrified screams of onlookers. Sixteen victims lay bleeding on the floor. Three were already dead, and two would not last long. Several minutes would go by before anyone even noticed Fong Wong, the waiter, lying mortally wounded off to the side. Someone turned him over and saw blood staining his chest. "I'm dying," he said.

Victims told the press it looked like a battlefield, and they weren't far from the truth. The gunmen had been from the Joe Boys, a street gang at war with the rival Wah Ching gang for control of the neighborhood's extortion rackets. Their target was gang leader Michael (Hot Dog) Louie and other members of the Wah Ching gang. But there was only one problem. The Wah Ching were unharmed. They had fled out the back of the Golden

The Golden Dragon restaurant in San Francisco's Chinatown, where five people were killed and eleven injured on September 4, 1977, in a clash between chinese gangs. (AP/Wide World)

The aftermath of the Golden Dragon massacre. This photograph was taken off a television monitor. (AP/Wide World)

Dragon before the Joe Boys even got in through the front. Calvin Fong and Robert Yuen were just neighborhood teenagers who happened to be sitting at the next table. The man picked out for execution on the main floor was a Louie look-alike. He was Paul Wada, 25, a Japanese-American student celebrating his graduation from law school with his girlfriend and two of her friends from Seattle. The revenge of the Joe Boys had been visited entirely upon innocents.[1]

For nearly half a century, organized crime in America had been dominated by Italians. Protection rackets, restaurant executions, gang wars—these had been almost exclusively the province of the nation's 24 Mafia families. The Mafia had emerged from Prohibition as the nation's premier crime group, and it spent a good part of the next 40 years getting rid of the competition. Italian criminals not only made an exclusive franchise out of such crimes as narcotics smuggling, gambling, loan-sharking, and extortion; they also put a choke hold on key sectors of the legitimate business world—the docks, the labor unions, the trash haulers, the concrete companies. Criminals from other ethnic groups were forced to stand back and watch, relegated to the lowest rungs of organized crime. Blacks operated illegal numbers games but they turned over their numbers bets to the Mafia. Puerto Ricans sold drugs, but they bought the drugs wholesale from the local mobster. When push came to shove, they all answered to the Italian mob. From New Orleans to Detroit, no major criminal enterprise could operate for any length of time without the Mafia's imprimatur.

But the Golden Dragon massacre signaled the end of the old order in organized crime. The sheer audacity of these Chinese gunmen belied the myth of Mafia supremacy. Not that Chinese gangs posed an immediate threat to the Italian mob. No mafioso watching the news in his social club in Brooklyn or South Philadelphia was likely to have lost any sleep over the massacre. But as a symbol it was awesome—immigrant gangsters invading a restaurant with automatic weapons. America had not seen anything like this since the St. Valentine's Day Massacre in 1929. Gangs like the Wah Ching and the Joe Boys preyed on their immigrant neighborhoods in much the same way as embryonic Italian mobs had in the 1890s. They demanded monthly tribute from restaurants and protected gambling dens—and they were doing it just blocks from an old Mafia stronghold in San Francisco's North Beach section. By the late 1970s, there was barely a mob left in North Beach. But there was one growing fast in Chinatown. Skinny kids in blue jeans and army jackets might not be Hollywood's idea of the gangster. But in a changing America, the

Golden Dragon gunmen spoke more about the future of organized crime than all the graying dons of the Mafia put together.

In the 1980s, while the FBI was locking up the bosses of Mafia
families around the country, the Golden Dragon's prophecy was
fulfilled. A new wave of ethnic gangsters swept across America's
urban landscape. Today, not only are Chinese criminals entrenched in gambling, extortion, and narcotics in at least 19
major North American cities, but a frightening array of other
groups has carved up the American underworld. Some of them
moved into our cities with all the stealth of a Panzer division. Jamaican "posses," graduates of their country's bloody political
wars, murdered more than 1,400 people between 1985 and
1988—many of them independent drug dealers—on their way
to controlling the crack trade in ghettos from Washington to
Kansas City.[2] Their methods were so brutal and their spread so
blatant that law enforcement mobilized and put the most notorious posses out of business by the early 1990s.

But other groups are more insidious, and more likely to play a
lasting role in American society. Russian gangsters emerged in
Brooklyn's Brighton Beach section in the 1970s and have surpassed even the Mafia in their cunning. Master forgers and confidence men, the Russians have engineered credit-card scams that
have netted them millions of dollars. They have also teamed up
with the Mafia in gasoline-tax evasion schemes so widespread
that federal agencies have assembled task forces to deal with
them. Marat Balagula, one of their reputed masterminds, is said
to have amassed $600 million in illicit profits from the bootleg
gasoline scam.[3] With the frightening explosion of organized
crime in the newly capitalistic nations of Eastern Europe, Russian influence in the American rackets will only grow larger.

José Miguel Battle is a Cuban mob boss whose name is spoken
with fear in Hispanic neighborhoods from Florida to New York.
And for good reason: He runs the nation's biggest illegal lottery
network, a syndicate that stretches up and down the East Coast
and controls hundreds of numbers outlets in New York City
alone.[4] He is bigger than the legendary numbers kingpin Dutch
Schultz, but Dustin Hoffman won't be playing him in a movie.

He is virtually unknown to the public—and to many law enforcement agencies.

Vietnamese robbery and extortion gangs move into cities quickly and without warning. They shake down merchants, terrorize the homes of Asian businessmen, rob jewelry stores—and then get back on the highway. By the time the police investigation gets underway, they are doing the same thing on the other side of the country. A Vietnamese gangster named Trung Chi Truong was typical. In 1987, Truong was living in Lowell, Massachusetts, near the New Hampshire border. But he was linked to a murder in Los Angeles and robberies in Virginia. He did a stint with the Ping On, a Chinese gang in Boston, but was thrown out for being too reckless. By 1992, he was the leader of a Vietnamese gang engaged in a brutal war for control of Toronto's Chinatown.[5]

If organized crime was once a seamless Italian garment, it is now a many-colored tapestry. Dominicans have become the junior partners of the Colombian cartels, controlling wholesale cocaine sales throughout the Northeast. Haitians operate illegal numbers games in Essex County, New Jersey. Vietnamese gangs steal computer chips in Silicon Valley. Korean gangs in Queens, New York, extort money from restaurants and control the traffic of "ice," or smokeable methamphetamine. Ukrainian crime rings steal cars in Chicago and smuggle them to Poland. Gypsy clans perpetrate insurance scams that run for years and amount to millions of dollars. Albanians in the Bronx smuggle heroin and operate gambling halls in partnership with the Italian mob.

In a report to a congressional subcommittee in 1987, the FBI recognized an Arab mob as a close ally of Detroit's Mafia. Christian Iraqis known as Chaldeans are a hard-working people who own hundreds of convenience stores in the Motor City. But among them are drug kingpins, insurance fraud artists, and moblinked gamblers. They supply some of the Mafia's most dependable bookmakers in the Detroit area and run illegal gambling casinos.[6] One Mafia-linked gambler who was a regular in Detroit-area gambling houses in the 1980s and 1990s was Imad Samouna, known on the street as Chaldean Eddie. Another

Chaldean crime figure, Fred Salem, was a top Detroit bookie suspected of being a key intermediary between the Italian and Chaldean mobs.

For years, experts on organized crime expected black crime groups to succeed the Mafia. After all, they had been linked to the mob as numbers operators for decades and lived in the poorest and most violent neighborhoods. Francis Ianni, a Columbia University professor who studied New York's underworld in the mid-1970s, was the most noted of these "ethnic succession" theorists. His book *The Black Mafia* found that "Italians are leaving or being pushed out of organized crime [and are] being replaced by the next wave of migrants to the city: blacks and Puerto Ricans."[7]

Black criminals *have* found a place in the new matrix of organized crime, though perhaps not the place Ianni and others envisioned 20 years ago. They have not taken control over a broad range of criminal activities or assembled into a few large, well-structured groups like Mafia families or even Chinatown gangs. They operate in small groups and deal almost exclusively in drugs. But that does not mean their threat is less organized or pervasive than Ianni had feared. Black gangs from a handful of big cities—New York, Chicago, Detroit, and Los Angeles—have gained a stranglehold on street-level cocaine dealing in smaller cities around the country. When competition becomes too fierce on their home turf, these gangs head for the American heartland. The Bloods and Crips, infamous Los Angeles street gangs, are as likely to control cocaine sales in Omaha, Nebraska, or Portland, Oregon, as they are in Watts or South Central Los Angeles. Detroit gangs handle most of the cocaine peddling in Columbus, Ohio, Fort Wayne, Indiana, and even as far away as Chester, Pennsylvania. Brooklyn drug gangs have invaded smaller communities across New York State, and are the dominant street cocaine peddlers in cities as far south as Washington, D.C.

These drug gangs spread violence like a virus. Many small-town police have beefed up manpower and formed special units to deal with the invaders. "These guys are a lot more violent than our local drug dealers," said Sergeant William Gavin, supervisor of intelligence for the Syracuse police. "We used to go a week with one or two shootings. Now we get five or ten a night."[8]

This new plethora of crime groups is the dark side of what former New York Mayor David Dinkins called the "gorgeous mosaic," the melange of races and ethnic groups that have recently flooded the nation's major cities. In the 1980s, immigrants poured into this country in greater numbers than at any time since the turn of the century. Between 1982 and 1989, 685,000 legal immigrants settled in New York City alone; perhaps another 200,000 came there illegally.

And California is bursting at the seams. The state's population grew by a staggering 6.1 million in the 1980s, and experts said that 37 percent of the newcomers were immigrants. (Much of the rest of the increase was due to the high birth rate of Hispanics.) More than 100,000 Vietnamese live in Orange County alone.

Despite the backlash against immigration that has been building around the country in the last decade—spurred on by events like the bombing of the World Trade Center in February 1993—immigration has been a boon for older cities like Boston, New York, and Chicago, helping to stem their population losses and bringing a new spirit of entrepreneurship to many depressed neighborhoods. Sections of the South Bronx that were bombed-out war zones in the 1970s have been reinvigorated by Dominican immigrants, who have moved in and opened video stores, beauty salons and small grocery stores known as bodegas. But immigration has also had its price. Some of these immigrants brought with them the criminal traditions of their countries, planting them in fertile ground in the teeming ethnic ghettos of American cities.

The most fascinating aspect of this new ethnic diversity in organized crime is how closely it parallels the underworld at the turn of the century, a period like our own in that it had seen America transformed by immigration. The Irish syndicates that had dominated racketeering in many cities in the latter half of the 19th century found themselves crowded by gangs of Italian and Jewish newcomers. As crime groups battled for control of the enormous bootlegging profits that flowed out of Prohibition, the nation saw the bloodiest gangland battles in its history.

The Mafia's emergence in the 1930s as the preeminent crime group brought stability to the rackets, helping to quell the gangland violence that had made the previous decade so sensational. By upsetting that stability, today's diverse crop of immigrant and minority gangsters has brought anarchy back to the underworld and ushered in an era of more gangland violence than the nation has ever seen before.

Indeed, the 1980s was a decade so drenched in blood that it made the Roaring Twenties look quaint by comparison. But the wars this time were over drugs instead of illegal booze—and we have no such magic wand as the lifting of Prohibition to bring them to an end. Drugs are the single biggest force behind the spread of new crime groups. The rulers of the syndicates behind the spread of crack in the mid-1980s were not Mafia dons but the bosses of the Colombian drug cartels. Drug barons like the late Pablo Escobar of the Medellín cartel and José Santa Cruz Londono of the Cali cartel smuggled tons of cocaine into the United States every year, earning profits that Mafia bosses could only dream about. One oft-cited estimate put the cartels' take at $10 billion to $14 billion a year.[9] To bring in that kind of money, they need multiethnic armies to distribute the cocaine once it arrives in the United States. Those armies are behind the epidemic of drugs, guns, and violence that has engulfed our nation's cities.

Some of the episodes of violence associated with drug gangs over the last decade have been mind-boggling. One such incident took place in 1987, after a notorious Jamaican posse known as the Spanglers had literally taken over two blocks of Edgecombe Avenue in Harlem. The posse was peddling crack from almost every apartment between 142nd and 144th streets. One spring afternoon, a police car drove up Edgecombe and—to the horror of two officers—saw what appeared to be a group of men playing soccer with a human head. The head belonged to a young drug buyer who had been caught trying to slip two extra "rocks" of crack into his pocket while making a purchase. In inimitable posse fashion, Spangler soldiers dismembered the thief in a bathtub—the posses call it being "jointed"—put the pieces in a bag and dumped them into a garbage dumpster. There a hapless scavenger came across the body parts and dropped the bag in horror. The grisly head rolled into the street. What looked like a soccer game was really a group of men kicking the head away from them so as not be implicated as the police pulled up. But the real shocker came as the police investigation led to the bath-tub, which was at 219 Edgecombe Avenue. There, investigators pulled up the drain trap and removed material that turned out to contain the DNA of some 14 people. "There were at least four-teen people cut up in that bathtub," said James Killen, a rackets investigator with the Manhattan District Attorney's Office who worked on the case.[10]

With mayhem like this taking place on the streets, drug gangs that murder dozens of people aren't even news anymore. Best Friends, a hit squad founded by a drug lord on Detroit's East Side, was suspected of up to 50 murders by the time its leaders were arrested or killed by 1993.[11] The gang was a modern-day Murder Inc., far more vicious than Detroit's legendary Purple Gang of the 1920s. But Best Friends wasn't a big story even in Detroit, let alone in the national media.

The new diffusion of organized crime has erased many of the subtle controls that once governed the underworld and kept a lid on the violence. After all, Italian mobsters in the 1950s and 1960s had played by certain rules. The most important of these was that they refrained from killing people outside their own mi-lieu. Mafia bosses kept tight controls over murder contracts and made sure the victims were not police, judges, lawyers, reporters, or even blatantly innocent victims. These rules, of course, were broken from time to time (such as when New York mobster Johnny DioGuardi had acid thrown in the face of syndicated labor columnist Victor Riesel, who was left blind). But they were largely observed, because they worked to the mob's benefit. If gangsters committed crimes that outraged the public, they found that the police came down hard on all their gambling operations, costing them millions of dollars. Killing some reporter or cop who had offended a gang boss was simply not worth the heat that followed.

This threat of a crackdown gave police a means of keeping the underworld in line. But those controls have broken down as anarchy has taken over the underworld. Several innocent bystanders have been killed in the cross fire of Chinese gang wars in New York and San Francisco. Black gangs have come up with the term "mushrooms" for innocents who have been killed by their stray bullets. Vietnamese gangsters have murdered Vietnamese reporters around the country. And a shudder went through the entire New York press corps when Manuel de Dios Unanue, former editor of *El Diario-La Prensa*, the city's biggest Spanish-language newspaper, was executed in a Queens restaurant in 1992 on the orders of a leader of Colombia's Cali cartel. It used to be that when the mob got out of hand, detectives could pay a visit to the clubhouse of the local boss and warn him to cool things down. Cops have no such recourse these days.

Organized crime is not only more violent these days; it is also more likely to end up costing the average citizen. More than ever before, crime groups are developing schemes that hit every taxpayer in the pocketbook. Many of the new crime groups, such as the Russians and Chinese, are deep into credit-card and insurance frauds that drive up costs for all consumers. Organized-crime groups are also becoming increasingly adept at stealing taxpayer dollars directly, by ripping off government agencies. The Russians have stolen hundreds of millions from the IRS through gasoline-tax scams. Vietnamese gangs have engineered multimillion-dollar Medicaid frauds. And federal authorities rounded up 29 Fujianese immigrants in New York's Chinatown in September 1994 for a massive food-stamp fraud. The conspirators redeemed $40 million in illegally obtained food stamps through fruit markets and other stores that in some cases were never even open for business.[12]

The fraudulent redemption of grocery coupons is found in metropolitan areas around the country, and in most of them it is controlled or dominated by Arab organized crime groups. In some cases, the proceeds from the coupon fraud have been funneled to Middle Eastern terrorist organizations. In 1986, the U.S. Postal Service rounded up 70 coupon fraud violators in South Florida who were accused of sending the money to Palestine Lib-

Manuel de Dios Unanue, a Cuban-born journalist who was assassinated on orders from Colombia's Cali drug cartel. (AP/Wide World)

eration Organization contacts in Europe and the Middle East. The ring had direct contact with other coupon-fraud networks around the country.[13]

The coupon caper is really very simple. The operators set up cutting houses where newspaper coupons stolen from manufacturers' plants or newsstands are clipped by the hundreds of pounds and wrinkled to look as though they have gone through stores. They are then shipped to manufacturers' clearinghouses, which send redemption checks to the stores. All the scam artists need are dozens of stores willing to lend their names and addresses to the scheme in exchange for a share of the illicit redemption money. Often, the fraud artists work with shady finance companies that will loan immigrants money to open stores at grossly inflated interest rates. The merchant then pays off the loan with his or her share of the coupon fraud. "This is a national network that siphons off hundreds of millions in dollars in corporate funds," said Benjamin Jacobson, a corporate security expert who has investigated coupon fraud for six years.[14]

New York, St. Louis, South Florida, and California are all major centers of coupon fraud. But the Chaldeans and their network of convenience stores have given Detroit the reputation of being the coupon-fraud capital of the nation. Often graduates of Detroit's coupon-fraud rings are the ones perpetrating the schemes in other cities. According to law enforcement officials, New York's top coupon-fraud artist is Radwan Ayoub, a 49-year-old Lebanese immigrant who got his start clipping coupons in Detroit. Ayoub is a smooth talker who knows the coupon business inside and out. He has often acted as a legitimate agent for grocery stores. An internal investigation in the late 1980s by the Seven Oaks coupon clearinghouse in El Paso, Texas, found that he claimed to represent 300 stores. But the investigation soon revealed that the stores were fronts for Ayoub's fraud and that he had been making cash payments to two of the clearinghouse's employees to ensure that his accounts were not questioned, according to Jacobson.[15]

Jacobson, a retired New York City detective, spent years tracking Ayoub for the A.C. Nielsen Company, the nation's largest agent for manufacturers' coupons. Jacobson set up surveillance on a cutting house that Ayoub allegedly operated in a first-floor apartment at 2 Pinehurst Avenue in northern Manhattan. His investigators watched women passing garbage bags filled with clipped coupons out of a first-floor window. His investigation also showed that stores linked to Ayoub had wild fluctuations in the value of coupons they sent to Nielsen for redemption. The total of coupons redeemed by a C-Town supermarket at 3320 Broadway in Manhattan jumped from $4,023 in 1986 to

$39,983 in 1988, and then dipped to $10,894 in 1989. Total coupons at another store, the 8th Avenue New Way, at 2204 Eighth Avenue in Manhattan, jumped from $1,845 in 1987 to $22,539 the following year; in 1990, its total was back down to $1,374. Such fluctuations in themselves were seen as strong evidence of coupon fraud.

Jacobson's investigation also showed that Ayoub arranged high-interest loans for people to open stores, loans that were then repaid with the coupon money. In his files, Jacobson has copies of dozens of clearinghouse checks that were first endorsed by stores and then signed over to Sea Crest Trading Company, a firm in Greenwich, Connecticut, that has lent money for the openings of scores of Dominican *bodegas* in Washington Heights, in northern Manhattan. Sea Crest is a finance company that has been investigated by federal agencies in the past for its lending practices. Neither Ayoub, Sea Crest, nor any of the stores were charged in connection with alleged company fraud.

The societal cost of these new white-collar crimes is enormous, but it is dwarfed by the amount of money spent on the drug war. No one really knows how much American taxpayers have spent to combat the drug trade. But we do know that the newer crime groups are the ones ringing up the charges. They, even more than the Italian Mafia, are leading the armies of drug smugglers and distributors laying waste to U.S. cities. The war on drugs is in large part a war on the new mobs, and it is consuming not only billions in taxpayers' dollars but also the energy of national leaders who are neglecting other pressing societal concerns, like the degradation of the environment, our ailing public schools, and the downward economic spiral of the urban poor.

The insidious spread of new ethnic crime groups means more violence and a greater societal cost than that wrought by the old Italian-American Mafia. Yet it is still the Mafia that gets the most attention from the media. The slaying of a major black or Hispanic drug dealer may not even make the papers; the murder of a Mafia figure in any city is front-page news. The Philadelphia press was agog for days when a rival faction ambushed Mafia boss Joseph Stanfa on a local expressway in September 1993.

Stanfa's 23-year-old son was injured, but the Big Man wasn't even hit.

The reason for this hype is simple. Within the law-abiding community, there is a reluctance to let the Mafia die. Prosecutors, newspaper reporters, authors, television-script writers, and others have too much invested in its myth. Italian mobsters may be as cold-blooded as any other gang of killers. But they have become a treasured American cliche, as romantic as the gunslingers of the Old West. In our mythology, they are men of honor and respect who never betray the secrets of *La Cosa Nostra*—"this thing of ours." They don't kill men in front of their families or cut down innocent bystanders. Mobsters are always good to have on the block—they keep the burglary rate down.

It doesn't matter that none of these images captures the true character of the mafioso. We have enshrined him in movies and novels. The image of the mobster will forever be that of the grandfatherly Don Corleone in his tomato patch. Or the avuncular Clemenza remembering to grab his wife's cannolis off the front seat after shooting a mob rat in the head. Some were even sorry to see John Gotti packed off to jail. Sitting on the courtroom bench with his $1,000 suits and delicious smirk, Gotti was a living embodiment of the myth.

The criminal world was much simpler when the Mafia controlled the rackets. Society could easily identify the culprits who were promoting gambling, loan-sharking, and illegal lotteries. If a man in a business suit was found murdered in the trunk of his Cadillac, police would have a pretty good idea of which organization was responsible. The perpetrators were neatly divided into 24 Mafia families, each with an identifiable hierarchy whose entire membership would be listed from time to time in congressional hearings. The chief public enemies were well known to law enforcement and the populace.

The world of crime these days is far more murky and byzantine. It has exploded into a vast constellation of ethnic gangs that defy not only the understanding of the public but the intelligence-gathering apparatus of law enforcement. We are left with potent new criminal conspiracies, like the Russian Mafia, that federal authorities are forced to admit they know little about. Crimes like credit-card fraud and insurance fraud often occur without authorities ever finding out that an organized-crime group was behind it. If a body is found in a car these days, it may bear the marks of a professional murder, but there are now any number of sophisticated crime groups that could take the blame. The only reliable guide is the nationality of the body, and even that does not always solve the mystery. In 1988 hearings before a congressional subcommittee, James Zazzali, head of the New Jersey State Commission on Investigation, testified that the agency had identified 29 organized-crime groups operating in the state, and only seven of them were traditional Mafia families.[16] We no longer know who is behind the organized crime being perpetrated on our streets. Formerly, when someone placed a bet on an illegal number, they knew the profits were going into the pockets of an Italian mobster. Now the numbers game in New York City is divided among Italian, Cuban, black, Puerto Rican, and Dominican gangsters.

Indeed, no one has been sorrier to see the demise of the Mafia than the FBI. The war against the Mafia in the 1980s was the Bureau's finest moment. After spending a decade infiltrating Mafia families with informants, laying wiretaps, and gathering street intelligence, the Feds pulled in the nets. Hundreds of Mafia members and associates across the country were indicted, including the heads of most of the nation's 24 families. The Mafia lost its control over the national Teamsters Union and was booted out of New York City's concrete industry. Now, having built up so much institutional knowledge about the mob, the FBI is reluctant to start from scratch with other criminal groups—especially when Mafia indictments still generate bigger headlines.

The federal bureaucracy has been slow to recognize the emergence of new criminal groups. The head of the FBI's organized crime unit in New York City told the author in 1994 that the Chinese were the only emerging organized-crime group. He had begun putting resources into Russian organized crime only because of pressure from Washington, he said. He viewed all the other ethnic mobs as small-scale outfits without strict hierarchies or far-reaching scope. He was asked about José Miguel Battle's organization—the Cuban mob—with its hundreds of members and vast policy operation. Of this group, he admitted, he knew very little.[17]

The view in federal law enforcement is beginning to change. The Justice Department's new antiviolence initiative, begun to satisfy politicians' growing preoccupation with street crime, means that more prosecutors will be seeking to bring cases against violent drug gangs. Mary Jo White, the United States attorney in Manhattan, has been especially active in targeting drug gangs. In May 1994, her office indicted 17 members of the C&C gang, which was renting out street corners to drug dealers in the South Bronx. When a group calling itself the Willis Avenue Lynch Mob took over the turf, she indicted its leadership two months later. Her office has also gone after the Latin Kings, a largely Puerto Rican gang, and brought a racketeering case against an alleged Harlem drug kingpin named Kevin Chiles. These are the kinds of cases that would have had a tougher time getting into federal court as racketeering cases in the Mafia-busting 1980s.

Since the early 1980s, there has been enormous emphasis in the Justice Department on the "enterprise theory" of investigation, which involves targeting entire crime groups under the Racketeer Influenced and Corrupt Organizations Act, commonly known as RICO. This Act allows prosecutors to encompass years of criminal acts in a sweeping racketeering indictment, and it has been used widely against Mafia families. But RICO is less effective against fluid organizations with hazy leadership and changing memberships—that is, against many of the nation's newer crime groups. Russian mob figures thrive on the deal of the moment and are not easy to pin down to one group. Dominican crime groups are as insidious a threat as exists anywhere, but no one in law enforcement has been able to identify a single organization behind the prolific spread of these dealers, so they have received limited federal attention.

Even in the case of Chinese crime groups, whose well-structured hierarchies are tailor-made for RICO, the Feds have been slow to act. Gangs like the Wah Ching and the Joe Boys had been terrorizing North America's biggest Chinatowns since the mid-1960s, accounting for more than 50 murders in San Francisco alone by 1977. But they were largely dismissed as a case of juvenile delinquency gone haywire. With their ducktail haircuts and black leather jackets, the earliest Chinese gang members seemed like something out of *West Side Story*, alienated city kids fighting for turf and honor. To compare these inscrutable Chinese youths with the Mafia would have seemed like lunacy. And yet anyone who took a closer look would have seen how starkly they differed from classic youth gangs. From their very beginnings, Chinese gang leaders in San Francisco and elsewhere were businessmen. They fought over turf, but only because turf meant profits: the right to extort money from neighborhood merchants and sell protection to gambling dens.

Moreover, these gang members since the 1960s have had tacit alliances with the "leaders" of American Chinatowns—the merchants' organizations, or *tongs*, that had helped found the districts in the 19th century. The war between the Wah Ching and the Joe Boys was not a mindless dispute between juvenile delinquents. It was a war over profits, over who would control the neighborhood's vice. These kids would soon own their own restaurants and muscle their way into legitimate businesses, such as the promotion of Asian entertainers in the Bay area. With each passing year, they began to act more like organized-crime figures, more like the heirs of Al Capone and Bugsy Siegel than the Jets and the Sharks.

But it was not until 1984, when the President's Commission on Organized Crime held a hearing on Asian organized crime, that the press and most people in law enforcement recognized the insidious spread of Chinese syndicates. By then they were already rivaling the Mafia in size and sophistication. The gangs and criminally-influenced *tongs* in North American Chinatowns had exploited their ties with Hong Kong crime groups in flooding the country with heroin. By the late 1980s, they would control 60 percent of the supply. Even the Mafia, with its European heroin pipeline crippled by law enforcement, had to take a back seat to the Chinese smugglers.

The gangs are following the prospering Chinese population out of the squalid inner city and into outlying neighborhoods in New York and San Francisco. They even operate in suburban areas like Bergen County, New Jersey, and Orange County, California. No Chinese restaurant in the New York metropolitan area is safe from a possible visit by gangs like the Ghost Shadows or the Flying Dragons. No Asian businessman is safe from the threat of a home-invasion robbery, one of the most brutal and frightening new tactics of the Chinese, Vietnamese and Korean gangs.

And it's not just robberies and shakedowns. Chinese gangs are deeply into classic organized-crime activities like loan-sharking, bookmaking, credit-card counterfeiting, and illegal video poker machines. Criminals from the Fujian province in southern China are behind the widespread people-smuggling schemes that are flooding America's Chinatowns with illegal aliens. Those who don't quickly come up with the money to pay for their passage are often kidnapped and enslaved until the families pay.

In short, the Chinese mob is acting a lot like a new Mafia. But in the face of these far-reaching criminal conspiracies the federal government has often been complacent. The first federal RICO case against a Chinese gang was a 1985 prosecution of the Ghost Shadows in New York City. But that was a New York City police investigation that state prosecutors brought into federal court. It would be six more years before the Feds brought their own RICO case against a local Chinese gang—the 1991 indictment of the murderous Green Dragons in Queens. Federal authorities in New York City have intensified their efforts against Asian organized crime in the 1990s, but only after giving the gangs some 25 years to become entrenched.

In California, the other center of Asian organized crime in the United States, the picture has not been much better. California Attorney General John Van De Kamp in 1987 publicly proclaimed that his state could no longer cope with Asian organized crime without federal help.[18] But as late as 1991, the FBI office in

Los Angeles had no one squad dedicated to combating Asian organized crime.[19] Yet it still had an active unit targeting the city's Mafia family, even though that organization was so enfeebled that it could not even get local bookmakers to pay attention to it. San Francisco has been more progressive than Los Angeles. In 1991, its FBI office became the first in the United States to publicly designate Asian gangsters as the top priority of its organized-crime unit.[20] It has since brought a successful racketeering case against the Wo Hop To, a Hong Kong-based crime group that had moved in on the Bay Area's rackets.

The federal government has the power to make a difference in the fight against organized crime. It has the RICO law and more resources and better equipment than local authorities. Federal agents are also less prone to corruption—an element that has been especially important in the battle against the Mafia. It took U.S. treasury agents to bring down Al Capone on an income tax rap, because Capone owned Chicago's mayor and police department.

And yet the Feds historically have been slow to respond to threats from organized crime. J. Edgar Hoover was notorious for his refusal to commit the bureau's resources to battling the mob. Historians disagree as to the reason. Some point to his fear that Mafia investigations would not produce the kinds of arrest statistics that he was so fond quoting to Congress. Others suggest that he had ties to the mob. Whatever the reason, his inaction was glaring. In 1957, some 30 years after Lucky Luciano and Meyer Lansky had built the Mafia into a national syndicate, the FBI in New York City had more than 400 agents assigned to rooting out Communist spies, but only four assigned to organized crime.[21]

Hoover did not understand the Italian criminal subculture, nor did he particular care to understand. He was of a generation that saw Italian-Americans as swarthy denizens of inner-city ghettos. The victims of their murders and shakedowns were more often than not also Italians. It was not an affair with much consequence for the WASPs who controlled the reins of power in Hoover's America. A similar element of ethnic chauvinism is present today. Chinese organized crime was never considered a major problem as long as it was confined to Chinatowns. In San Francisco's Chinatown, youths had been killing each other with increasing frequency since 1965. But it was not until the Golden Dragon massacre, when white suburbanites got caught in the cross fire, that police put together a task force to deal with the problem. Federal authorities took an interest in the Chinese gang problem only after the commission hearings in 1985 disclosed that gang members had begun peddling heroin in the community at large.

Too often, this enormous threat posed by new ethnic crime groups is used as an argument for tightening up our national borders. Ethnic crimes are cited as evidence that immigrants are bent on taking what they can from America and giving back little in return. In Lawrence, Massachusetts, a battered old mill town that has been overrun by Dominican drug dealers in recent years, an Italian-American detective told the author he was fed up with his home town. "The Italians and the Irish came here to work hard and make a better life for their children," he said. "These people don't give a shit. They're here to make some quick cash and then it's back to the Dominican Republic." It is a view held by many Americans, but is hardly new. Americans have been branding immigrants as shiftless and immoral since colonial days. Many Americans choose to forget that they themselves are just a few generations removed from the ghetto, and that among their Irish, Jewish, and even Polish forebears were pimps, hit men and drug dealers. Periods of mass immigration have always brought a new dynamism to the American underworld, a new flowering of crime. We have a tendency to think of our new mosaic of ethnic crime groups as a distinctly modern phenomenon. But as we shall see, it is in a sense a very old story, one that began with a potato famine and ships filled with Irish immigrants.

2: "All That Is Loathsome Is Here"

The Irish had fled their country with pestilence and death licking at their backs. A strange blight had infected the potato crop in 1845, reducing plump potatoes to a greasy black pulp. Without the staple that fed their families and livestock, hundreds of thousands of Irish peasants died from starvation and disease. Many more scraped up a few coins, crammed into the holds of filthy and disease-ridden ships, and sailed unhappily for the New World. More than 850,000 Irish arrived in New York City alone between 1847 and 1855.[1]

Most of these peasants came penniless and malnourished. They came with the dirt of barren potato farms still caked on their boots, a rural people ill-prepared for life in growing American cities. Their families had been torn apart. Their sense of community, which was rooted in small rural villages, was lost. The Irish who embarked for America were a ravaged people, and neither they nor their adopted land would ever be the same again.

They might have fared well enough if there had been an effort by Americans to welcome them. But these predominantly Roman Catholic immigrants—the first "ethnics" to disrupt the country's English homogeneity—were despised by the Protestant majority from the day they stepped off the boats. "No Irish Need Apply" signs went up on storefronts, driving the newcomers into back-breaking labor that no one else wanted, like canal digging and railroad building.

Irish women were good enough to work as domestics for the rich, but not to live in their neighborhoods. In New York, Boston, Philadelphia and other cities, when Irish moved into neighborhoods, Americans moved out. Irish immigrants crowded into the first ethnic ghettos of the New World, districts far worse than today's urban slums. Many Irish families crammed into single rooms in buildings without running water or bathrooms. They relied on public baths and makeshift outhouses in back alleys cluttered with sewage and garbage. Cholera epidemics ravaged big-city Irish neighborhoods in the 19th century. Drunkenness and fighting were so common the term "paddy wagon" was coined for the vehicles police used to cart Irish hooligans off to jail.[2]

The most notorious Irish slum was New York's Five Points district, named for an intersection of five streets near what is now Foley Square in lower Manhattan. Paradise Square, a teeming red-light district, lay in the middle of the Points, with dozens of dance halls and saloons and greengroceries fronting for speakeasies. From the square radiated corridors of sagging clapboard buildings whose overcrowded apartments held the most desperate of the Irish poor. Known by such names as "Gates of Hell" and "Jacob's Ladder," the tenements were gruesome affairs with broken windows, leaking roofs and connecting underground tunnels where robbers murdered and buried their victims. Even Charles Dickens, the great chronicler of London slums, found the Five Points frightening. "The coarse and bloated faces at the doors have counterparts at home and all the whole world over," he wrote in *American Notes*. "Debauchery has made the very houses prematurely old. See how the rotten beams are tumbling down, and how the patched and broken windows seem to scowl dimly, like eyes that have been hurt in drunken frays . . . all that is loathsome, drooping and decayed is here."[3]

This Dickensian nightmare yielded the New World's first gangsters. Irish gangs began appearing around 1830 in Paradise Square greengroceries, which dispensed bootleg liquor in their back rooms. The Forty Thieves, the first of the major gangs, made its headquarters in the back of Rosanna Peer's grocery store. Soon to follow were the Kerryonians, Chichesters, Roach Guards, Shirt Tails and Plug Uglies, the latter named for the tall plug hats they used as helmets. Most important of the Five Points gangs was the Dead Rabbits, a breakaway faction of the Roach Guards. The gang was born during a quarrelsome meeting of the Roach Guards, when a heckler threw a dead rabbit in the middle of the room. Taking it as an omen, the faction formed a new gang and adopted the rabbit as its mascot, brandishing the lifeless beast on a stick whenever its brawlers charged into battle.[4]

The original Five Points gangs were little more than bands of thieves and roughnecks. Their wild brawls with the later gangs of the Bowery were legendary, engulfing entire neighborhoods in civil unrest. They could summon hundreds of men within minutes, armed with muskets and bludgeons, ready to kill for a few square blocks of turf. The most fabled battles were between the Dead Rabbits and the Bowery Boys, sworn enemies throughout the mid-19th century. On July 5, 1857, some 800 to 1,000 members of the two gangs went at each other with bludgeons, paving stones, axes, pitchforks, and pistols near the corner of Bayard Street and the Bowery. Eight men were killed and 100 injured in fighting that raged for hours and required the dispatch of three Army regiments.[5]

But for all the thuggery of the early Irish gangs, some of their activities clearly met today's definition of organized crime. They had stables of prostitutes and operated many of the gambling establishments that sprang up along the Bowery. They also were the first to forge what would become more than a century of alliances between the underworld and crooked Democratic bosses in Tammany Hall. An estimated 30,000 New Yorkers were loyal to Irish gangs in the 1850s, giving them an influence that politicians could not ignore. In return for cash, jobs, and protection from the law, the gangs would deliver votes, stuff ballots, and serve as candidates' private armies on Election Day. Corrupt politicians began using gangs as sluggers and repeaters at the polls as early 1834. But it took Fernando Wood, a Tammany boss in the 1850s, to bring the corrupt alliances to a new level. Wood was dubbed "the king of the Dead Rabbits" by one opponent after the gang flagrantly abetted his reelection as mayor in 1857. With the Bowery Boys supporting a candidate of the rival Know-Nothing Party, the Rabbits were out in force at the polls, making sure Wood's forces were not denied the right to intimidate voters, steal ballots, and file fraudulent votes.[6]

The Dead Rabbits and the Bowery Boys disappeared after the Civil War, but they were replaced by others of their ilk. The Whyos gang, an offshoot of the Chichesters, started on Mulberry Street near the Five Points and eventually extended its territory as far as Greenwich Village, about a mile to the northwest. With names like Red Rocks Farrell and Baboon Connolly, its derby-wearing loyalists were the most vicious gangsters of the era. No one could join the gang without first having killed a man. One of the Whyos' most colorful leaders, Dandy Johnny Dolan, wore a copper hook on his thumb like a ring, specially designed to gouge out a victim's eye. Burglars, pickpockets, whoremasters—the Whyos had a place for everyone. One of the gang's members specialized in exacting tribute from stuss card games—a derivative of faro—that appeared after the Civil War. They also were eager to hire themselves out as leg-breakers, furnishing a price list to prospective clients:[7]

Punching	$ 2
Both eyes blacked	4
Nose and jaw broke	10
Jacked out [knocked out with a blackjack]	15
Ear chawed off	19
Shot in leg	25
Stab	25
Doing the big job	100 and up

The Whyos' most prominent contribution to the city was Big Tim Sullivan. Sullivan was a kid from the Irish slums who used the Whyos' influence to get elected to the state legislature at the tender age of 23.[8] Sullivan was a two-fisted politician who became one of the greatest rogues ever to rule Tammany Hall. His ideal voter was a man with a two-day stubble who could go home, shave and come back and vote again. Legend has it that Sullivan had the ballots in his district perfumed so he could tell if the paid repeaters were going to the polls. Even while holding political office, Sullivan never gave up his extensive interests in illegal gambling. Big Tim was a towering figure in the history of New York City graft, whose hand would guide three generations of underworld leaders—Irish, Jewish and Italian. But for all his sins, Sullivan was the picture of the lovable Irish pol. When he went insane and committed suicide on a railroad track in 1913, more than 25,000 mourners followed Big Tim's body to the grave.[9]

The great brawling Irish gangs afflicted New York through the 1880s and 1890s. Succeeding the Whyos were such notorious gangs as the Hudson Dusters and the Gophers, both of which plagued Manhattan's West Side. The Dusters ruled over the west side of Greenwich Village and plundered the Hudson River docks. Their most sensational crime was the stomping of a patrolman from the Charles Street station who had vowed to smash the gang. Waylaying the patrolman while his back was turned, the gangsters beat him with blackjacks, took his badge and revolver, and gouged his face with the heels of their boots.[10] The Dusters' archenemies, the Gophers, were the "lords of Hell's Kitchen," controlling an area bounded by 13th and 42nd Streets and Seventh Avenue and the Hudson River. Among their graduates was Owney Madden, an English-born gangster who became a famous bootlegger in the 1920s.

The Irish immigrant experience in New York City was hardly all one of crime and corruption. But the Irish suffered the consequences of being the first ethnic minority to immigrate to this country in mass numbers. They were the first to be dumped like unwanted trash in neighborhoods on the fringes of polite society. It is hardly surprising that their ranks produced the first gangsters. So many first-generation Irish-Americans took to lives of crime that there emerged a popular notion that the Sons of Erin were racially disposed toward villainy. In the 1850s, more than half the people arrested for crimes in New York City were Irish born.

But the Irish would not stay in the ghetto, thanks in no small part to their phenomenal success in politics. By the late 1800s, the Irish controlled political machines in New York, Chicago, Boston, San Francisco, Milwaukee and many other cities. Political power meant jobs as policemen, fire fighters and inspectors, and a path out of the slums. Waves of Italian and Jewish immigrants took the place of the Irish on the bottom rungs of the social ladder, providing new faces in the criminal underworld. Irish would continue to play a role in the rackets, both as gangsters and corrupt political bosses, and would furnish some of the most prodigious Prohibition bootleggers. But the era of rampant Irish lawlessness—the seminal epoch in American organized crime— was over by the turn of the century.

Just before midnight on July 16, 1912, a gambler named Herman (Beansey) Rosenthal walked into the café of New York's Hotel Metropole. He had a copy of the *New York World* tucked under his arm. Beads of sweat clung to his brow. Beansey was nervous and it showed. He was a regular in the café, a guy who usually attracted little notice. But tonight a hundred pairs of eyes watched as he walked into the hotel. The bellhops stole discreet glances. So did the waiters and bartenders. Even some shady men hiding in the shadows out on West 43rd Street were watching Beansey that night. He was something most had never seen before: a walking dead man.

Rosenthal was a stubborn guy who felt he'd been wronged. A gambling joint he operated at 104 West 45th Street had been raided by the police a few weeks before. For some gambling halls, this would have been merely a cost of doing business. But Rosenthal was supposed to have protection. His secret partner in the establishment was none other than Lieutenant Charles Becker, head of the police department's vice squad. Part of their deal was that Becker would keep the cops away from the place. Beansey smelled a double cross and he planned to do something about it. So he did the unthinkable. He went public.

First he went to the *World*, dictating an affidavit on July 13 that detailed his entire arrangement with Becker. The paper splashed it across the front page the next day. Then he made a deal with Charles Whitman, the New York County district attorney, to tell everything he knew about crooked cops and politicians. And he knew plenty. Rosenthal was deeply wired into the city's Democratic establishment. One of his buddies was Big Tim Sullivan, the Tammany boss and friend to a thousand mobsters. Beansey had an appointment with the grand jury on the morning of July 17. Ignoring his wife's pleas that he stay in the house the night before, Rosenthal joined several associates in the café.

At 1:56 A.M., Rosenthal was drinking coffee and reading the paper, its headlines trumpeting his betrayal of the underworld, when a man approached his table. "There's someone outside who wants to see you, Herman," he said. Rosenthal put down the newspaper and headed for the door. No sooner had he stepped outside than four men jumped from a touring car parked across 43rd Street. The first shot hit him in the chest. Another bullet struck him in the face, tearing away his nose and cheek. Beansey died on the sidewalk in a pool of blood.[11]

The Rosenthal murder set off one of the city's great police corruption scandals. But beyond what it revealed about graft, the slaying was notable for another reason: it brought Jewish organized crime into the limelight for the first time. By the turn of the century, Jewish gangs were fast replacing the Irish as the new scourge of the underworld. Becker had given the murder contract to Big Jack Zelig, a notorious Jewish gang leader from the Lower East Side who sold protection to many of the gambling joints in Midtown. Three of the four men who stepped from the touring car were young Jewish thugs from Zelig's gang: Louis (Lefty Louie) Rosensweig, Harry (Gyp the Blood) Horowitz and Jacob (Whitey Louis) Seidenshner. For their part in the crime, they joined Becker in the gas chamber.

New York's Jewish leaders were horrified by the scandal. They feared a backlash against Jews if the public began to grasp what they themselves had ignored for so long: that crime and gangsterism were an undeniable part of the Jewish-American experience.[12] Jewish gangs had been operating on the Lower East Side of Manhattan since the 1890s, but respectable Jews preferred to

sweep the problem under the rug. If there were Jewish prostitutes or craps games lining a street, good citizens would simply
walk another route. "It is better to stay away from Allen, Chrystie
and Forsyth Streets if you go walking with your wife, daughter or
fiancée," the *Jewish Daily Forward* wrote in 1898. "There is an official flesh trade in the Jewish quarter."[13]

Crime was not a problem to which Jews were accustomed.
Their communities in Europe had been among the most peaceful
and law-abiding. And the first wave of immigrant Jewry, largely
Germans who arrived between 1850 and 1880, was no different.
German-Jewish immigrants made up a hard-working community
that was spread among the population in New York and other
cities, not clustered in ghettos. By the end of the Civil War, many
German Jews were bankers, real estate developers or businessmen. They had become an accepted part of American life, a
community applauded for its respect of the law. "If we enter a
penitentiary or prison of any description," wrote a nineteenth-
century journalist, "the marked face of the Israelite is rarely to be
seen within its walls."[14]

But things began to change toward the turn of the century.
The 1880s saw the beginnings of a flood of Jewish immigrants
from Russia, Poland and other Eastern European countries. The
estimated 2,000,000 Eastern European Jews who entered the
country over the next four decades were a different breed than
their German predecessors. They had faced much harsher repression in Europe and arrived poorer and less educated. Many had
been driven from Russia by mobs that rampaged through Jewish
villages, setting fire to homes and killing men, women and children. Whereas most German Jews practiced Reform Judaism, the
new immigrants were Orthodox Jews who adhered strictly to religious law. The men wore earlocks, skullcaps and beards, while
the women wrapped scarves around their heads. Their language
was Yiddish, a Russianized German dialect that sounded guttural
to Americans and even to some German Jews. Many established
Jews, eager to meld quietly into American life, treated the new
immigrants as an embarrassment.

Like the Irish, the Eastern European Jews were rural villagers tossed into the big cities of America. The majority crammed into Manhattan's Lower East Side, a neighborhood more crowded than the worst slums of Bombay. By the end of the century, more than 300,000 people lived in a small district bounded by Allen, Essex, Canal and Broome Streets. Most lived in filthy, overcrowded tenements plagued by fires and disease. Many families slept three or four to a room in apartments so cramped that mattresses and pillows had to be stored on fire escapes during the day. Most buildings had one toilet per floor and no showers or baths. Dr. George Price, a city sanitary inspector who worked in the Jewish ghetto, described the apartments as "filthy, foul and dark," with buildings so disease-ridden that "children dropped like flies."[15]

Even under these conditions, the Jewish tradition of self-reliance flourished. Many immigrants ended up slaving in garment-factory sweatshops and working as rag pickers or organ grinders. But a significant portion went into business as peddlers or operators of the neighborhood's famous pushcarts. In 1900, the Lower East Side was estimated to have 25,000 pushcarts, stacked with everything from fruits and vegetables to clothing.[16] Lined up side by side at the curb, the pushcarts gave thoroughfares like Hester Street the flavor of an outdoor bazaar, so crowded that horse-drawn carriages could barely pass through the street. Besides operating pushcarts, Jewish immigrants opened hundreds of cigar shops, laundries, tailor shops, delicatessens and other businesses. If the earnings from such businesses were often meager, they nonetheless laid the groundwork for what would be the remarkable upward mobility of immigrant Jews.

But not everyone on the teeming, filthy streets of the Lower East Side was so interested in honest labor. Crime flourished in the neighborhood well before the turn of the century. The torching of overinsured buildings was so common that arson became known as "Jewish lightning." Forty-four percent of the arson cases reported by the New York Times in the 1890s were linked to Jews.[17] Horse poisoning was also a common crime, a threat used by Jewish extortionists to get cash out of merchants and peddlers, who depended on the animals. Prostitution was so widespread that *McClure's* magazine in 1909 called the Lower East Side "the world's brothel."[18] Jewish pimps would grab young immigrants off the boats and put them to work on street corners and in seedy dance halls. "On sunshiny days the whores sat on chairs along the sidewalks," author Michael Gold wrote of his childhood in the Jewish ghetto. "They sprawled indolently, their legs taking up half the pavements. People stumbled over a gauntlet of whores' meaty legs."[19]

The Jewish quarter was also a fertile ground for gangs. They were on nearly every corner and every block, as natural a social outlet for youth as Little League would be for their grandchildren. Authorities estimated in the early 1900s that the Lower East Side had 336 gang hangouts in a single square mile.[20] The neighborhood had no parks, playgrounds or baseball fields, none of the recreation programs available to today's urban youth. They couldn't congregate with friends in apartments that were too cramped even for their own families. Their playground was the streets, and on the streets gangs ruled. Gangs gave kids an identity. They provided protection from the taunts of other youths—and from the Irish and Italian kids who stood ready to pummel any Jewish youths who wandered a few blocks out of their neighborhood. Many of the gangs were fairly harmless, a place for kids to engage in teenage mischief before going on to live legitimate lives. But the Lower East Side also harbored serious criminal gangs that would help spawn the great Jewish syndicates of the succeeding decades.

Among the first notorious Jewish gangsters was Monk Eastman, who organized an assortment of gangs into one of two criminal federations that ruled over Manhattan's East Side in the 1890s. (The other was the rival Five Pointers, an Italian-led successor to the old Irish gangs of the Five Points.) Born Edward Osterman in the Williamsburg section of Brooklyn around 1873, the son of a respectable restaurant owner, Eastman was one of the most feared gangsters of the 19th century. With a mat of unkempt hair, drooping jowls, a broken nose, cauliflower ears and knife scars on his face and neck, Eastman was a fearsome-looking character. Long before he founded the Eastmans, he was a bouncer in a Lower East Side dance hall, where he cut a notch into a bludgeon every time he used it to eject a patron. Once he clubbed an innocent old man quietly sipping his beer. "I had 49 nicks in me stick," he explained later, "an' I wanted to make it an even 50."[21]

From his headquarters on Chrystie Street, Eastman ruled a territory that spread from the Bowery to the East River, and from 14th Street to Monroe Street. When he was not commanding his legions of pickpockets and burglars, he operated whorehouses and demanded protection money from the neighborhood's push-carts. The Eastmans also engaged in regular wars with the Five Pointers, usually centered around the gangs' practice of robbing each other's stuss games. Eastman himself was shot and wounded by a group of Five Pointers as he walked along the Bowery in 1901. The most deadly battle between the two gangs occurred on a stifling night in mid-August 1903, when six Eastmans came across a group of Five Pointers about to rob a stuss game on Rivington Street. They shot and killed one Five Pointer and traded gunfire with the others. In the next several hours, scores of gunmen from both gangs fired at each other from behind pillars of an elevated railway on Allen Street. Eastman was among those arrested, but the case against him was dismissed.

If Eastman seemed to be a crude heir to the brawling gangs of the Five Points, he also had one foot planted in the 20th century. He had close ties to Big Tim Sullivan and other Tammany Hall leaders, who brokered a short-lived peace treaty between the Eastmans and the Five Pointers after the 1903 shootout. His protection racket was a prototype for the kind of extortion schemes that have become standard fare for immigrant gangsters. And he was also among the first of the city's racketeers to supply muscle to unions and employers in labor struggles. But he met his downfall in the most ignominious of ways: he was sentenced to 10 years in Sing Sing in 1904 for a simple street robbery. His victim turned out to be a Pinkerton detective.

During Eastman's imprisonment, his gang was run for a time by a legendary gangster called Kid Twist (real name Max Zweiback or Zerbach), who was murdered in Coney Island by a

Five Pointer in 1908. The gang then split into thirds, with a key faction falling into the hands of Big Jack Zelig. Another son of respectable parents, Zelig was a handsome and wiry man who cut his teeth as a pickpocket and jewelry thief in the bustling Chatham Square area of Lower Manhattan. He was one of Eastman's trusted associates and had learned plenty. Zelig took over Eastman's protection and gambling rackets and become almost as notorious as his mentor.

But Zelig had a much better image in the Jewish community, largely because of his reputation as a guardian of the Lower East Side. Italian thugs from neighborhoods to the west often marauded through the Jewish community, robbing merchants, taunting bearded Jewish immigrants and mistreating Jewish prostitutes. One of the first notches on Zelig's pistol was the shooting death of an Italian whose gang had crashed a party held by Jewish prostitutes. Once he became a major underworld figure, he posted guards on the neighborhood's periphery to keep out Italians. One contemporary called him "the great emancipator of the East Side."[22]

By the 1920s, Jewish mobsters would dominate organized crime not only in New York but also in Detroit, Cleveland, Boston, and Newark, New Jersey. Among the greatest Jewish villains was Arnold Rothstein, who would become renowned for fixing the 1919 World Series. Rothstein didn't need the underworld for cash. His father had gotten out of the Lower East Side through a dry goods and cotton-converting business and had become a wealthy member of the Orthodox Jewish community on the Upper West Side. His son had a lucrative career waiting for him in the family business—if it hadn't been for his insatiable gambling habit. Rothstein began his gambling career by hanging around Lower East Side stuss parlors, where he became acquainted with Monk Eastman and Herman Rosenthal. The two introduced him to Big Tim Sullivan, who was so impressed by the young man's intellect that he took him under his wing, personally instructing him in the art of gambling.

In 1910, while still in his 20s, Rothstein opened his own gambling establishment on West 46th Street—an area of Manhattan that had previously been off limits to Jewish racketeers. He later began a series of floating crap games whose locations were widely known on the street but which stayed one step ahead of any police who weren't bought off. Rothstein's clientele came to include big-time Broadway gamblers, politicians, wealthy businessmen, and sports figures like Charles Stoneham and John Mc-Graw of the New York Giants.[23]

His wealth and political clout grew so immense that he became an underworld legend, the inspiration for Meyer Wolfsheim in F. Scott Fitzgerald's *The Great Gatsby* and numerous characters in Damon Runyon stories. Known as "The Brain" or "The Man Uptown," Rothstein had no gang or army of sluggers. His muscle lay in political connections and the cash he made available for such underworld ventures as bootlegging and dope smuggling. The list of men he trained in the finer points of racketeering reads like a *Who's Who* of organized crime: Meyer Lansky, Lucky Luciano, Dutch Schultz, Frank Costello, Waxey Gordon, Legs Diamond and others.

The Brain reached his peak of notoriety in the famous "Black Sox" scandal, in which eight players of the Chicago White Sox threw the 1919 World Series. Rothstein was accused of masterminding the scandal—in truth, he only gave it financial backing—and was vilified in the press for corrupting the national pastime. Soon after, Rothstein publicly announced his retirement from the rackets. But it wouldn't last. Rothstein would stay active in the rackets well into the 1920s, when his money would back the entrance of many Jewish gangsters into Prohibition-era bootlegging.

It would have been hard at the turn of the century to predict the Italian dynasty in organized crime. Sicilian secret societies had been operating in this country as early as 1855, and poor Italians banded into street gangs as readily as the Jews and Irish. But they initially played a smaller role in racketeering. They lacked the political connections of the Irish and the labor-union ties of the Jews. Their main competitive edge was a reputation for ruthlessness, an attribute that made all the difference in the underworld.

Irish gangs might have been fond of street brawls and quick with a bludgeon, but Italian gangs were much more likely to reach for a gun or a knife. "The most vicious of all the gangs were easily the Italians," wrote Daniel Fuchs, a former member of a Jewish gang in Brooklyn. "They were severe in their methods, seldom willing to fight with their fists or stones, but resorting unethically to knives and guns. After all, the Irish could be said to fight almost for the fun of it, while the Jews always fought in self-defense. But the Italians went out definitely to maim or kill."[24]

They also had a growing numerical advantage over the Irish and the Jews. More than 4,000,000 Italians arrived in this country between 1880 and 1920, mostly poor tenant farmers from Sicily and southern Italy driven from their lands by plummeting agricultural prices. Seeing greater opportunity in urban jobs than in rural farming, the immigrants massed in the industrial cities of the Northeast and Midwest. Most settled in Eastern cities like New York and Boston, but significant numbers migrated to Cleveland, Chicago, Buffalo, and even New Orleans.[25]

They crowded into squalid ghettos in most cities, places like the famous Little Italy in Lower Manhattan, where the "alleys and yards were so narrow they remained dark even on sunny days."[26] Conditions were hard, but Italians were more successful than other immigrants in transplanting the communal bonds of village life to the big cities of America. In many cases, newly arriving immigrants joined their fellow villagers, who were clustered in the same neighborhood or even on the same street. People from San Fratello, Sicily, settled on 107th Street in Manhattan; Western Avenue in Chicago was peopled by immigrants from the Tuscan village of Colle di Compito; just about everyone in Pen Argyle, Pennsylvania, was from Vittorio Veneto in Venice.[27]

If the Little Italys of America were thriving communities—bejeweled with outdoor markets, street theater, festivals, and Catholic churches—they also had their dark side. Italian immigrants had to cope with a criminal element far more insidious than that found in Irish and Jewish neighborhoods. Secret criminal organizations were part of the culture that Italians had left behind in the old country. The Mafia, in particular, had a long and inglorious history in Sicily, where it originated in the private armies that large landholders maintained to protect their property and privilege from peasant uprisings. It had its Neapolitan counterpart in the Camorra, a criminal society whose roots dated back to the sixteenth century. Both organizations wielded enormous influence in their regions, acting as unofficial local governments in periods when the Italian states were under foreign occupation. They exacted iron-clad oaths of loyalty and secrecy from their members, which made them impenetrable to outsiders. The mafiosi and the camorristi pledged to value the "Honored Society" above all else. It came before family, country or God.

Italian peasants who ventured to America during the peak immigration years may have thought they had left all this behind. Imagine their shock at finding that their old oppressors had already been at work in some U.S. cities for several decades. The New Orleans press stumbled across its first Mafia conspiracy while the city was still cleaning up from the Civil War. "There is now in the second district of this city a band of about twelve well-known and notorious Sicilian murderers, counterfeiters and burglars," the *True Delta* newspaper reported in 1869, "who in the last month have formed a general co-partnership or stock company for the plunder and disturbance of the city."[28]

The first Italian crime groups to attract widespread attention in this country were the so-called Black Hand societies. Bands of extortionists who plagued Italian businessmen, the Black Handers were often portrayed as a monolithic group, an American incarnation of the Sicilian Mafia. In reality, the Black Hand threat was used by countless freelance extortionists who wanted victims to think they were the dreaded Mafia. Their methods were the same in city after city; the victim would receive a threatening extortion letter stamped with skull and crossbones or a black imprint of a hand. The letters were usually polite, even poetic, such as the one received by a Chicago businessman near the turn of the century:

Most Gentle Mr. Silvani,

Hoping that the present will not impress you too much, you will be so good as to send me $2,000 if your life is dear to you. So I beg you warmly to put them on the door within four days. But if not, I swear this week's time not even the dust of your family will exist. With regards, believe me to be your friend.[29]

The Black Hand first showed up in this country in January 1855 when the body of a Sicilian farmer was found on a Louisiana riverbank with 18 stab wounds and a slit throat. His wife turned over to police an extortion letter stamped with the dreaded black hand. Black Hand extortion was a rarity for the next 30 years, but became a widespread form of terror toward the end of the century. Chicago police estimated that 400 Black Hand victims were killed by guns, knives, bludgeons, or bombs in their city between 1895 and 1925. The *Chicago Daily News* reported that 55 bombs had been detonated in that city's Little Italy in the first three months of 1913. The paper quoted a detective who estimated that for every Italian who stood up to the Black Hand, ten quietly turned over the cash.[30]

Similar plagues afflicted Italian enclaves in New York, Cleveland, Boston, and other cities. They created hysteria in the press, which proclaimed that the Mafia had been transplanted to the United States as an evil cabal linked across the country. Anglo-America branded Italians with the same stigma it had attached to the Irish and the Jews—that they were criminal by nature. The U.S. Commission on Immigration (the Dillingham Commission) in 1911 called Italians moral degenerates and said Sicilians were "excitable, superstitious and revengeful."[31]

On March 4, 1888, Buffalo police rounded up 325 Italians— virtually the entire community—in a search for weapons after one Italian murdered another. Only two weapons were found. The Italian ambassador in Washington lodged a letter of protest with the Buffalo authorities. When New Orleans Police Chief David Hennessey was murdered in 1890, probably by Sicilian immigrants, authorities told of a plot "to assassinate all city and state officers who acted contrary to the wishes of the Mafia."[32] Of the 10 Italians charged in the crime, seven were acquitted and the jury deadlocked on the others. Outraged, a lynch mob broke into the jail and murdered every Italian in sight, including several who weren't even being held in the chief's murder.

While the Mafia threat was exaggerated in the press, its growth in this country was real. Criminal societies were active in most major Italian communities by the 1890s. A Mafia–Camorra war broke out in New York in 1889, sparked by an offhand remark from the city's chief of detectives, Thomas Byrnes. Fed up with a spate of killings in Italian ghettos, Byrnes said the gangsters could "go ahead and kill each other" and the police would not interfere. The gangsters took Byrnes at his word. By the end of the first year, 47 people were dead. The war continued for the next 27 years, costing 1,400 people their lives. When it was over in 1918, the Camorra had been absorbed into the Mafia, making the Italian underworld a Sicilian-Neapolitan alliance.[33]

For all their butchery, Italian secret societies were not easily able to break the Irish and Jewish grip on New York's underworld. Indeed, the city's best known Italian gangster at the turn of the century, Paolo Vicarelli, had risen through the ranks of the Irish mob. Better known by his alias, Paul Kelly, the former prizefighter was a member of the Whyos gang in the 1870s before he split off and formed his own group, the Five Points gang. The Five Pointers were one of Manhattan's last great fighting gangs. Its 1,500 members included Irishmen and Jews as well as Italians. Kelly's only requirement was that they remain loyal to him and be ready to battle the Eastmans, the Five Pointers' archenemies. The Five Pointers controlled the territory between Broadway and the Bowery, 14th Street and City Hall Park, a realm just west of the Eastmans' turf. The deadly struggle between the Eastmans and the Five Pointers had begun over rights of plunder in the Bowery entertainment district.

Kelly was far more refined than the brawling Monk Eastman. Though he was a former bantamweight boxer, Kelly rarely took part in fighting himself, preferring to give orders from his headquarters, the New Brighton Dance Hall on Great Jones Street. A soft-spoken man who favored neat and conservative clothes,

Kelly was fluent in French, Spanish, and Italian and conversant with the arts. Yet he was able to command respect from cut-throats with names like Eat 'Em Up Jack McManus and Louis (Louie the Lump) Piloggi. Among those fiercely loyal to Kelly was Johnny Torrio, head of the James Street gang. Emulating Kelly's understated style, Torrio would later move to Chicago, where he and a subordinate named Al Capone would take over that city's underworld in the 1920s.

Not all of Kelly's men remained loyal. Two of his toughest gun-men, Biff Ellison and Razor Riley, had a falling out with the leg-endary mob boss and vowed to kill him. One night they got their chance. Stumbling drunkenly into the New Brighton Dance Hall, they spotted Kelly at a rear table with Bill Harrington, Rough House Hogan, and Harrington's girlfriend. Riley fired off a shot and killed Harrington, but Kelly dove under a table. As the lights in the tavern went out, Kelly blasted away in the darkness with two revolvers. He was struck by three shots. When the police ar-rived, the dance hall was dark and empty, except for Harrington's body. The establishment never reopened, and Kelly took a month to recover from his injuries.[34]

The first major Italian gang leader in Chicago was Big Jim Colosimo, who was Johnny Torrio's uncle. Colosimo had been brought to the United States from Naples at age 10. His family settled in the middle of the Levee, the wicked red-light district on Chicago's South Side, giving the young immigrant an early intro-duction to crime and vice. A pickpocket and a pimp as a teenager, he was a Black Hand extortionist by his early 20s.[35]

Colosimo married a well-known madam at the turn of the cen-tury and together they opened a string of bordellos in the Levee. In 1910, they opened Colosimo's Café on Wabash Avenue, a le-gitimate nightclub that—even though it lay in the middle of the city's vice district—became a popular destination for the more daring members of Chicago's gentry, who were attracted by the most beautiful chorus girls and the finest entertainers in the Mid-west. Gathered under its gold and crystal chandeliers on any given night would be anyone from singer Al Jolson and depart-ment store magnate Marshall Field to the notorious Black Hander Vincenzo (Sunny Jim) Cosmano. None of them were under any illusion about their host. Colosimo was little more than a glorified whoremaster. The biggest share of his estimated $600,000 annual income came from gambling and the white slaves he put to work in his bordellos.[36]

Few Sicilian gangsters were as well known as Kelly and Colosimo in the early 1900s. But they were a malevolent presence in their own neighborhoods, not only in New York and Chicago but in other large cities as well. Many of their murders were committed with such stealth that they were never tied to the rackets. A series of bodies found stuffed in barrels in Brooklyn and Manhattan in the first part of the century at first baffled police. They were later linked to Ignazio Saietta, a Sicilian boss known on the streets as Lupo the Wolf. The Wolf was so feared in Sicilian neighborhoods that law-abiding citizens would make the sign of the cross when they mentioned his name. Saietta and a sidekick, Giuseppe Morello, operated a stable on East 125th Street where at least 23 men were believed to have been murdered between 1900 and 1917. It became known as "Murder Stable."[37] The two gangsters were originators of the Italian lottery, which would be a windfall for the Mafia for decades to come. Among Saietta's protegés was Ciro Terranova, who took over Italian numbers in Harlem and the Bronx after Sajetta went to prison in 1910. For a time, Terranova was the city's most notorious Italian gang figure. The press dubbed him the Artichoke King after he used intimidation to become New York's sole supplier of artichokes.

Another of Saietta's underlings, Giuseppe Masseria, would eventually outstrip Terranova in importance. In the 1920s, Masseria headed the most powerful of what had evolved into five major Italian gangs in New York. Nicknamed Joe the Boss, the fat, unkempt Masseria was despised by his enemies but had survived their numerous attempts to kill him. Masseria's gang, which included Sicilians, Neapolitans and Calabrians, was studded with some of the biggest future stars of the Mafia. His protegés included Charles (Lucky) Luciano, Frank Costello, Willie Moretti, Vito Genovese and Joe Adonis.

The second most powerful of the Italian gang leaders was Salvatore Maranzano, an immigrant from the Castellammarese region of Sicily. Maranzano was as refined as Masseria was coarse. The tall and muscular mafioso wore conservative gray pin-striped suits and spoke in a smooth, powerful voice that mesmerized his followers. "I felt honored and privileged just to be near him," legendary mobster Joseph Bonanno wrote in his memoirs. ". . . When I was around Maranzano, I felt more alive, more alert, more called upon to fulfill my potential."[38]

The two gang leaders were destined to clash. When they did, it provided one of the most dramatic moments in the evolution of Italian organized crime. The conflict started when Masseria, seeking to take over New York's Italian underworld, issued death sentences for all gangsters from the Castellammarese region. Maranzano's entire gang was on the list, along with his loyalists in cities as far away as Buffalo, Detroit and Chicago. Most of the fighting, though, took place in Brooklyn. Sixty people were murdered before Luciano, Masseria's second in command, ended the war by cutting a deal with Maranzano. Luciano invited his fat boss to a Coney Island restaurant called Scarpato's on April 15, 1931. When Luciano excused himself to go to the men's room, gunmen walked in and shot Masseria in the back of the head.[39]

Maranzano would not be around long to savor his victory. But in his brief reign he determined the shape of the American Mafia for the rest of the century. Not long after Masseria's death, Maranzano summoned hundreds of Italian gangsters to a meeting hall in the Bronx, where he announced the formation of New York's five Mafia families. Modeling the families after the armies of ancient Rome, he decreed that each would have a boss, underboss, *consigliere* (adviser), *caporegimes* (lieutenants), and soldiers. (The five original bosses designated by Maranzano were Luciano, Tom Gagliano, Joseph Profaci, Joseph Bonanno and Vincent Mangano.) This prototype soon spread to other cities, giving the nation the 24-family Mafia consortium that still exist today.

As a final touch, Maranzano named himself *Capo di tutti Capi*—"Boss of all Bosses." It was this lust for power that sealed his doom. He made the mistake of plotting the murders of Luciano, Genovese and a host of other young mobsters whose ambitions he feared. Just days before Genovese and Luciano were to be knocked off by an Irish killer named Vincent (Mad Dog) Coll, they turned the tables on the stylish old don. On September 10, 1931, Maranzano was shot and stabbed to death in his office at 230 Park Avenue by several killers posing as policemen on a raid.[40]

The younger mafiosi who arranged Maranzano's murder regarded him as a "Mustache Pete," an outmoded Sicilian don whose views had no place in the modern American underworld. But the traditions that he and other Sicilian-born gangsters brought to this country continued to govern the Mafia for decades. No member of the Mafia would violate the vow of secrecy for the next 30 years, despite the thousands that must have been arrested and pressured by police. Only when mob turncoat Joseph Valachi agreed to testify before a congressional committee in 1963 did America learn that Italian mobsters referred to their organization as *La Cosa Nostra* (Our Thing), that one must be a full-blooded Italian to belong, and that the Mafia was broken up into "families," each with a well-defined hierarchy.

Some scholars have expressed doubts over the years that Mafia families across the country have national links or that the Mafia even exists. But the parade of informers that law enforcement has developed since the 1980s, and their revelations about the mob's origins, have laid most of that skepticism to rest. Some of the evidence has been striking. Valachi's description of the Mafia initiation ceremony that he underwent in New York in 1930 was virtually identical to the ceremony mob informer James (Jimmy the Weasel) Fratianno underwent in Los Angeles in 1947, and to the Mafia initiation that the FBI secretly tape-recorded in Providence, Rhode Island, in 1989. In each of the cases, the inductee's fingers were pricked, a dagger and pistol were displayed on the table, a ritual paper was burned, and the new member uttered the vow of *omerta*, or secrecy. More frightening still, the ritual was strikingly similar—right down to the pistol and dagger and the letting of blood—to a Camorra initiation in Naples that was recorded by a historian in 1872.[41]

For all their diamonds, touring cars, and nightclubs, men like Salvatore Maranzano, Big Jim Colosimo, Paul Kelly, Big Jack Zelig—and countless other Irish, Jewish and Italian gang leaders—were small-timers compared to the criminals who would succeed them. The chintzy gambling joints, bordellos and neighborhood protection rackets would give way to huge suburban mansions, multi-million-dollar bankrolls, international investments and political clout reaching all the way to the White House. All this was possible because of a national experiment called Prohibition.

Prohibition turned organized crime into big business. Before the Eighteenth Amendment took effect in January 1919, ethnic criminal gangs were relatively small outfits that operated in well-defined turfs in seedy neighborhoods. They made their biggest money from the same street-corner rackets that had sustained gangsters since the Five Points days: gambling, prostitution and extortion. Peddling illegal booze not only generated vast new profits, transforming the biggest gangsters into virtual moguls of crime; it also brought masses of thirsty but otherwise law-abiding citizens into league with the underworld. Anyone who visited one of the ubiquitous speakeasies of the day, or served a few drinks at a cocktail party, was patronizing the local mobster. When Al Capone called himself a "public benefactor," he was not too far from the truth.

Irish gangsters were the first to turn Prohibition into a windfall. Big Bill Dwyer, a New York dock worker, was the genius behind Rum Row, an unloading point for booze-laden ships just outside the Coast Guard's three-mile limit. Dwyer grew up in a tough neighborhood on Manhattan's West Side, in the middle of Gopher and Hudson Duster territory. And he used alumni of both gangs to help build his bootlegging empire. The ruddy-faced stevedore had a fleet of vessels that would pick up liquor from ports in Latin America and Europe and then unload it onto speedboats outside the U.S. three-mile limit. Big Bill was actually an average-sized man. His colorful nickname stemmed more from the scope of his operation. By the early 1920s, he owned two hotels, several nightclubs, casinos, racetracks, and a brewery in Manhattan that netted $7 million a year. When it was time for entertaining, he retired to an estate in Belle Harbor, Queens.[42]

Jewish bootleggers in New York, Cleveland, Boston, Detroit, and Philadelphia would eventually outpace their Irish competitors, becoming for much of the 1920s the dominant group in American organized crime. With some exceptions, they achieved this dominance less through violence than by their superior business instincts. Arnold Rothstein, who had the biggest bankroll in the New York underworld, supplied bootlegging capital to more than a few gangsters. Waxey Gordon, a Lower East Side gang member, used a Rothstein loan to become a Prohibition legend. Initially a partner of Big Bill Dwyer, Gordon acquired interests in 13 illegal breweries and became a supplier of booze across the Northeast. His ally was Newark's top mobster, Longy Zwillman, who provided the Gordon syndicate with his muscle. Another Jewish protegé of Rothstein's, Dutch Schultz, jumped into the liquor business with Dwyer as his supplier. Years before he became the numbers kingpin in black Harlem, Schultz opened up a string of beer joints in uptown Manhattan and the Bronx.

Moe Dalitz was the top bootlegger in Cleveland, moving so much booze across Lake Erie from Canada that it became known as "the Jewish Lake." In Detroit, the all-Jewish Purple Gang shipped booze across the Detroit River and distributed it across the country. The Purples' chief competition was another Jewish gang, the Third Avenue Navy, which took its name from the boats it used to transport liquor. But the competition did not last long. The Purple Gang was one of the most homicidal—some say suicidal—gangs of the Prohibition era. Its members used to tear up bars frequented by Italian gangsters just for the fun of it. When one of the Purples' liquor shipments was hijacked in September 1931, a top Purple named Ray Bernstein lured three Third Avenue Navymen to the Collingwood Manor apartments. The unarmed trio were gunned down in what became known as the "Collingwood Massacre."[43]

Italians initially played a smaller role than the Irish or the Jews in rum-running. Italian bootlegging began with the illegal kitchen stills that filled the streets of many a Little Italy with the sour stench of cooking alcohol. In Chicago's Little Italy, the Terrible Genna Brothers, a feared Sicilian gang, turned home-alcohol cooking into a lucrative enterprise. They installed stills in the kitchens of hundreds of Italian immigrants, paying them $15 a day for booze that would fetch the gang a great deal more on the illegal market.[44]

The Gennas' efforts were paltry compared to the schemes cooked up by Johnny Torrio. The New Yorker had given up his James Street gang around 1909 and gone to Chicago to join the organization of his uncle, Big Jim Colosimo. Torrio was originally brought in to arrange the murders of Black Hand figures who had been shaking down Colosimo, but he decided to stay on in the Windy City. In 1919, he brought along Al Capone, who had been an apprentice in the James Street gang and needed to get out of Brooklyn to beat a rap for shooting a man in a barroom brawl. Capone started out in some lowly jobs like dumping bodies and acting as a doorman at the Four Deuces, a brothel Torrio had opened at 2222 Wabash Avenue. But the Capone-Torrio partnership would soon turn the Chicago underworld upside down.

Their first victim would be Colosimo himself. Big Jim, happy with his gambling and prostitution rackets, waved aside Torrio's urging that they tap into the big money flowing out of Prohibition. It was a lack of ambition that Torrio couldn't forgive. On May 11, 1920, a day when both Torrio and Capone had unshakable alibis, Colosimo was shot once behind the ear as he stood in the vestibule of his café. It was Chicago's first major gangland rub-out of the Prohibition era, but it would be far from the last. Of more immediate importance, it freed Torrio and Capone to move into the lucrative bootlegging business.

Torrio turned out to be one of the great criminal visionaries of the Prohibition era. Using organizing skills he had picked up from Paul Kelly, Torrio convinced leaders of Chicago's gangs to cooperate in distributing illegal booze. The Genna brothers would get to control alcohol production in Little Italy stills; Dion O'Banion, an Irish gang boss who at one time was the dominant crime figure in the city, would have exclusive rights to import whiskey from Canada; and Torrio and Capone would brew beer. Other gangs could run speakeasies with these gangs as their suppliers. It was no small feat bringing these brutal forces together, and the cooperation would eventually fall apart. But while it lasted the combine would gross $12 million a year and flood Chicago and its environs with booze.[45]

Torrio's sights, however, were not limited to Chicago. In his zeal to make organized crime a corporate-like structure, he reached out to like-minded gangsters around the country. In New York, his natural partners were Lucky Luciano and Frank Costello, who had been the chief bootleggers in Masseria's gang but who had much bigger plans than their slovenly boss. Independent of Masseria, Costello had maintained partnerships with Big Bill Dwyer and Arnold Rothstein. Luciano had cut deals with the Bugs-Meyer Mob, a Jewish gang headed by Rothstein protegés Meyer Lansky and Benjamin (Bugsy) Siegel. This multiethnic partnership would combine to transform bootlegging into a national syndicate.

Their first big step was uniting a series of Eastern and Midwestern bootlegging mobs into a loose partnership that would join in purchasing, shipping and distributing liquor. The group became known as the Big Seven Combination after the seven bootlegging outfits that formed it. Among the seven gangs were the Bugs-Meyer mob; a Luciano-Costello-Torrio partnership; Waxey Gordon's organization; and the northern New Jersey crime group headed by Willie Moretti and Longy Zwillman. The others were Charlie Solomon in Boston; a Brooklyn group headed by Joe Adonis; and Enoch (Nucky) Johnson, the Democratic boss in Atlantic City who oversaw the landing of liquor on the Atlantic coast.[46]

The Big Seven group would eventually grow to include 22 mobs, some as far south as Florida and as far west as the Mississippi. Bootlegging had made organized crime a national corporation, with fleets of trucks, huge warehouses and offshore bank accounts. It even came to have its own security division, Murder Incorporated, a gang of Jewish and Italian killers formed by the syndicate in the 1930s to eliminate anyone who stood in the way of

Mafia visionary Charles (Lucky) Luciano, center, is led into Manhattan Supreme Court in 1936 for sentencing in a prostitution case. (AP/Wide World)

the mob's inexorable march. More than 400 killings were laid to Murder Incorporated before its leader, Abe (Kid Twist) Reles, was arrested and turned state's evidence in 1940. As the heads of this new combine, people like Luciano, Costello, and Capone became as well known as sports figures and screen stars. The murderous exploits of these gangsters were in the papers every day, and yet the public treated them like celebrities. When Capone went to Chicago's Comiskey Park, photographers would gather around as ballplayers like Gabby Hartnett of the Chicago Cubs would personally come to his seat and sign an autograph for his son.

The syndicate's galling power reached its greatest manifestation in May 1929, when the nation's top gangsters openly held a

Meyer Lansky, the Jewish gangster who helped create the national crime syndicate, being booked for questioning at a Manhattan police stationhouse in 1958. (AP/Wide World)

three-day conference at the President Hotel in Atlantic City. The meeting, held under the protection of Nucky Johnson, was called to reach agreement on reducing the gang warfare that was putting too much heat on the syndicate. It included the biggest names in the Italian and Jewish underworlds. (Few Irish gangsters now figured in the national syndicate.) Besides the Big Seven group, there was a dazzling array of other gangsters from around the country. Al Capone was there with a Chicago delegation that included his business adviser, Jake Guzik. Moe Dalitz was there from Cleveland and Abe Bernstein from Detroit's Purple Gang. The meeting was a heady affair for the nation's gangsters, a summit of some of the world's greatest criminal minds; and it was covered by newspapers, which actually photographed Al Capone strolling on the boardwalk with Nucky Johnson.[47] It also represented the peak of ethnic cooperation in organized crime.

There would be other summits and even more spectacular displays of power. Mobsters would control national labor unions, supermarket chains, concrete companies, Las Vegas casinos, and entire industries like garbage hauling and trucking. They would acquire global reach in the narcotics trade. But few of these new moguls of crime would have Irish or Jewish names. Big-time racketeering would become almost an exclusively Italian affair in the decades succeeding Prohibition. Meyer Lansky, who inherited Arnold Rothstein's role as underworld financier, helped set up the national bookmaking syndicate that replaced rum-running as the mob's chief source of income. But he was the only Jewish gangster who retained any real clout, and even he had to defer to his Italian overlords. His chief partners in the Italian underworld, Lucky Luciano and Johnny Torrio, passed from the scene in the mid-1930s. Torrio, who lost his taste for the gangster life after being seriously wounded in a gun battle in 1925, retired and turned over his interests to Al Capone. Luciano was imprisoned by mob-busting prosecutor Thomas E. Dewey in 1936 and then deported to Italy. Their successors were less accommodating of other ethnic gangs, often finding it easier simply to kill them.

Many of the most sensational mob killings in Prohibition's aftermath involved Jewish and Irish victims. Capone set the pace in Chicago. The truce between Chicago's gangs had broken down, turning the city's underworld into a bloody free-for-all. Some of Capone's most bitter enemies did him the favor of killing each other off. His biggest nemesis, Dion O'Banion, was murdered in his flower shop in 1924 by the Genna Brothers. But Capone had no qualms about removing enemies on his own. Chicago's Irish mob was all but wiped out on St. Valentine's Day in 1929, when Capone's men lined up eight survivors of the O'Banion gang in a Chicago warehouses and cut them down with Tommy guns.

Detroit's Purple Gang also did not survive long after Prohibition. Several of its leaders went to jail and others were killed by Sicilian and Neapolitan gangs. Similar fates awaited top Jewish mobsters in other cities. Arnold Rothstein was shot to death on November 4, 1928, at the Park Central Hotel in Manhattan, a murder that has never been solved. Dutch Schultz was slain in the upstairs of a Newark restaurant after Italian mob bosses were taken aback by his insane plot to murder Dewey. Bugsy Siegel was shot through the eye in his Las Vegas hotel room in 1947. Waxey Gordon was forced out of the mob because of Italian threats. Longy Zwillman held on longer than most Jewish mobsters, committing suicide in his New Jersey home in 1959. Besides Lansky, the only major Jewish mobster who lasted well past World War II was Cleveland's Moe Dalitz.

With their rivals out of the way, the country's 24 Mafia families set out to build their criminal dynasty. The underpinning of that empire would be illegal gambling, which was firmly under the Mafia's control by the end of World War II. In most of the nation's major cities—and even the smaller mill towns of the Northeast and Midwest—no one could make big money in sports betting, illegal casino gambling, loan-sharking, or street lotteries without a mob connection. Estimates in the late 1970s and early 1980s put the mob's gambling earnings at $2 billion to $12 billion a year, the lion's share coming from a national bookmaking syndicate that reached down to the lowliest small-town bookie. It was not uncommon by the 1970s for a single mob bookmaker to bring in $1 million a week in sports bets, clearing a profit of $100,000.[48]

But even that impressive sum paled compared to the money that mobsters were taking in from heroin importation. After his deportation to Italy, Luciano did his Mafia friends the favor of setting up the Turkey-Marseilles-New York heroin pipeline that flooded America with the drug for decades. Many Mafia families had an internal rule against dealing in drugs, but most bosses were ready to turn their heads if they were in on the enormous profits.

The American Mafia has made its biggest money from gambling and narcotics, but its malevolent hand has reached into nearly every corner of criminality. Mobsters have been involved in truck hijackings, bank robberies, pornography, extortion, fencing of stolen goods, toxic-waste dumping, credit-card fraud, securities fraud, marijuana dealing, auto-theft rings, counterfeiting, postage-stamp ripoffs, theft of goods from Kennedy Airport, arson for profit, illegal fireworks sales, and a thousand other rackets. The profits from all these crimes, even if committed by the lowliest soldier, have flowed to the top echelons of Mafia families.

The Mafia has also had vast influence over legitimate business. Mobsters' control over garbage carting in New York, Tampa, New Jersey, Boston and numerous other cities has allowed them to fix the bidding for municipal contracts, hitting taxpayers squarely in the pocketbook. In New York City, the mob's legendary control over the concrete industry drove up the cost of public construction projects for years. The mob has controlled the Fulton Fish Market, the city's largest wholesaler of seafood, since the 1930s. It has deep interests in parking garages, trucking, topless bars and supermarket chains. A 1970s investigation of the nation's food industry found 50 figures from 12 crime families linked to 30 food and food-service companies. The mob-influenced food companies were said to have combined annual sales of $400 million.[49] Many smaller businesses have been acquired by mobsters when their owners could not pay off gambling debts. An often-told story in Detroit is that mobster Vito Giacalone won the Home Juice Company in a crap game.

The labor racketeering pioneered by Jewish and Irish mobsters had become an Italian stronghold by World War II. Mafia influence over the Teamsters' Union became so total by the 1960s that mobsters could give orders to the union's national president. When legendary Teamster president Jimmy Hoffa attempted to regain his position, his mysterious disappearance in 1975 was almost certainly the work of gangsters from Detroit and New Jersey. The prevailing theory, the one subscribed to by the FBI, is that Hoffa's body was fed into an incinerator in Hamtramck, Michigan, owned by the late Mafia soldier Jimmy Quasarano.[50] Former Teamster President Roy Williams testified in a 1986 prosecution that he took orders from Kansas City Mafia boss Nick Civella. In 1974, Williams said, he approved a loan from the Teamsters' pension fund to the owners of two Las Vegas hotels where Civella and other Mafia leaders skimmed off gambling winnings. The mob has had control over numerous other national unions. Carlo Gambino, the top Mafia boss in New York in the 1960s and 1970s, had such total control over the International Longshoremen's Association that he could produce a labor walkout and paralyze the East Coast shipping industry with a nod of his head. The cost that organized crime placed on shipping is blamed for the decline of New York's port.[51]

Mob territories have been carefully apportioned since the 1930s. Most crime families control not just cities but entire regions. The Buffalo family's territory, for example, covers Rochester and the entire city of Toronto. New England's Mafia, traditionally headquartered in Providence, controls Boston and most of Connecticut. Disputes between families over these territories have been settled by a national commission that has varied in size over the years. Police surprised a meeting of the Mafia's national commission in 1957 at a mobster's home in the western New York town of Apalachin. Fifty-eight top mobsters from across the country were detained, including the bosses of four New York families, and five others were later firmly identified as having been there. "Well, I hope you're satisfied," Chicago boss Sam Giancana later told Buffalo boss Stephano Maggadino in a wiretapped phone call. "Sixty-three of our top guys made by the cops."[52] The commission grew smaller in later years, when it became dominated almost entirely by leaders of the New York families.

In most of the country, the Mafia has ruled the rackets with relatively little internal conflict. Most killings have been directed at people outside the leadership of the families: disobedient soldiers, deadbeat money borrowers, businessmen who resisted Mafia infiltration, low-level drug pushers. Outside New York and Chicago, the slaying of Mafia bosses has been a rarity. Men like Joseph Zerilli in Detroit, Maggadino in Buffalo, Santo Trafficante in Tampa, Carlos Marcello in New Orleans, and Raymond Patriarca in New England ruled over their families without challenge for decades. Angelo Bruno, the longtime boss of the Philadelphia family, was one exception. Known as "the Gentle Don" for his success at keeping peace in Philly's underworld, Bruno was shot to death in his car in 1980, probably by New York mobsters who wanted to move in on Atlantic City rackets after gambling was legalized.[53]

Only in New York, where five families have divided up the rackets for 60 years, have violent transfers of power been a regular feature of the underworld. Vito Genovese made a bid to become "Boss of all Bosses" in the 1950s, rubbing out Albert Anastasia—head of what is now the Gambino family—and New Jersey rackets boss Willie Moretti. He also attempted to kill Frank Costello in the doorway of his Park Avenue apartment building, but the gunman's bullet just grazed Costello's head. Genovese's bid ultimately was thwarted by his imprisonment on federal narcotics charges. In the early 1960s, renegade Mafia soldier Joseph (Crazy Joe) Gallo led a rebellion against his family's boss, Joe Profaci, beginning a war that left more than a dozen people dead. The family finally caught up with Gallo in 1972, when he was gunned down in Umberto's Clam House in Little Italy. Famed Mafia boss Joseph (Joe Bananas) Bonanno had plotted the murder of other family leaders in 1964 and was first kidnapped and then forced into retirement. One of his successors as boss of the Bonanno family, Carmine Galante, also had plans to take over the New York underworld. He was bumped off in a Brooklyn restaurant in 1979. John Gotti made one of the most sensational power plays in mob history when he took over as boss of the Gambino family by having Paul Castellano gunned down outside a Manhattan steakhouse in 1985.

These dramas have fascinated the American public. They have been the fodder for sensational front-page news stories, best-selling books and blockbuster movies. The Mafia's dominance of organized crime was accepted as a fact of life. Who would challenge them for control of the rackets? The Mafia never expected real trouble from the black and Hispanic pushers who clung to the periphery of the underworld in many cities in the 1950s and 1960s. They were kept on the margins, without any connections in the white-dominated police departments and political machines to pave their way into the bigger world of organized crime.

But the criminals on the lowest rungs of the underworld wouldn't wait forever for a piece of the action, especially when the action was increasingly taking place in their own neighborhoods. The Mafia is said to have greatly feared the Kennedy administration's introduction of wiretapping and other new methods to control organized crime in the 1960s. But the most important challenge to the Mafia's criminal monopoly had nothing to do with new law enforcement technology. By the dawn of the 1970s, the biggest threat was the changing face of the inner city.

3: Mr. Untouchable

talian control over organized crime in many inner-city neighborhoods had taken on a colonial aspect by the 1960s. Much of
the Mafia's profits were flowing out of black and Hispanic communities, where the local hoodlums greatly outnumbered their
Italian masters but lacked the organization and firepower to
expel them. Like a colonial power, the Mafia used the indigenous
crooks to help administer its criminal empire and to keep the lid
on any potential insurgencies. Thus black and Hispanic criminals were used to run numbers, peddle heroin and handle other
low-level racketeering. But they were never admitted into the
inner circles of the Mafia, and any murders or beatings meted
out in the ghetto in the name of organized crime were carried out
by Italian-Americans.

The Mafia had begun as an immigrant phenomenon, controlling racketeering in Sicilian and Neapolitan ghettos in the nation's largest cities. Criminals might not have a natural right to
plunder any community, but the Mafia's activities at least fitted
neatly into the social order of the Italian ghetto. The mafiosi who
ran the crap games, sold illegal numbers and cooked alcohol in
Italian neighborhoods in the years before World War II were not
always seen as neighborhood pariahs. They were offering amuse-
ment and the chance of a windfall for ghetto dwellers who had
few other diversions. Once the days of Black Hand terror had

past, the local Mafia don was even able to be seen as a respectable figure in his community, making up for his misdeeds with acts of charity. (The tradition lives on in Queens, where neighbors of John Gotti used to look forward to his annual Fourth of July block party.)

But in the years after the war, no such benevolent window-dressing existed in black and Hispanic ghettos. Black people might enjoy playing the numbers, but they were under no illusion that the mafiosi had anything but ill will toward their community. Especially when the mob was the supplier of heroin that turned hundreds of thousands of ghetto children into hopeless addicts. The vast migration of blacks from the South after World War I—and to a lesser degree the migration of Hispanics from Puerto Rico, beginning in the 1930s—had transformed many northern cities. The Italian mobster no longer lived in Bedford-Stuyvesant, Chicago's South Side, North Philadelphia, or Detroit's East Side by the 1960s and 1970s. These areas had become huge black ghettos. Like the colonial master, the mobster was merely there to siphon off whatever wealth he could from the territory and take it somewhere else. No one is likely to have found this more galling than the resident criminal, who no doubt took to wondering why the white man was calling the shots in his neighborhood. As the passions of the civil rights movement galvanized the ghettos in the 1960s and 1970s, the message was not lost on black gangsters. They began to push for control over their neighborhoods. They even began to hazard armed skirmishes with Italian mobsters.

Experts began to see the underpinnings of a vast new criminal force taking shape in American ghettos. In the 1970s, many journalists and academics treated it as a given that blacks—and to a lesser extent, Hispanics—would replace the Mafia as the dominant figures in organized crime. Books like Francis Ianni's *The Black Mafia* and Donald Goddard's *Easy Money* argued compellingly that the transformation had already begun, that black and Hispanic gangsters were already handling most of the narcotics distribution and a good share of the policy operations in their own neighborhoods, fast replacing the mafiosi who had controlled both spheres for decades. These observers were only partly correct in assessing the future of black and Hispanic organized crime. They underestimated the tenacity of Italian mobs in holding onto key territories and missed the significance of other ethnic crooks, such as the Chinese. But they were correct in predicting a dramatic new role for minorities in the rackets. For black criminals, the climb up the ladder of organized crime was especially dramatic and often brutal. The flowering of the black underworld in the 1970s represented the first of what would become a series of challenges to the Mafia's criminal monopoly.

The first black gangsters of any significance were policy operators. From small rural communities in the South to big northern ghettos, poor blacks have always been eager players of the illegal numbers game. In the 1920s, blacks in Harlem, Chicago's South Side, and other urban areas operated their own policy wheels, unmolested by Irish, Jewish or Italian gangsters, who were so busy making money bootlegging that they hadn't time to worry about little old ladies and their 10-cent numbers bets. A West Indian woman named Madame Stephanie St. Clair was known as the "Policy Queen" of Harlem during most of Prohibition—a time when, she later recalled, "there were at least 30-odd Negro banks doing a good business" in the neighborhood.[1]

But the mob discovered in the late 1920s that these 10-cent bets added up to a lot of money. Beer baron Dutch Schultz, looking for a new racket after the end of Prohibition, moved in on the Harlem numbers game and began murdering black operators. St. Claire resisted the incursion and found herself being hunted by Schultz's henchmen. On one occasion, she said, "I had to hide in the cellar while the super, a friend of mine, covered me with coal." St. Claire dodged the gunmen and ended up getting the last laugh. She sent a telegram to Schultz's hospital room after he was shot and mortally wounded in 1935. It read, "As ye sow, so shall ye reap."[2]

But black criminals did not regain control over New York's numbers racket after the Dutchman's death. Instead, it fell under the control of Italian mobsters in East Harlem, first Trigger Mike

Coppola and then Anthony (Fat Tony) Salerno, who later became boss of the Genovese family and controlled the uptown lottery racket into the 1970s. Mafia families also took control of policy operations in most other black communities around the country. And as marijuana and heroin became popular in the ghettos, Italians also took care of the dope dealing. Most of the heroin that Italians smuggled into the country from Marseilles and Palermo found its consumers in black and Hispanic neighborhoods.

Italian gangsters had no choice but to rely on black people to help them penetrate the ghetto. Blacks pushed drugs for the Italian dealers and handled the streets for the Italian-run policy banks, acting as numbers runners and controllers, positions that often made them wealthy and influential underworld figures in their own right. Black numbers controllers lived in expensive apartments and drove luxury automobiles. They bought nightclubs and loaned money to businesses. In places like Harlem and Chicago's South Side, the black numbers runner was often the wealthiest man in the neighborhood.

One of these black racketeers was Ellsworth Raymond (Bumpy) Johnson, who is sometimes called the first black gangster and was the model for the Harlem kingpin depicted in the "Shaft" films of the 1970s. From the 1940s to the 1960s, Johnson was the middleman between the Italian mob and a host of black criminals. "Suave, well-spoken, always well-dressed, he was an avid reader and more than competent chess player as well," Francis Ianni wrote. "Fellow prisoners at Dannemora, the New York State penitentiary where Johnson once did time for a drug charge, were accustomed to calling him 'The Professor.' Yet Johnson worked essentially as a middleman for the Italian syndicate. When a black person wanted to buy a franchise to establish a numbers bank, he went to Bumpy Johnson, who arranged it for a fee. When a black drug dealer wanted to buy a large quantity of drugs, Johnson arranged the sale. Italian racketeers knew him as a 'persuader,' one who could settle underworld quarrels before disputes erupted into violence, and violence into the publicity they naturally wanted to avoid."[3]

But this arrangement—the black gangster as vassal of the Italian mob—was not to last. The continuing black migration to northern cities and the movement of Italians and other whites to the suburbs changed the demographics of many inner-city neighborhoods. The civil rights movement and the increasing emphasis on "black power" encouraged black people to take control of commerce in their own neighborhoods, an inducement that was not lost on black racketeers. Black criminals wanted greater control of the underworld, and they began by pushing for control of the numbers. In city after city, black thugs graduated from runners and controllers to independent numbers bankers. Mafia families tried to stem the tide by murdering independent numbers operators, but eventually they accepted the inevitable. Detroit Mafia boss Joseph Zerilli ceded the city's numbers racket to black operators in the 1960s in exchange for a percentage of the proceeds. Buffalo's Mafia family demanded a 10-percent tribute from black operators, but then got none at all. In Newark, the mob suffered an even bigger indignity: blacks temporarily pushed the Genovese family out of the numbers business at gunpoint, robbing and even shooting at the Italian operators.[4] New York's mob was more difficult to dislodge from the numbers, and even in the 1990s has remained deeply involved in the racket. But by 1974, 14 of New York's 60 numbers operations were controlled by blacks.[5]

Black operators had a harder time doing without the Italians in narcotics, since the mob controlled the overseas supply of heroin. But some black dealers became so powerful that it was almost a case of the tail wagging the dog. The most important of the early black heroin kingpins was Frank Matthews. Matthews began his criminal career in the late 1950s in the poorest part of Durham, North Carolina, where as a 14-year-old known as Pee Wee he organized a group of younger boys to steal chickens. When he assaulted a man who caught him robbing his henhouse two years later, Pee Wee did his first stint in prison. But he was hardly rehabilitated. In the mid-1960s, Matthews moved to Bedford-Stuyvesant, Brooklyn's oldest black ghetto, where he found work as a collector-enforcer for a numbers operation.[6]

Matthews' entrance into the world of narcotics came around

1967, when he purchased a kilogram of cocaine from a major Cuban drug dealer named Rolando Gonzalez for $20,000 and turned it into instant profit. Not long after, he began buying heroin from the Mafia's Gambino family, and by 1968 had developed a major cocaine and heroin distribution network. Matthews headquartered the operation at "the Ponderosa," an apartment at 925 Prospect Place in Brooklyn where he paid workers $100 a day to cut, bag and bundle narcotics for street sales. Fortified with steel and concrete and protected by guards with shotguns and automatic weapons, the Ponderosa became the nerve center of a drug operation that eventually covered much of the East Coast. Matthews was a key supplier for black drug dealers in Boston, Philadelphia, Baltimore, Washington, Atlanta, Baton Rouge, Miami, Detroit, Chicago, St. Louis and other cities. By the early 1970s, he had become the first black drug dealer to circumvent the Mafia and import his own heroin. He bought heroin from Corsican gangsters and smuggled it into this country through Caracas, Venezuela, with the help of Rolando Gonzalez, who had relocated to the South American country.[7]

Matthews became a giant in the drug world. At the height of his operation in 1972, he was operating several drug mills in Queens and Brooklyn, some of them employing as many as 50 people on the assembly line. Only 28 years old, he strolled around in ankle-length sable coats, maintained at least five stylish apartments and owned a fleet of luxury cars. He bought a $200,000 mansion on Staten Island's exclusive Todt Hill for his wife and three children. During all this, Matthews thumbed his nose at the Italian mob, once telling a Gambino family soldier, "Touch one of my people and I'll load my men into cars and drive down Mulberry Street and shoot every wop we see."[8] His audacity reached its height in October 1971, when he assembled the 40 biggest black drug dealers from around the country for a business convention in Atlanta. The main topic of discussion was how blacks could break the Mafia's near monopoly on heroin importation.[9] Despite his insolence, the Mafia never moved against him, probably fearing the publicity that would arise from a war

Heroin kingpin Frank Matthews shown outside a Las Vegas court-house in January 1973, six months before he skipped on $325,000 bail and disappeared, reportedly with $20 million. (AP/Wide World)

between black and Italian gangsters. Instead, the mobsters bided their time and waited for Matthews' inevitable downfall.

It didn't take long. On August 30, 1973, Gonzalez and 11 other men were seized in Caracas with more than 26 pounds of cocaine bound for Matthews' operation. Some of the people arrested cooperated with authorities and Matthews was arrested on drug conspiracy charges. But the wily old chicken thief would never come to trial. Free on $325,000 bail, Matthews disappeared with $20 million and has never been seen since.

By the time Matthews' operation was dissolving in Brooklyn, another legendary black heroin kingpin, Leroy (Nicky) Barnes, was reaching the zenith of his power in Harlem. Barnes was more of a Mafia creation than Matthews. He began his career as a pusher for an Italian heroin gang in Harlem and then went on his own in 1964 with the mob's blessing. By 1965, Barnes had 50 people working for him and was selling more heroin in Harlem than his Italian mentors. But since he was buying his heroin from the Lucchese and Bonanno families, no one in the Italian underworld complained.

Barnes' career suffered an early interruption in 1965, when he was arrested with $500,000 worth of heroin and shipped off to Greenhaven prison. There, the 33-year-old hoodlum made an acquaintance that would have an enormous influence on his criminal career. Joseph (Crazy Joe) Gallo, a renegade soldier in the Profaci family—now known as the Colombo family—was doing a 14-year stint in Greenhaven for extortion and immediately took a liking to the Harlem kingpin. The short, fiery, blond-haired gangster was running low on friends in the Italian underworld. His gang in South Brooklyn had staged a bloody rebellion against family boss Joe Profaci, kidnapping several high-ranking members of the family and demanding a bigger share of the rackets. In the ensuing warfare, more than a dozen mobsters were killed and Gallo's life was probably saved only by his conviction and imprisonment. But he was finished in the Mafia. If he were ever again to play a role in the underworld, it would have to be through a new criminal network.

In his long chats with Barnes in prison, Gallo had a brainstorm. The two agreed to organize all of the city's top black gangsters into a well-organized crime family to rival the Mafia. They figured that New York's ghettos, bristling with weapons and hungry young hoodlums, had more than enough muscle to depose the Italians. All they needed was a mastermind like Gallo to school them in the fine art of racketeering, in much the same way that Meyer Lansky had served as an adviser to the early Italian mob. First they would organize New York, and then they would put together a nationwide syndicate of black gangs.[10]

Gallo, who was released from prison in 1971, was so enthusiastic about the plan that he arranged for a lawyer to work on Barnes' appeal, and the drug dealer's 25-year sentence was thrown out. Soon after he was released, Barnes called for a meeting of Harlem's top black racketeers to discuss Gallo's proposal. The meeting was set for a bar at 125th Street and Eighth Avenue. Going into the meeting, Barnes already had the support of two other kingpins, Hollywood Harold Munger and Sonny Woods. But he was not able to convince anyone else. Ten black mob bosses showed up at the meeting; they defeated the idea for a Gallo-sponsored syndicate by a 7–3 vote.[11] It is the closest the nation has ever come to having a true "Black Mafia."

Rebuffed in his plan for a black syndicate, Barnes rededicated himself to the task of becoming the city's leading heroin merchant. Many of his workers had stayed on his payroll while he was in prison, and once he was back in charge the organization grew. Using Mafia families as his model, Barnes organized other black kingpins into a seven-member council that carved up drug-dealing territories around the city. Like Matthews, he also made contacts in other cities, supplying heroin to dealers in Canada, Arizona, Pennsylvania, Chicago and upstate New York. He, too, would have heroin mills with dozens of women lined up at a glass table cutting and bagging the powder. But Barnes' mills had a twist. The women worked naked so they would not be tempted to stick any of the bags in their pockets.[12]

Barnes was ruthless with those employees he suspected of stealing. One of those who may have incurred his wrath was Reginald Isaacs, his chauffeur-bodyguard and one of his most trusted employees. In November 1972, Isaacs was assigned to bring 16 kilos of heroin to the courier for a Detroit drug dealer who had paid $250,000 for the drugs up front. Isaacs returned an hour later and told Barnes that he had been held up at gun-

Leroy (Nicky) Barnes, at right, celebrating his birthday in 1976 at New York's Time-Life Building. He is with Frank James, left, and Ish-mael Mohammed, members of a seven-person council that controlled heroin distribution. (AP/Wide World)

point and relieved of the drugs. According to police investigators, the boss apparently didn't buy the story. On December 3, 1972, police found Isaacs' body stuffed in the trunk of his Lincoln Continental, which was parked off Gun Hill Road in the Bronx. Barnes' intuition about his employee's betrayal was apparently sound. Five days after his body was found, police arrested a man walking out of Isaacs' apartment with 16 kilos of heroin.[13]

Joseph (Craze Joe) Gallo, a renegade Brooklyn mafioso who plotted with Barnes to set up a national black syndicate, testifying before the McClellan committee in 1963. (AP/Wide World)

As Barnes' power and wealth grew, he became a legend in Harlem. The kingpin stood only five feet five, but he had a powerful build and a thick beard that made him look menacing. Chauffeured around in his Mercedes-Benz limousine or his Maserati, Barnes made his rounds in Harlem bedecked in finery from his vast wardrobe: 300 suits, 100 pairs of shoes, 50 leather jackets, 25 hats, all custom tailored and color coordinated.[14]

He was a regular in Harlem nightclubs, including those owned by celebrities such as Wilt Chamberlain and Sugar Ray Robinson. "I spent several nights hopping from nightclub to nightclub with Nicky," recalled Donald (Tony the Greek) Frankos, a Mafia hitman. "He took me to a place he co-owned that . . . featured beautiful Cuban waitresses and a high stakes dice game in the back. Nicky was always 'giving' me girls, and often I accepted."[15]

By his own admission, Barnes made millions in the heroin business. He put his money in gas stations, travel agencies, car washes and an apartment complex in Detroit. He maintained apartments in upper Manhattan, the Riverdale section of the Bronx, and Hackensack and Fort Lee in New Jersey. On the tough streets of Harlem, his flamboyant style and finery made him a folk hero. He would greet neighborhood kids with a broad smile and stuff a $20 bill in their pocket. One Christmas he stood on 126th Street at St. Nicholas Avenue handing out turkeys to the poor, a modern-day Robin Hood whose message to the black poor was unmistakable: crime does indeed pay.

Barnes was even more legendary for his in-your-face attitude toward police. He had been arrested 13 times since 1950, but had beaten so many raps for so long that he became known in Harlem as "Mr. Untouchable." First there was the 25-year sentence thrown out in the early 1970s. Then, in August 1973, police raided his apartment at 100 Haven Avenue in upper Manhattan and found hashish under the carpet, five handguns, a sawed-off shotgun and $50,000 in cash. Barnes was arrested in the basement, but he beat the charges after it was ruled that none of the evidence linking him to the upstairs was admissible. Between 1975 and 1977, he was acquitted of a fatal stabbing in the Bronx and offering a bribe to a police officer, and had charges thrown out in two separate gun-possession cases.[16]

None of this was for lack of trying by the authorities. The Police Department's intelligence division had listed him as a "major narcotics violator" since the mid-1960s and had voluminous files on him, some code-named "Operation Slick." Barnes was frequently followed by investigators and once spent eight months in 1973 under 24-hour surveillance. He knew he was being tailed and played games with investigators, making series of U-turns or driving 100 miles an hour on the West Side Highway. Once, he pulled his car into some tall weeds and then pulled out behind the surveillance team and flashed his lights in their rear-view mirror.[17]

Federal authorities finally caught up with Barnes in March 1977, indicting him, five of his lieutenants and 12 others with selling more than 40 pounds of heroin a month out of the Harlem River Motor Garage at 112 West 145th Street. The indictment, which charged Barnes with ordering a series of murders to keep drug dealers in line, was considered such a major blow against heroin trafficking that President Jimmy Carter sent a letter to the New York DEA chief congratulating him. After a two-month trial, he was convicted and sentenced to life in prison. But Mr. Untouchable still had one more rabbit to pull out of his hat. In 1982, he became a federal informant, working undercover in prison and supplying authorities with enough information for indictments against 44 high-level drug dealers, including several former associates who had taken over his organization. The 50-year-old inmate, looking almost professional with his balding pate and glasses, appeared in court and renounced the evil of drug dealing. "I've made an attempt to re-evaluate myself," Barnes testified, adding that he had decided "my whole life was shallow."[18] His former associates put an $8 million contract on his head, but Barnes managed to stay alive and had his sentence reduced to 35 years. With time off for good behavior, Barnes is due to be released in October 1998. He will be 66 years old.

The 1970s saw black gangs in other cities also modeling themselves after Mafia families and moving in for a piece of the rackets. Garland Jeffers, a 24-year-old black gangster in Gary, Indiana, proclaimed himself "the godfather" of the city's tough Midtown neighborhood in 1971 and recruited more than a dozen other hoodlums into a group he called The Family. Jeffers' henchmen, dressed in wide-brimmed hats and leather jackets, forced pimps and drug dealers to pay protection money, killing anybody who refused. Over a year, The Family was linked to 22 murders, including that of a well-known drug pusher who was found in his gold Cadillac with two bullet holes in his head. "They just got tired of the small stuff," one federal investigator told a reporter in 1972, trying to explain the gang's rise. "They figured they could make more money through protection than ripping off hubcaps."[19]

Another explanation is that Jeffers had seen *The Godfather* too many times and got it into his head that he could be the black Don Corleone. When federal agents began raiding The Family's hideouts, they found logbooks with the group's bylaws, meeting notes and expenses. Among the expense entries was $40 for tickets to *The Godfather*. Gary Mayor Richard Hatcher—himself an African-American—was outraged when he heard about that. "Any black person who goes to see *The Godfather* and doesn't come out with some kind of revulsion is the worst sort of Uncle Tom," he said. "Remember the line, 'Let the niggers have the drugs; they're animals anyhow.' The Family should get one of the international awards for Tomism."[20]

But the image of "the godfather" unfortunately intrigued aspiring black gangsters in other cities as well. Wayne (Akbar) Pray, a young Newark gangster, also called his organization The Family. The organization started in the early 1970s as an offshoot of a Muslim sect in Newark and initially limited its criminal activities to supporting bank robberies. It even operated a bank-robbery school. But before long, Pray was selling drugs, first in Newark and then in other areas of the country, including Ohio, Michigan, New York State and southern Florida. The Family, which has been tied to a slew of murders in the Newark area, is one of the longest-running black crime groups in the country. Pray went to prison in 1989, but his lieutenants were still running the organization in the mid-1990s.[21]

One of the most important of the black crime groups of the 1970s was Philadelphia's Black Mafia, whose violent legacy would haunt the City of Brotherly Love for the next two decades. The Black Mafia was unique among black crime groups in that it participated in a wide variety of racketeering, not just narcotics. By its peak in the mid-1970s, the gang was involved in extortion, auto-theft rings, loan-sharking, illegal lotteries, credit-card fraud, and a wide array of other crimes, all carried out without any interference from Philadelphia's powerful Italian Mafia family.

The group started in September 1968, when a group of thugs who hung around South Philadelphia street corners began robbing crap games and shaking down merchants. They took the name Black Mafia so they would be instantly recognizable when they walked into a store and asked for money. The gang originally had about 11 members, most of whom were graduates of smaller street gangs and already had lengthy police records. Their leader was Eugene (Bo) Baynes, 30, and his right-hand man was Samuel Christian, 29, a bull-necked young gangster who became the gang's most notorious member. Christian's lengthy arrest record dated to at least 1953, when as a 15-year-old he was picked up with three other kids for burglarizing and ransacking a real estate office in South Philadelphia.[22]

From the beginning, the Black Mafia dealt harshly with members who didn't follow the rules. On April 19, 1969, a Black Mafia member named Nathaniel Williams staged the robbery of his own crap game over a barbershop at the corner of 14th and South Streets. Several other members of the gang were in the game when two gunmen burst in and robbed the players. But Williams was conspicuously absent, and word immediately spread on the street that he was behind the robbery. About 90 minutes later, witnesses saw him being led from a nearby bar at gunpoint. His bullet-ridden body was found in an isolated spot near the Naval Base in South Philadelphia.[23]

The Black Mafia extorted money from drug dealers, pimps, storefronts and even black and white numbers bankers, although they carefully avoided the banks controlled by Philadelphia's Mafia family. By the early 1970s, the gang was sending squads into suburban Delaware County to rob and sometimes murder white racketeers who were not connected to the Mafia.

Around 1970, the group moved into the trafficking of heroin and cocaine, expanding out of its stronghold in South Philadelphia and into the black ghettos of West and North Philadelphia. Angelo Bruno, Philadelphia's Mafia boss, had pulled his family out of narcotics in 1957, leaving the field wide open to black pushers. By threatening or murdering other drug dealers, the Black Mafia gained control of about 80 percent of the city's heroin traffic, carving up the ghettos into four territories. Each of the four territories was run by a Black Mafia lieutenant who had autonomy in his region but had to turn over a share of his income to the Black Mafia's coffers.[24]

Among the Black Mafia's associates was a drug dealer named Fat Tyrone Palmer, known on the street as Mr. Millionaire. Only 24 years old, Palmer was a big player in the heroin trade, a middleman between heavyweight Frank Matthews in New York and the drug retailers in Philadelphia. Palmer led a delegation that included Black Mafia members to Matthews' historic Atlanta business conference in October 1971. But not long after that meeting, Palmer began to run afoul of the Black Mafia. It has never become clear exactly what Palmer did to alienate the gang. The dispute is believed to have been linked to Palmer's having ordered the murder in March 1972 of James (P.I.) Smith, a drug dealer who was not able to pay for $240,000 worth of cocaine that he had gotten on consignment. Palmer apparently didn't care that the reason Smith was not able to pay for the drugs was that he himself had been stiffed by Richard (Red Paul) Harris, who had already paid with his life a month earlier. Somehow this sequence of events is believed to have put the Black Mafia at odds with Palmer, either because the gang was angry over the Smith murder or because the gang too was shortchanged in the cocaine deal.

On April 3, 1972, Palmer was on his way home from a trip to Bermuda when he stopped in Atlantic City to see singer Billy Paul's Easter night performance at the glitzy Club Harlem. Paul had just finished his opening number, "Magic Carpet," before a crowd of 600 to 800 people when a big man—believed to be Christian—walked up to a large table near the stage and said he wanted to talk to Palmer privately. Palmer's entourage reached for their guns, but they were too late. Gunfire came from every direction. Palmer and three others at his table were killed. Eleven other people were injured, one of who died 10 days later.[25]

Christian was charged in the killing and fled, appearing a year later on the FBI's 10-Most-Wanted List. But the Black Mafia's reign of terror was hardly over. Around 1971, the gang had become affiliated with Philadelphia's Black Muslim mosque. Christian and some of the other Black Mafia members were involved with the mosque as early as 1967, becoming captains in the Fruit of Islam, the movement's highly disciplined enforcement arm. After the merger in 1971, the Black Mafia used the religious organization as a convenient front for its criminal activities. Their unholy alliance led to a crime that was even more heinous and sensational than the Club Harlem shootings.

On January 18, 1973, eight Black Muslims from Philadelphia burst into the Washington, D.C., home of Hamaas Abdul Khaalis, a renegade Muslim leader who had sent to the sect's ministers across the country a letter labeling national Black Muslim founder Elijah Muhammad a "false prophet." Khaalis was not home at the time of the attack, but several of his followers would pay for his blasphemy. The marauders, armed with sawed-off shotguns and a .38-caliber revolver, bound and shot two adults and a child and drowned four babies in a bathtub. Two other shooting victims survived and gave descriptions that led police to the killers. One of those convicted in the massacre was Black Mafia enforcer Ronald Harvey.[26]

The Black Mafia was still around in the mid-1970s, after most of its original founders were dead or in jail—a durability rare among black crime groups. But it was crippled by a federal crackdown on its leaders in 1974. It was further wounded when Wallace Muhammad, who took over the national Black Muslim leadership after his father died in 1975, cleaned the gangsters out of the Philadelphia mosque as part of his reform efforts. The gang attempted a revival in 1977, when member Clarence (Squeaky) Hayman started firebombing the homes of drug dealers to regain control of the heroin trade. But Hayman was shot to death in July 1978 in a dispute over money, and no one stepped forward to see that the killer paid for Hayman's death.[27] No further evidence was needed that the Black Mafia was a thing of the past.

By the 1980s, talk of a black syndicate fell out of vogue with academics and journalists. It was not that no other gangsters tried to follow Frank Matthews, Nicky Barnes, Wayne Pray and Garland Jeffers in building a black Mafia. Their chances of success just seemed to grow dimmer. As we shall see in a later chapter, succeeding generations of black gangs became less organized and more reckless, engaging in internecine turf wars that hampered their efforts to build a criminal legacy. But an even bigger reason why ethnic succession theorists stopped focusing on blacks is that the face of the inner city was once again in flux. America was in the middle of a tidal wave of immigration that would turn the world of organized crime upside down.

4: The Rainbow

Louie Rossi owns a record shop in New York's Little Italy. It has been at the corner of Mulberry and Grand Streets since the 1920s, the days when the famous Italian community sprawled across Lower Manhattan. E. Rossi & Co., as it was named by his grandfather, made its name selling sheet music for old Italian songs that immigrants could find nowhere else in America. To this day, the sheets for old forgotten songs are stacked neatly behind the counter waiting for an old-timer to come by. But E. Rossi & Co.'s business is not really about music these days. It is about souvenirs. Sweatshirts with the words "Little Italy" emblazoned in red and green are lined up in the front window. There are Little Italy banners and Little Italy key chains. There is even a mock no-parking sign that says, "PARKING FOR ITALIANS ONLY. ALL OTHERS WILL BE TOWED."

Life on Rossi's corner is ostentatiously Italian. Stabile Brothers, a real estate firm, stretches a huge red-and-green banner across Grand Street around Christmas time every year, announcing "Buon Natale"—Italian for "Merry Christmas." The cafés and restaurants lining Mulberry Street—with names like Luna, Fratelli, and Positano—pipe Italian music into the street. For its 100th anniversary in 1992, the famous Ferrara's café on Grand Street even had engraved on the sidewalk several diamond-shaped markers showing an Italian man in a chef's hat.

If the denizens of Mulberry and Grand are not shy about asserting their traditions, it may be because the past is all the neighborhood has left. Little Italy is now little more than a motif for tourists. It runs no more than a block or two from the center of that garishly appealing street corner. Few Italians even live there anymore. Chinatown has moved north like a great tide, spilling over from the south of Canal Street and engulfing the little Italian enclave. Shops that 20 years ago housed Italian butchers now have glistening roast ducks and cuttlefish hanging in the windows. Even Ferrara's now rents its top floors to a Chinese-owned garment factory. The sidewalks outside the Italian cafés may swarm with tourists at night, but by day they are crowded with Chinese rushing to and from their abodes on all sides of the enclave.

Rossi, 83 years old, sat in his shop on a cold day in January 1995 repairing a wooden box with guitar-like strings used for cutting macaroni dough. It's true, he admits, the neighborhood isn't really about macaroni anymore. He believes the true Little Italy died when Mayor Fiorello LaGuardia took the pushcarts off the streets in the 1920s. When asked about the state of the neighborhood 70 years later, Rossi stops work and peers out from under his old black driving cap, the brim pulled close over his eyes. "It used to be the best neighborhood in the city of New York," he says grimly. "But they all moved out. They've gone to Brooklyn, New Jersey, Long Island. If you ask me, 18th Street in Brooklyn is Little Italy now. Over here it's all Chinamen. Italians don't come around here anymore. They're all gone."

Little Italy is caught in the tail winds of a changing America. People like Louie Rossi—America's traditional "ethnics"—have watched the slow ebbing of a world they had known their entire lives, a world where the great urban melting pot was an amalgam of Jews, Irish, Italians, Poles, blacks, Puerto Ricans and Mexicans, groups that may never have coexisted comfortably—often not even peaceably—but nonetheless had grown accustomed to each other's ways. The world slowly emerging on the streets of American cities today is far less recognizable. It is a collision of languages, cultures, customs, races and religions unlike anything the nation has seen since the turn of the century. The melting pot is once again fully molten, and it will stay red-hot for at least a generation, before it forms into something resembling a cohesive national identity, a new American persona that promises to be fresh and exciting but can hardly be divined in advance. In the meantime, Louie Rossi won't be the only one feeling a little nonplussed when he looks out his front window. All Americans, new and old, rich and poor, urban and rural, black and white, Asian and Occidental, are awash in the tides of mass immigration and not entirely sure what they will find when the waters recede.

In the last two decades, the changes in American demographics have been astounding. America is closing out the century in much the way we began it—with a vast influx of people from the poorer regions of the world. What we are seeing today is even more dramatic, even more tumultuous than the tidal wave of immigration that transformed U.S. cities a hundred years ago. The 1990 census counted 19.7 million foreign-born people in the United States, the largest number in U.S. history. And these are not the Europeans who made up the majority of immigrants up until the late 1950s. The "huddled masses" of the 1990s are Chinese, Cambodians, Salvadorans, Filipinos, Hmong, Asian Indians, Jamaicans, Brazilians, Mexicans, Nigerians, Russian Jews, and others. One in four Americans was found by the census to be of African, Asian or Hispanic ancestry, a profound shift from the 10 percent of Americans who claimed such ancestry in 1970. The number of Asians in the United States doubled between 1980 and 1990 to 7.3 million; the Hispanic population jumped by 56 percent to 22.3 million (not including the vast numbers of illegal aliens who evaded census takers), so that Hispanics now make up at least 20 percent of the population in all of the nation's 10 largest cities except Detroit. As recently as 1970, no top-10 city except Los Angeles could claim anywhere near a fifth of its population as Hispanic. With an average 600,000 immigrants establishing residency in the United States every year, this seismic shift in our demographics is far from over.

We can hardly foresee what contributions these immigrants and their progeny will make to American society, but we know they will be significant. It is hard to imagine an America without the impact of the Irish, Jews and Italians who dominated previous waves of immigration. Jews built Hollywood and made enormous contributions to commerce, law, government, and medicine; the Irish gave us the first great spread of American Catholicism; the Italian influence on the arts, literature, entertainment, cuisine and other elements of our culture has been equally profound. Though there have been blacks in America for centuries, their emancipation in the 19th century and their migration to northern cities before World War II placed an indelible stamp on American culture, especially on popular music, entertainment, fashion and athletics. And these contributions are just the tangibles. It is far more difficult to assess the even greater impact that this synergy of Irish, Jewish, Italian and black culture has had on the American personality: its manners, its humor, its sense of honor, its mating rituals—yes, even its villainy. The new mix of peoples planting their seeds in American soil in the 1990s will not disappoint us—their cultural hybrid will be just as rich and layered as the old.

To see this synergy taking shape, one only need look at the nation's biggest cities and their suburbs. New York is hardly the same place it was 25 years ago. With more than a quarter of its population foreign born (a figure that does not include the city's 950,000 Puerto Ricans), New York's landscape has become a patchwork of ethnic enclaves. Chinatown was once just a few blocks surrounding Pell and Doyers Streets, but it has slowly crept across lower Manhattan, engulfing Little Italy and the Jewish Lower East Side and even nipping at adjacent Soho and Tribeca. At the same time, bustling Chinese neighborhoods have emerged in Brooklyn and Queens. Flushing, Queens, is home to a Chinese community bigger than the Chinatowns of Boston and Chicago put together. A neighborhood of sturdy brick apartment buildings in the shadow of the Long Island Rail Road, downtown Flushing was for many years a bastion of the Jewish, Irish and Italian working class. A local civic group still strings gay "Merry Christmas" signs and plastic wreaths across Main Street around the holidays. But they look out of place amid the Chinese produce stands, dumpling houses and jade stores that give the neighborhood the look of central Hong Kong or Taipei.

Queens may be the most ethnically heterogeneous place on earth. A study by the New York City Planning Department found that the Elmhurst section alone absorbed 17,200 immigrants from 118 countries between 1983 and 1989.[1] Roosevelt Avenue snakes through several miles of Queens under the No. 7 elevated subway tracks, but it might as well be traversing the continents of the world, so diverse are the communities that it visits along the way. In Jackson Heights and Woodside, all these ethnic worlds seem to run together, giving the street's shops and restaurants the aspect of an international bazaar. Though this area is far off the beaten track for tourists, here a visitor can find the cuisine of Colombia, Ecuador, Uruguay, Argentina, Thailand, South Korea, Ireland, Italy, Hong Kong, Taiwan, the Dominican Republic, Mexico, El Salvador and a dozen other nations in the space of two miles.

New York has two neighborhoods that bear the name "Little Korea." One is cheek-by-jowl with Flushing's Chinatown, so close that the non-Asian visitor is jarred when the characters on the latticework of vertical signs suddenly shift from Chinese to Korean. The other Little Korea is in the lower part of Midtown Manhattan, where Koreans and Asian Indians control a wholesale jewelry, cosmetic and apparel district that supplies retailers around the country.

The five dozen blocks north of 150th Street in Manhattan may well be called Little Santo Domingo. The beat of *merengue* pounds through its streets and Caribbean culture spills onto the sidewalks. Tropical vegetables like *yuca* and *platano* (green bananas) are stacked several feet high in front of *bodegas*. The cluck of live chickens emanates from the meat and poultry shops along such thoroughfares as 181st Street, Broadway and St. Nicholas Avenue. Through the 1960s, Puerto Ricans made up the vast majority of the city's Hispanic population, but now they comprise only a little more than half. Dominicans are the fastest-growing immigrant group in the city, now numbering several hundred thousand. The 1990 census counted 332,000 Dominicans, but no one believes that to be an accurate number. Many Dominicans have come to this country with forged Puerto Rican birth certificates and are likely to have claimed ancestry from that island, not their own, if cornered by a census taker.

South of 150th Street, Harlem has been forever transformed by the influx of immigrants from Jamaica and Trinidad in the Caribbean and from any number of African countries. Indeed, one in four of New York's black residents is now foreign born, with 391,000 of them claiming ancestry from the West Indies. The presence of these Africans and West Indians is most apparent in the flocks of peddlers who sell jewelry, clothing, oils, incense and other trinkets on Manhattan streets. They became so dense on 125th Street in the fall of 1994—up to 1,000 of them gathering on peak shopping days—that Mayor Rudolph Giuliani ordered them removed from the street, prompting understandable cries of racism from Harlem leaders, who argued that no such action had been taken against similar unlicensed peddlers in Chinatown and other ethnic enclaves.

The ethnic mosaic unfurls like a great banner across the city and its suburbs. The new face of the metropolis is Liberian immigrants slaughtering deer in the hallway of a Staten Island housing project. It is the great pots of *borscht* boiling in the kitchens of Russian restaurants in Brighton Beach, Brooklyn, a neighborhood so packed with Jewish emigrés that it is known as Little Odessa by the Sea. It is a crowd of 200 Colombian men cheering a volleyball game in a schoolyard in Jackson Heights, Queens. It is the newly arrived Polish of Greenpoint, Brooklyn; the Greeks of Astoria, Queens; the Albanians of Belmont in the Bronx. Across the river from Manhattan in Hudson County, New Jersey, tens of thousands of Cubans who have made the area home since the 1960s have recently begun sharing their communities with an influx of Colombians, Ecuadoreans, Brazilians and others. Newark's Ironbound section is home to the Portugese, and Jersey City has absorbed thousands of Asian Indians.

Fort Lee, New Jersey, a quiet community of 32,000 people just across the George Washington Bridge from Manhattan, has perhaps the most startling ethnic mix of any New York suburb. Once dominated by Irish and Germans, Fort Lee attracted upwardly mobile Italians after World War II and then absorbed an influx of affluent Jews when luxury high-rises began popping up in the 1960s. Then came a new wave in the 1980s—a flood of Japanese and Koreans and a lesser sprinkling of Eastern Europeans, Arabs and Hispanics. Fort Lee has become a paradigm of a new American phenomenon—the suburban melting pot. Some immigrants, Koreans among them, have enjoyed so much economic success in this country that they often claw their way out of the city in the first generation. Suburbs for the first time are experiencing the kind of rapid ethnic transformation and accompanying stress that traditionally have affected inner-city neighborhoods. While there is little overt racial or ethnic tension in Fort Lee, neither is there much mixing among the groups. Each seems to have found a separate niche: Italians and Irish control the Police Department and other municipal jobs; Koreans and Chinese run most of the shops on Main Street; and Jews predominate among teachers and school administrators. The community's new diversity is reflected most strikingly in its elementary schools, where bilingual courses are offered in nearly a dozen languages and each classroom looks like a student United Nations. On the first day of school in 1994, the local PTA introduced ethnic liaisons for parents who didn't speak English. There were liaisons for speakers of Spanish, Arabic, Korean and Japanese, and separate liaisons for two Chinese dialects, Mandarin and Cantonese.

Immigrants have injected new energy and entrepreneurial vigor into New York City. Perhaps most importantly, immigration is given credit for reversing its long population decline. New York's population plummeted from 7,895,000 to 7,071,000 between 1970 and 1980 as the middle class headed for the suburbs and people left the Northeast to look for jobs in the Sun Belt. But between 1980 and 1990, the city's population rebounded to 7,312,000, largely because of immigration. Many neighborhoods given up for dead have been turned around by the entrepreneurship of hungry immigrants. Dominicans have taken stretches of upper Manhattan, the South Bronx and Brooklyn that were pockmarked by boarded-up stores and turned them into prosperous commercial districts. Koreans have opened thousands of produce stores and nail salons in every corner of the city and taken control of the wholesale beauty-supply business. Chinese own thousands of restaurants and control the downtown garment industry. Asian Indians run most of the city's newsstands, and Arabs have opened hundreds of minimarkets. The foreign-language press thrives in New York, with scores of newspapers serving ethnic communities, from *El Diario-La Prensa* in upper Manhattan to the *Novoye Russkoye Slovo* (New Russian Word) in Brighton Beach, Brooklyn.

Ethnic change is not limited to New York City. Every region of the country is being touched in some way by immigration. In the 1960s, Little Havana used to be a Miami neighborhood sur-rounding the intersection of Flagler and 8th Streets. Now that term can just as easily be applied to the entire city. Cubans now make up close to 40 percent of Miami's population, and people from other Latin American countries make up an additional 20 percent. One can spend an entire day in Miami—including a trip downtown, a stop at a government building, a visit to a major tourist attraction—and never hear a word of English. The popu-lations of major Texas cities like El Paso, Corpus Christi, and San Antonio are more than half Mexican-American. Between 1980 and 1990, Chicago's Asian population nearly doubled to more than 100,000 and its Hispanic population increased by more than 100,000 to well over half a million—all this while its *total* population dropped by more than 200,000. East Dearborn, Michigan, has so many Arabs that one can walk the early-morn-ing streets and hear the call to prayer emanating from its mosques. Even tiny Garden City, Kansas, surrounded by wheat-fields and more than 1,500 miles from either ocean, has seen an influx of immigrants. This little town has within its borders a tor-tilla factory, a Vietnamese-run karaoke bar, a Laotian market that sells Thai videos, and a Vietnamese restaurant.

And then there's California. As dazzling as the ethnic mosaic is in New York City, it is even more spectacular in California. In the last decades of the 1900s, California has taken over the role that New York played at the turn of the century—that of the Promised Land for the world's hungry. It is now the freeways of

Los Angeles, not the cobblestone streets of New York, that peasant lore describes as being "paved with gold." Of the more than 9 million immigrants who were admitted to the United States between 1989 and 1993, roughly a third settled in California—more than in New York, Texas, Florida and Illinois combined. These newcomers, mostly Mexicans, Central Americans and Asians, have redrawn the ethnic map of the state, especially in the Los Angeles area. Greater Los Angeles now has a Little Saigon in Westminster, a Little Phnom Penh in Long Beach, a Koreatown and Little Tokyo in central L.A., and a new suburban Chinatown in Monterey Park. It has Russians in Hollywood, Armenians in Glendale, Iranians on L.A.'s West Side, and sprawling Mexican barrios from East Los Angeles to East Compton.

America's future beckons from places like the western San Gabriel Valley, a monotonous sprawl of suburban communities east of Los Angeles. In 1970, the western Valley was an emblem of middle-class America, where whites made up 78 percent of the population and the only "foreigners" were Mexican-Americans, who often lived in dingy, isolated neighborhoods. But an explosion of Asian immigration over the last two decades has transformed the region. The white population of the area has dipped to less than a third, while the proportion of Asians has climbed from almost none to more than 30 percent. Asians have profoundly affected the tenor of life in the Valley. Energetic Asian entrepreneurs have pumped life into listless commercial districts in Monterey Park, Alhambra, and other cities. Many of the Valley's schools now send home announcements to parents not only in English but also in Vietnamese and Mandarin. The influx of Asians has affected life in ways one might not expect. An Alhambra city planner told of his surprise in the late 1980s when he found that many developers consulted the compass of a *fung shui* master—a practitioner who finds auspicious locations—before choosing the layout of a building. In Chinese tradition, storefronts that face north or south are thought to be more prosperous. The planner came up against one Chinese restaurant owner who was furious that the city planned to close off a street next to his business. "He said the location of his front door, the cash register, and the main dining room were all decided by the compass of the *fung shui* man," the planner recalled. "He said closing off the one street would be analogous to cutting off one of the heads of a five-headed dragon."[2]

The Asian influx in Monterey Park, a city of 60,000 people five miles east of Los Angeles, was especially dramatic. Monterey Park is now nearly half Asian, and its downtown is studded with so many Chinese banks, restaurants, gift shops, groceries and other businesses that it could pass for a street in Taipei. In the space of a decade, longtime residents watched their community become the nation's first suburban Chinatown—and not everyone liked it. A 1985 survey of 263 Monterey Park residents found extreme racial tensions. Anglos and Latinos expressed anti-Asian sentiments while Chinese talked of ethnic prejudice in the schools and elsewhere. The City Council in 1987 further heightened tensions by passing a resolution proclaiming English the nation's official language. It also banned the raising of the Taiwanese flag over City Hall on Taiwan's National Day. Much of the transformation of the city began when a Taiwanese developer, Frederick Hsieh, began buying up land in 1977 and proclaimed the beginnings of a new Chinatown. He even had the temerity to set out his vision before 20 of Monterey Park's most prominent civic and business leaders. "Everyone in the room thought he was blowing smoke," said Harold Fiebelkorn, then a member of the city Planning Commission. "Then when I got home I thought, 'What gall!' He was going to come into my living room and change around my furniture?"[3]

Such anti-immigrant sentiment has long been exploited by California's political demagogues, who warn that the state cannot afford to feed, clothe, and educate the world's poor. They managed to make immigration the dominant issue in the 1994 elections. By a comfortable margin, voters approved the now famous Proposition 187, which was intended to deny any government assistance to illegal aliens, even to the point of excluding 300,000 children from the public schools. As of this writing, the law has been held up in federal court and is considered unlikely to ever be fully implemented. But its passage alone was evidence of the dramatic impact that immigration is having on American society.

Such a massive demographic shift cannot help but also bring sweeping change to American organized crime. As we have already seen, mass immigration has long been a precursor of upheavals in the criminal underworld. Neighborhoods where the immigrant poor struggle with poverty, overcrowded housing and juvenile delinquency turn a small but constant percentage of their citizens into gangsters. It stands to reason, then, that ethnic groups that migrate out of the inner city should also begin to lose control of organized crime. It was true of the Irish and the Jews and is also proving to be true for the Italians.

Italian-Americans have maintained a steady climb up the social ladder. Many families among the second generation of Italians had made their way out of the most crowded inner-city neighborhoods by the 1940s and 1950s, buying homes in working-class sections of New York, Chicago, Detroit, Philadelphia and other cities. In the early postwar years they were still to be found overwhelmingly in the blue-collar trades; Italian names were not commonly found on the shingles of law firms or doctor's offices. But even those last barriers to the upward mobility of Italians have fallen in recent decades. Italians are no longer consigned to manning a jackhammer or swinging a policeman's baton. They are just as likely to be found in the corporate board room, in the law office or on the floor of the stock exchange. Lee Iacocca, Mario Cuomo, Rudolph Giuliani, and Antonin Scalia are only a few of the Italian-Americans who have reached the highest levels of political power and economic might in this country.

As more and more Italians join the professional classes, they are abandoning the Little Italys of America—weakening the urban subculture that gave rise to *La Cosa Nostra*. The Italian enclave in East Harlem—the neighborhood that gave New York one of its most beloved mayors, Fiorello LaGuardia, and also yielded such feared mobsters as Ciro Terranova, Joseph Valachi, Fat Tony Salerno and John Gotti—has all but vanished. It was crowded on all sides and then engulfed by Spanish Harlem. Many of East Harlem's Italians moved on to quieter lives in the central Bronx, where thriving Italian communities then existed in a number of locations. But those enclaves are also a thing of the past. The

Italian presence in the central Bronx has been reduced to a tiny neighborhood surrounding Arthur Avenue in the Belmont section. This is a pristine little community where the sidewalks are clean enough to eat off, but one gets the sense there of a culture slipping away. New York's Italians have ceded their traditional neighborhoods to other ethnic groups. Those that have remained in the city have withdrawn to residential neighborhoods in Queens, Staten Island and southern Brooklyn, far from the core of the city. And for many, these neighborhoods are just a stepping-stone to the suburbs.

Italian-Americans today are even less of a presence in other big cities. Boston's North End, a fabled Italian neighborhood, was too quaint for its own good. Young professionals of all ethnic groups invaded the neighborhood in the 1980s, "gentrifying" it and diluting what was the city's last Italian stronghold. Detroit no longer has an Italian neighborhood in the inner city; most of its residents or their offspring have settled in the Macomb County suburbs. Gone are the Little Italys of Milwaukee, Kansas City, Cleveland and Buffalo, all cities that have traditionally had strong Mafia families.

As Italians have become suburbanites, so has the Mafia become an increasingly suburban phenomenon. Detroit's Mafia is now largely headquartered in Macomb County and other suburban areas. A huge Mafia gambling operation that Michigan authorities shut down in 1992 was based neither in some Detroit warehouse nor in the city's Eastern Market, a meat and produce district that was once a nerve center for Italian sports-betting operations. These gangsters were operating at the Wolverine Golf Club in Macomb Township, a rural community 25 miles from downtown Detroit. In Chicago, one of the biggest mob prosecutions in recent years was the arrest of Albert Tocco, whom the press called the suburban crime boss. His terrain covered Chicago's southern suburbs, reaching all the way to northern Indiana. Much of the Philadelphia Mafia has moved from the City of Brotherly Love to southern New Jersey, where many of the city's top mafiosi have their homes.

New York's five Mafia families still have plenty of interests in the inner city. But their headquarters are increasingly in residential sections of southern Brooklyn, Staten Island or eastern Queens. John Gotti's headquarters were at the Bergin Hunt and Fish Club in Ozone Park, Queens, a quiet residential neighborhood far from the teeming streets of East Harlem and East New York in Brooklyn, where he had learned the art of murder and racketeering. Northern New Jersey's mobsters are no longer heavily concentrated in Newark, Paterson and other cities that were once their prime turf. They are now in small towns like Garfield and South Hackensack, where local police and municipal officials have been willing to turn their heads if the local taverns are hosting sports betting or card games.[4]

The Mafia's withdrawal from the inner cities is the first phase of Italians' withdrawal from the control of organized crime. Like any criminal enterprise, the Mafia has relied on street toughs to survive. It has counted on hungry young criminals ready to kill and maim for their bosses. Henry Hill, the mobster turned informant who told his story in the book *Wiseguy*, wrote that what few people understand is that the Mafia is really just a system of protection.[5] Top Mafia figures make the lion's share of their money by collecting tribute from an assortment of criminal franchises. For the cost of that tribute, independent crooks get assurance that other criminal predators will stay away from their business rather than risk a clash with the Mafia. It is a system based on fear. And the Italian hoodlums who inspire that fear have traditionally grown up on the streets. Many ran with street gangs as teenagers. They learned to handle a gun or a knife long before they were inducted into a Mafia family. It's not the kind of education one gets in Macomb County, Michigan, or Garfield, New Jersey.

Nor is an Italian kid living out the middle-class dream going to be inspired to embark on a life of crime. Mafia informers who tell their stories to journalists invariably describe their introduction to the mob as a natural extension of life in their tough neighborhoods. Hill fell in with Lucchese family *capo* Paul Vario as a teenager hanging around the cab stand Vario owned in East New York. These kinds of experiences are not easily available to Italian-American youths growing up in the 1990s, especially if they happen to live out on Long Island or in suburban New Jersey. Joseph Pistone, an FBI agent who spent years undercover in the Mafia, said he discovered that the Italian criminal subculture that sustained the Mafia, while hardly extinct, was growing more feeble over time. "With each generation, the Mafia subculture moves closer to mainstream America," he told a congressional subcommittee in 1988. "The old-timers are aging and slowly dying off. They are being replaced by younger wiseguys, 25 to 35 years of age, who do not possess the same strong family values."[6]

But as that criminal subculture wanes in the Italian community, it is growing in black, Hispanic and Asian communities. The decline of the Italians' organized-crime dynasty is leaving a vacuum that is being filled by new ethnic gangsters. In the city neighborhoods that are producing the toughest young gangsters, the Mafia is increasingly irrelevant. Italian mobsters are no longer a source of fear and admiration. They no longer have all the guns, all the money, all the sources of supply for drugs, and all the connections to corrupt public officials. New immigrant gangsters are gaining these tools for themselves. The new ethnic map of America's cities is quickly putting them at the helm of organized crime, at least in their own neighborhoods.

Italians are still major players in organized crime, but they don't own the streets. The world of organized crime is now as diverse and multicultural as the face of the inner city. It is not hard to find examples of the ways the underworld has changed. All one has to do is to pick up a newspaper to read about a Jamaican drug murder, a raid on a Chinese gambling house, a seizure of a Colombian cocaine shipment, or the arrest of a Cuban numbers kingpin. Non-Italian organized crime can be as close as the neighborhood *bodega* or your favorite Russian restaurant, but it remains something of an enigma for the American public. What follows is a look at the dominant new ethnic crime groups in America. It is a story that transcends the boundaries of any one region of the country and even the borders of the United States. But it is unfolding most dramatically in a teeming New York City neighborhood known as Chinatown.

5: A Myriad of Swords

The death of Benny Ong in August 1994 was a cause for public mourning in New York's Chinatown. People of all ages stood silently on the sidewalks as his 120-car funeral procession snaked through the neighborhood's narrow streets. A huge photograph of his smiling and grandfatherly face, framed in white carnations and red roses, rested on a mound of flowers in an open-back limousine. Men and women looked somberly out of tenement windows as the procession slowed and halted in front of Ong's favorite places in Chinatown. One woman lined the ledge of her second-floor window with flowerpots marked with the words, "Big Bucks, Benny Ong," in keeping with the Chinese tradition of wishing the dead prosperity in the afterlife.

Uncle Seven, as he was known by most people in Chinatown, was an old man of 87 when he died of prostate cancer. He walked with a cane and had been in and out of Beekman Downtown Hospital. But he had lost none of his grit. When the *Daily News* checked out a false rumor a few months earlier that he had died, he shot back through his lawyer, "What son of a bitch say I'm dead?"[1] Ong could afford to be blunt. As "adviser for life" to the Hip Sing—a powerful *tong*, or fraternal association—he was long considered one of Chinatown's most important elders. With a nod of his head, he could give permission for the opening of a restaurant on Pell or Doyers Streets or settle a dispute between

Benny Ong, the "godfather" of New York's Chinatown before his death in August 1994. (New York Daily News)

two businessmen. If a new immigrant was looking for a job or needed a business loan, he would seek an audience with Uncle Seven in the Hong Shoon, the Pell Street restaurant where the old man held court every day at lunchtime. Ong was given a place of honor at community banquets and frequently appeared on the front pages of New York's Chinese newspapers gripping the hands of other important businessmen.

To what did Ong owe this enormous influence? Anyone watching the funeral procession could see that he was no ordinary civic leader. One clue might have been the plainclothes police who mixed with mourners outside the Wah Wing Sang Funeral Home on Mulberry Street. Or the uniformed cops who were posted on Chinatown street corners for days afterward, ensuring that there would be no violent effort to fill the power vacuum left by Ong's death. For Uncle Seven was not just a pudgy, bespectacled old man who shook people's hands at banquets. In 1991, a

Ong's funeral procession on Mulberry Street in Chinatown.
(AP/Wide World)

Senate subcommittee told the rest of the world what everyone on Pell Street had known for years—that Benny Ong was the "godfather" of organized crime in Chinatown.[2]

Even in his waning years, Ong took a cut of every last dollar that flowed from gambling, loan-sharking and extortion in the Hip Sing's territory, which covered scores of restaurants and other businesses on Pell and Doyers Streets and the Bowery. For all the favors and charity he might have bestowed on others over the years, Ong's real claim to influence was his control over the

Flying Dragons, a vicious street gang that has been affiliated with the Hip Sing since the early 1970s. The Dragons guarded the Hip Sing's gambling dens on Pell Street and exacted protection payments from businesses in the *tong*'s territory—only sparing those with close ties to Uncle Seven. Many people in Chinatown may have had real affection for Ong, but others gave him respect because it was simply healthier to do so. If anyone dared to question his power, they did so at the risk of getting a visit from the Dragons.

Herbert Liu learned that lesson the hard way. Liu was a former Hip Sing member who left the *tong* in the early 1980s and founded his own association on East Broadway. He designated it as a chapter of another *tong*, the Chinese Freemasons, and opened a gambling house. To add final insult, he recruited former members of the Flying Dragons to protect the gambling. It was an open challenge to Ong's authority—and one that would not go unanswered. On December 23, 1982, several members of the Freemasons gang and their allies in the White Tigers gang were drinking sodas in the Golden Star bar on East Broadway when several masked gunmen stepped into the doorway. The assailants opened fire, killing three gang members and wounding eight others. Ong was never officially tied to the killings, but his later statements to *New York* magazine were revealing. "Sixty year I build up respect," Ong said, "and he think he knock me down in one day?"[3]

In the new world of organized crime, no ethnic gangsters have a bigger future than the Chinese. While they may not yet approach the power of the Mafia in its heyday, Chinese crime groups are rapidly gaining power in cities around the country. In San Francisco, they are recognized by the FBI as the dominant organized crime group. They are second only to the Mafia in New York. Whereas Chinese criminals were once known for penny-ante restaurant shakedowns and a little harmless gambling, they now form an international crime syndicate that moves heroin and illegal aliens across continents and lords over sophisticated white-collar swindles that are the envy even of the Mafia.

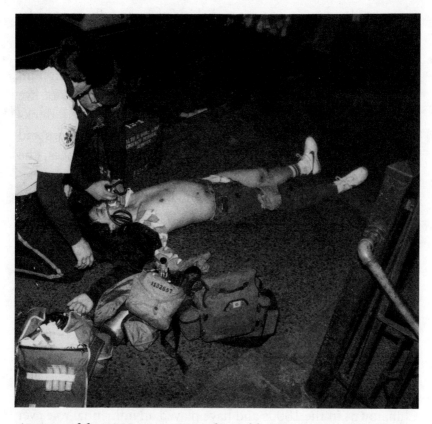

A victim of the 1982 massacre at the Golden Star restaurant in New York's Chinatown. (AP/Wide World)

But perhaps the most startling thing about Chinese gangsters is how deeply woven they are into the fabric of their own community. Benny Ong personified the duality of life in most American Chinatowns, the invisible line between the legitimate and the illegitimate, the chasm between what the tourist sees on the wondrous streets and what goes on just behind the storefronts. It is an open secret that many of the *tong* leaders who make up the legitimate power structure of most Chinatowns—who portray themselves as the leading lights of the community—are also the sponsors of the local gambling halls and whorehouses. Those very civic leaders who shake hands with the mayor or the governor one day are often ordering the murder of a rival the next. With its leaders on the take, the community is conditioned not to report the crimes that go on behind the carefully erected facades of most Chinatowns. Indeed, nothing seems threatening or amiss in the images that make New York's Chinatown such a tourist attraction: the old women playing mah-jongg in Columbus Park, the outdoor seafood stands with their buckets of live bullfrogs, turtles, and crabs; the glistening barbecued ducks hanging in the front windows of groceries, and the pig faces and dried cuttlefish stacked on their counters; the lion dances; the fireworks peddlers; the *dim sum*, the jewelry shops, the cheap souvenirs. But there is a second Chinatown that tourists rarely see. This is a place of secret societies and ancient feuds, where teenage gangsters kill each other over a few squares of sidewalk, where kidnapped illegal aliens are held captive in basement dungeons, where women are enslaved as prostitutes, where men bet tens of thousands of dollars in somber, smoke-filled gambling dens, and where merchants pay protection money just to stay in business. Blame for these hidden horrors must be laid at the doorstep of the *tongs*, the business elite of Chinatown.

Tongs like the Hop Sing and Suey Sing in San Francisco and the Hip Sing and On Leong in New York helped found American Chinatowns in the 1800s and have played an influential role ever since. They control the Chinese-language press and sway votes on the quasi-public bodies that govern America's two largest Chinatowns: the Chinese Consolidated Benevolent Association in New York and the Six Companies in San Francisco. Historically, *tongs* have done a lot of good in American Chinatowns. They dole out credit to merchants, find jobs for new immigrants and mediate business disputes. If the average *tong* leader's only crime were the operation of gambling casinos, he would be no bigger a villain than New York real-estate mogul Donald Trump.

But the *tong*'s crimes have not stopped there. *Tongs* fostered the growth of street gangs in the 1960s, using them to protect gambling dens, and they have retained these alliances ever since. *Tong* leaders not only turn their heads when gangs commit robberies and shake down businesses; they have worked behind the scenes in some of the bloodiest gang wars. When the Ghost Shadows gang went to war with the White Eagles to take control of New York's Mott Street in the mid-1970s, prosecutors say the On Leong *tong* supplied the Shadows with guns.[4]

Tong leaders use the gangs as muscle in their criminal ventures and as a way to maintain influence in the business community. As long as a gang is on the payroll, no one questions the *tongs'* right to control who opens businesses on their turf. In exchange, the *tongs* give the gangs legitimacy and financial backing. They supply lawyers when gang members are arrested, or whisk them out of town when they are hunted by police. In many cases, gang members are inducted into the *tongs*. Kenneth Chu, a former Ghost Shadow in New York, told a congressional subcommittee that he was inducted into the gang and the *tong* almost simultaneously in 1974. When he shot a rival member of the now-defunct Black Eagles gang on Mott Street in March 1975, the On Leong put him on a bus to Boston, where the *tong's* national president took him under his wing. He was paid $90 a week "long pay" for having done his duty in the shooting. Eventually, he ended up as a ranking member of the On Leong in Houston, where he claimed the *tong* was raking in $1 million a year in gambling parlors.[5]

These alliances are found in cities across the country. In San Francisco and Portland, the Hop Sing *tong* is linked to gangs. The Chee Kung *tong*, another name for the Chinese Freemasons, sponsored a gang in Boston known as the Ping On, which controlled the city's Chinese rackets throughout the 1980s. In New York, the bonds between *tongs* and gangs run especially deep. Each of Chinatown's four major gangs is paired with a *tong*. Together, they hold down territories that have changed little since the 1970s. The Ghost Shadows gang and the On Leong *tong* control the heart of Chinatown—Mott, Bayard and Mulberry Streets. The Hip Sing *tong* and the Flying Dragons control Pell and Doyers Streets and the Bowery. The Tung On *tong* and the Tung On gang control East Broadway and Division and Catherine Streets, east of the main tourist section. Still further east, in the newest and least prosperous section of Chinatown, is the territory of the Fukien American Association and the Fuk Ching gang, whose strongholds are Eldridge Street and a portion of East Broadway.

Because of their power in New York, the Hip Sing and the On Leong also sponsor gangs in numerous other cities around the country, including Boston, Philadelphia, Chicago and Dallas.

Not all *tong* leaders are as notorious as Ong. Some are actually able to pass themselves off as legitimate businessmen. Paul Lai, president of a *tong* called the Tsung Tsin Association, posed as a legitimate restaurateur and civic booster. Former New York Governor Mario Cuomo appointed him to a 10-member state panel on Asian affairs. "He's a generous man and has donated much time and money to the community," said John Tung, president of Chinatown's Sino-American Chamber of Commerce.[6] But police knew Lai as something else. He was indicted in December 1993 as one of the *dai lo dais*, or biggest brothers, of the Tung On gang and charged with operating gambling dens and ordering the murders of rival gang members.

By sponsoring gangs, the *tongs* have unleashed a plague on American Chinatowns. In three decades, Chinese gangs in New York, San Francisco, Chicago, Boston, Los Angeles, and many other cities have gone from two-bit shakedown operations to sophisticated criminal enterprises. When the gangs emerged in the mid-1960s, they protected gambling dens and extorted money from Chinese merchants. But their tentacles have since reached into a vast array of other criminal schemes: heroin smuggling, loan-sharking, bookmaking, counterfeit credit cards, money laundering, illegal gambling, smuggling of illegal aliens, and food stamp fraud. In some cases, the strength and sophistication of Chinese gangs now rivals that of the *tongs*. One of the gangs' most frightening innovations is home-invasion robberies. Gang members follow Asian businessmen to their homes and force their way in with guns, often torturing or raping family members if they fail to turn over cash and valuables.

In the last two decades, Asian gangs have engaged in brutal wars for control over their territories in New York, San Francisco, Boston, Toronto and other cities. Many of the killings in New York are not even mentioned in the press or are dealt with in small, back-page articles, even when an important gang leader is slain. But some of the killings have been horrendous enough to become national news, such as the Golden Dragon massacre in San Francisco and the Golden Star shootings in New York. In 1982, 13 patrons of a gambling den in Seattle's Chinatown were shot to death by robbers. More recently, five men were shot to death on January 12, 1991, in a social club in Boston's Chinatown, part of an ongoing struggle for control of that city's Asian rackets.[7]

The gang culture in American Chinatowns has spawned a Fagin-like figure known as the *dai lo*, a Cantonese term meaning "big brother." The *dai lo* is the street boss of the gang. He is an insidious character who recruits teenagers by alternating threats and beatings with promises of wealth and a life filled with adventure. Sometimes the *dai lo* stages an incident in which he appears to be rescuing an innocent teenager from a gang beating, earning the victim's gratitude and admiration. This is followed by gifts and exposure to attractive women and the promise that no one will ever dare to bother the victim again if he joins the gang. He will have instant respect on the streets. In some gang subcultures, the gang leader is merely the most violent and charismatic of the group. In Chinese gangs, the equation is more complicated. The *dai lo* must have the business skills to generate enough money to take care of his followers. He must be able to feed and clothe them and provide a safehouse for them to live in times of warfare. In some cities, he must also have the political skills to win the backing of a *tong* to lead the gang.

Sonny Chan was one gangster who put all the pieces together. In the early 1990s, he was recognized as the *dai lo* of Grand Street in New York's Chinatown. He walked along the block like he owned it—and in a sense he did. Even though he was only a young man in his 20s, he was treated like a neighborhood elder. Most of the restaurants paid him tribute to stay in business. He ate for free in the block's cramped little noodle houses and never even paid for a pack of cigarettes. Thousands of dollars worth of 24-karat gold draped from his wrists and fingers, a glittering complement to his expensive Italian suits. He drove around Chinatown in a sleek white Jaguar until someone blew it up.

A short wiry gangster with stringy black hair, Chan is not physically imposing. But other gangsters know not to underestimate him. He spent his teenage years as an enforcer for the Flying Dragons gang on Pell Street. "Sonny's got a good rep," said a police investigator who knows him well. "He's known as a good fighter. If you look at his fists, all the knuckles on both hands are broken; when the bones come back, it makes your fist harder. All the kids respect this guy."[8]

And not just for his rock-hard fists. Chan set himself apart in the Flying Dragons gang by bringing illegal video poker machines to Chinatown. Video poker is the high-tech equivalent of slot machines. People stand in stores and feed quarters into the arcade-style machines in the hope of hitting the jackpot. As with slot machines, their illegal distribution is controlled by the Italian Mafia. Anybody who has one in a store pays the mob 50 percent of the take or gets the thing smashed on the sidewalk. Chan cut a deal with some mafiosi to put the machines in Chinatown. He forced them on restaurants, video stores, and bars, giving the owners a percentage of the take and warning them not to complain. Pretty soon he had several dozen machines on the street, each pulling in up to $250 a day.

The video poker racket was Chan's ticket out of Pell Street. "He did this while he was a Flying Dragon," explained the investigator, "but he built up a lot of capital. That's what you need to start a gang. Nobody's going to follow a poor guy who can't feed them and has no respect." In 1989, Chan won the approval of the Hip Sing to start his own gang. He settled on a stretch of Grand Street east of the Bowery, where a growing Chinatown had recently sprawled into the Lower East Side. Sonny's Boys, as the gang became known, was given free rein to shake down businesses, eat for free in restaurants and otherwise treat Grand Street as its personal fiefdom. Chan, meanwhile, expanded his video poker racket to the new Chinatown in Flushing, Queens. He also started a fruit-and-vegetable business that forced stores and restaurants to buy his products. When federal authorities cracked down on the Flying Dragons and Sonny's Boys in 1994, Chan disappeared and was believed to have fled to Hong Kong.

But there are hundreds of other young Chinese gangsters in New York who are striving to match his success.

In the feudal system of power that governs New York's Chinatown, the widespread practice of extortion is perhaps the greatest injustice. Extortion payments to gangs, known as "lucky money," are an accepted cost of doing business for Chinese merchants. A recent study by Rutgers University researcher Ko-lin Chin found that 81 percent of the restaurants in New York's Chinatown and two-thirds of its businesses over all pay tribute to gangs.[9] In the mid-1980s, an undercover police officer wore a wire while posing as a waiter in Chinatown's Golden Boat nightclub. He watched the manager pay $100 a week to not one gang but two—the Ghost Shadows and the Flying Dragons. When the officer asked why the nightclub paid the hoodlums, the manager said anyone who doesn't know the answer "doesn't know shit about business."

"If you only pay one gang, then the other one will come and make trouble for you. They'll come up here and put their feet on the table and curse. How many customers will you have then?" You have to be patient to make money in Chinatown, the manager explained, because everyone pays. Restaurants and bars pay. Street vendors pay. Gang members eat for free, drink for free, and even get free movie tickets. "The China Theater, the Pagoda Theater, they give them free tickets," the manager said. "You can have a security guard there to watch, and then they'll pay to go in. But once they are inside, they'll cut up the seats. How are you going to catch them? That's why in Chinatown you have to pay these two gangs."[10]

His resignation may seem appalling, but the usual rules don't apply in Chinatowns. The lines between the legitimate and illegitimate have always been hazy, and sometimes they are nonexistent. Gambling, for example, has long been a passion of many Chinese, and parlors offering traditional Chinese games like *pai gow, mah-jongg* and *fan tan* are an accepted part of life in any Chinatown. In most Chinatowns, the schedules of games are posted outside gambling dens like banking hours. When Boston police raided gambling clubs during the Chinese New Year celebration in 1982, the community was up in arms, calling police culturally insensitive for interrupting holiday festivities. An attorney for one of the gamblers told the judge: "Trying to take gambling away from the Chinese is like trying to take pasta away from the Italians."

The enormous influence that gangs and *tongs* wield in China-towns is almost incomprehensible to outsiders. For many years, police had difficulty understanding why extortion victims would not turn to them for help. Or why no one ever seems to see anything when gang members are murdered. Or why residents continue to treat murderers and vice lords like civic leaders. But these questions become easier to answer when one views them through the prism of Chinese history and culture.

Criminal life in China, Hong Kong and Taiwan has been under the control of secret societies, known as "triads," for hundreds of years. In their 20th-century incarnation, triads in Hong Kong and Taiwan are Mafia-like gangs that control every facet of organized crime—and have worked their way into control of legitimate industries like entertainment and labor unions. In Hong Kong, it is a crime just to belong to a triad. But that hasn't stopped their growth. Hong Kong authorities estimated that the colony has up to 120,000 triad members, though only about 15,000 to 20,000 are active.[11] By contrast, the American Mafia is said to have had 4,500 members at the height of its power in the 1960s.

Historians have recorded the presence of secret societies in China since at least the year 9 A.D., when a group known as the "Red Eyebrows" rebelled against the conqueror Wang Mang, who had overthrown the Western Han dynasty. A Buddhist sect known as the White Lotus Society played a key role in installing the Ming Dynasty in 1368 and was influential in imperial circles for much of the dynasty's 300-year reign. By the 1600s, Chinese imperial rulers were coping with a vast array of political and religious organizations with names like the White Lily Society, the Incense Burning Society, the Origin of Chaos Society, the Origin of the Dragon Society or the Hung Society.[12]

The origins of modern-day triads date to 1644, when Mongol tribesmen swept across the Great Wall of China, overthrew the Mings and set up the Manchu Dynasty. The Manchus subdued northern China without much trouble, but they encountered fierce resistance in the southern provinces of Kwangtung and Fujian. In 1674, imperial forces destroyed a monastery near what is now the Fujianese capital of Fuzhou to flush out 128 monks who were leaders of the opposition. Described in triad legend as fierce warriors and masters of martial arts, the monks were betrayed by one of their own and nearly all were hunted down and killed. Five survivors of these purges are said to have founded a resistance group known as the Hung Mun, sometimes called the Heaven and Earth Society. Whether this story is apocryphal or not, it is to this group that Hong Kong's triads and their progeny the world over trace their lineage.[13]

The Hung Mun and what would eventually become hundreds of other triads were in the vanguard in the 250-year struggle against the Manchu Dynasty, acting as unofficial local governments in many rural areas. Most southern Chinese had no faith in their imperial rulers, so they turned to the triads for justice against criminals, the settling of disputes, and even loans of money. While not the instigators, triads were key participants in the famous Taiping Rebellion, which began in 1851 and raged for 13 years, nearly toppling the Manchus. The rebellion was finally suppressed and many triad members were forced to flee abroad. But the dynasty had only bought some time. Among the triad members who had fled abroad to regroup was a Kwangtung native named Sun Yat-sen. In 1911, Sun Yat-sen led an army that overthrew the hated Manchus and set up the Chinese Republic. With Sun Yat-sen as the Republic's president, the triads gained access to the corridors of power. Sun Yat-sen had been a triad member since his teenage years and by the time of the coup was a senior official in Hong Kong's Chung Wo Tong Society and the Kwok On Wui Society in Honolulu and Chicago.[14]

This new "triad state" was by no means to China's benefit. Triads were no longer the heroic patriotic organizations that had begun the fight against the Manchus. The years underground had forced them into criminal activities to survive. By the end of the 19th century, they were more criminal then patriotic. Sun Yat-sen and the triad member who succeeded him, General Chiang Kai-shek, gave the triads almost free rein to run extortion, prostitution and dope-smuggling rackets. Chiang also used the triads as hired thugs for any Kuomintang repression that was too dirty to involve the army. On April 12, 1927, gangsters from the Green Gang triad in Shanghai marauded through the city massacring members of Communist-led labor unions. The gang's ruthless leader, Tu Yueh Sheng, known as "Big-eared Tu," was rewarded handsomely for his service to the KMT. He was made a major general in the army and given a free hand to illegally export opium from China.[15]

Triads had been migrating to Hong Kong since the early 19th century, especially after the enclave was ceded to Britain in 1842 and became a convenient refuge from the Manchus. After Mao's takeover of China in 1949, Hong Kong became the triads' prime base of operations. The triads that had been controlling the city for decades—the Wo group, the Yee On, the Kuk Yee Hing and others—were suddenly inundated with competing gangs that had fled Communist China. Big-eared Tu and other leaders of the Green Gang transplanted their operations to Hong Kong. So did the 14K triad, a gang from Kwangzhou, the capital of Canton province. The 14K was to become one of Hong Kong's most important crime groups. Headed by a former KMT general named Kot Siu Wong, the 14K triad ruthlessly expanded its influence in the rackets and established a near monopoly on the flow of heroin from the Golden Triangle. Hong Kong's police, alarmed by the growing power of the 14K, initiated a crackdown in the mid-1950s. The 14K did not take it lying down, fomenting an anti-British riot in October 1956 that left 59 people dead, more than 400 injured and some $20 million in property damage.[16]

In recent decades, the dominant Hong Kong triads have been the 14K, the Sun Yee On and the Wo group, the latter made up of some 40 smaller gangs, like the Wo Hop To, the Wo Shing Tong and the Wo Yung Yee. These groups have a disturbing grip on the colony and an even more alarming reach across the globe. Not only are they the lords of vice and the worldwide heroin traffic, but they also control Hong Kong's entertainment industry and have repeatedly infiltrated the Hong Kong police.

Though they evolved into modern criminal syndicates, the triads never abandoned their roots. New members still go through an elaborate Hung Mun initiation ceremony that involves the drinking of blood and swearing to 36 oaths. The initiate vows never to betray the society's secrets, and to die from "a myriad of swords" if the vow is betrayed. Triad members are given rankings that correspond with numbers that have deep significance in the Hung Mun's history. The leader—known as Shan Chu, or Hill Chief—is given the number 489. The Heung Chu, or Incense Master, handles ceremonial duties and is 438. The White Paper Fan, number 415, is an adviser and financial administrator; the Red Pole, number 426, is a fighter or enforcer; the Straw Sandal, number 432, is a messenger and liaison to other groups; ordinary members are given the number 49. These rankings may seem almost childish, but they are taken with deadly seriousness by triad members, who to this day kill for the traditions of the Hung Mun.

Those criminal traditions unfortunately are also part of the Chinese-American experience—and have been for more than 150 years. Chinese immigration began during the California Gold Rush in the 1840s. News that gold was being sifted from the hills and rivers of Northern California first reached Chinese ears in a district of Kwangtung province known as Toishan. The Toishanese, who lived in a rocky, mountainous region unsuitable for farming, had been a seafaring people for generations. They were the first to pick up news from the outside world in their travels to other ports, and they were far less apprehensive than other Chinese about long journeys. Thousands of Toishanese took to the South China Sea for the voyage to the Mountain of Gold—as they called California—and in the process became the founding fathers of Chinatowns across the country.

The first American Chinatown took root in San Francisco. Its earliest record dates to 1849, when 300 Chinese met on a restaurant on Jackson Street to elect an "adviser" to lead their community. Three years later, the 300 had turned into 25,000, centered around Dupont Street, which is now Grant Avenue, the main drag of San Francisco's modern Chinatown. Chinese were at first greeted warmly by San Franciscans, who admired them for their work ethic and humility. Chinese helped fill labor shortages, taking the jobs that native Americans didn't want. Some 10,000 Chinese helped build the Central Pacific Railroad, working faster than the Irish laborers who built the Union Pacific.[17] The joining of the two railroads at Promontory Point, Utah, in 1869 linked commerce on the two coasts and opened the door for the West's explosive growth.

But in the 1870s, as the Gold Rush died out and depression gripped California, the Chinese accomplishments were forgotten. They became scapegoats for unemployed workers who unfairly saw the Chinese as taking away American jobs. Dennis Kearney, a former sailor who had been financially ruined by the collapse of gold mining, started a new career as a political demagogue. Armed with the slogan "The Chinese must go," Kearney whipped Californians into a frenzy that turned murderous. Chinese were lynched and driven from small towns. Many abandoned the Mountain of Gold and headed East, founding Chinatowns in New York, Boston, Philadelphia, Chicago and numerous smaller cities. In these eastern cities, they opened laundries and cigar shops but mixed little with whites. It is this legacy of racism—together with a historical Chinese suspicion of Westerners—that is partly to blame for the traditional unwillingness of Chinatowns to open their arms to non-Asians.

Secret societies corrupted American Chinatowns almost from the start. In this country, they didn't use the Chinese term for "triad." They called themselves *tongs*, a word that means "meeting hall" in the Cantonese dialect. But they were the same. In fact, the first Chinese secret society to take hold in San Francisco, the Chee Kung Tong, was the American arm of the Hung Mun Society.

In 1854, at about the time the Taiping Rebellion was driving triad members abroad, San Francisco police received a tip that something was afoot in Chinatown. The city's police chief raided a meeting hall on January 4 and found 400 Chinese men engaged in some kind of ceremony. Most fled across the adjoining rooftops, but 159 of them stayed in their places. Not knowing exactly what he had stumbled across, the chief hauled them in. "As a means to bring them quietly to the station house, they were tied together by the tails of their heads, in half-dozens, and in this manner marched to the station house," reported a local newspaper.

In court, the men insisted they were members of a benevolent society. But other members of the Chinese community told a different story. They said the men were part of a gang that extorted money from merchants and brothels. The trappings in the raided meeting hall, these witnesses said, were identical to those used by secret societies in China. Though the police surely didn't know it at the time, they had stumbled onto a triad initiation ceremony.[18]

The meeting hall raid was probably the first contact American authorities had with a Chinese secret society. But it would not be the last. In October of that same year, police responded to a disturbance at a little hotel on Dupont Street. This time, there was no mystery as to what was happening. Police arrested several Chinese who were attempting to extort money in the name of the Triad Society, another name of the Hung Mun.[19]

The Chee Kung's affairs would not stay this low-key. Chinatown soon became a notorious center of vice and graft. Brothels sprang up to serve the neighborhood's ubiquitous bachelors, who had no other access to Chinese women. By the 1860s, the neighborhood was beset by opium dens and gambling parlors. The San Francisco Call once estimated that there were 300 opium dens in the city, most of them in Chinatown. They bore names like Blind Annie's Cellar (718-20 Jackson Street) and Ah King's (730 Jackson).[20] Chinatown had become such a spectacle by the 1890s that shiftless entrepreneurs organized guided tours through its streets for Caucasians who wanted to see its wickedness first hand.

Tongs were the overlords of all this seediness. The Chee Kung and more than a dozen of its offshoot *tongs* sold the opium, kid-napped the women for prostitution, and paid off police to pro-tect the gambling dens. Inevitably, the competition between the *tongs* would turn violent. Each society maintained a cadre of "salaried soldiers"—*boo how doy*—who were ready to protect the *tong*'s honor with hatchets and guns. The hatchet men, as they became known in the press, were said to eat wildcat meat to prime themselves for battle. And some of their killings indeed seemed the work of animals. In 1875, several members of the Suey Sing *tong* attacked members of the Kwong Duck *tong* on Waverly Place, killing three of them and wounding six others. A year later, 50 *tong* members burst into the Yee Chuy Lung & Co. merchandise store at 810 Dupont Street and attacked 12 men eating at a table. One man was fatally chopped with a hatchet and several others were badly hurt. At the scene, police found iron bars and clubs, a revolver, a meat cleaver and four razor-sharp hatchets. The killings became so common that newspapers literally began reporting them in box scores. On March 6, 1900, the *Call* reported that seven had been killed and eight wounded in the latest Suey Sing–Hop Sing war.[21]

The most legendary of San Francisco's *tong* bosses was Fong Ching, better known as Little Pete. Born in a small town outside Canton in 1864, Little Pete was brought to San Francisco as a 10-year-old and grew up to be a handsome and refined young man. Proficient in English, he became an interpreter for one of the Six Companies, a group of business and civic organizations that ran things in Chinatown. Through this connection, he scraped to-gether enough money to open a shoe business with several rela-tives. It grew to have 40 employees. Had he stopped there, he could have grown to be a wealthy old man. But Little Pete had too much ambition. He turned to smuggling illegal aliens and prostitutes from China and eventually opened a string of gam-bling dens. While still a young man, he had founded the Gee Sin Seer tong and assembled his own complement of hatchet men. Little Pete became the King of Chinatown, the only man who ever attempted to claim that title in the 19th century. But his reign was to be short. Members of the rival Bo Sin Seer *tong* had been after him for months and they finally got him on January 23, 1897. He was shot to death while he sat waiting for a haircut in a Washington Street barber shop.[22]

The *tong* wars started later in New York's Chinatown, but the story was much the same. A Pell Street shop owner named Wah Kee had been running gambling joints and opium dens in the neighborhood since the late 1860s. But the violence between *tongs* began about 1899, when the On Leong and the Hip Sing started battling over the district's vice trade. In the mid-1890s, there were said to be 200 gambling establishments in the three-block triangle of Pell, Mott and Doyers Streets. There were so many opium dens that the pungent fumes of the foot-long pipes hung over every corner. The dope dens and gambling joints paid police $17.50 a week and turned over a smaller but significant chunk to the *tongs*.[23]

The early *tong* wars were a mismatch. Tom Lee, the On Leong chief, initially dominated the neighborhood's gambling—thanks in part to his political ties—and encountered little trouble from the weak Hip Sing. A Hip Sing leader named Wong Get had made several inept attempts over the years to loosen Lee's grip on the gambling houses, but he never succeeded. The situation changed around 1900 when a hatchet man named Mock Duck came to town. Duck, a short, fat gambler who carried two guns and a hatchet, wanted a part of Chinatown's gambling revenues and clashed with the On Leong. His ambitions brought him into alliance with Wong Get, who before long helped Duck gain control of the Hip Sing. From then on, it was war. Hatchet men from the two *tongs* went at each other for more than 20 years. Much of the killing took place at a sharp bend in Doyers Street where assassins would wait for their prey to turn the corner and then strike. The spot became known as the "Bloody Angle." Legend has it that more men were killed at the Bloody Angle than at any other spot in America.[24]

The city's authorities and even the Chinese government intervened on a number of occasions to stop the bloodshed. In 1906, Judge Warren Foster of the Court of General Session brokered a peace agreement between the leadership of the two *tongs*. The treaty created a division of the neighborhood's spoils. The Hip Sing would control Pell Street and the On Leong would control Mott Street.[25] (Incredibly, the division still exists today and is the basis for turfs claimed by the Ghost Shadows and Flying Dragons.) But the treaty did not last. Even worse killing was still to come. In 1909, the *tong* wars flared again, claiming some 50 lives over a few short years. Tom Lee, the *tongs'* elder statesmen, appealed for an end to the killing, but even he could not control the wild young hatchet men. The new Chinese Republic helped arrange another treaty in 1913, but it also was broken. The battles raged into the 1920s, sometimes spilling over into Brooklyn and the Bronx.

It is startling to compare this war-torn image of American Chinatowns with the peaceful communities that emerged after World War II. After the last of the great *tong* wars petered out in the 1930s, America's Chinatowns launched a massive effort to change their image. Gambling never stopped flourishing in basement warrens and some *tong* members remained criminals. But no longer were Chinatowns renowned for debauchery. Gone were the acrid fumes emanating from opium dens and the enslavement of Asian women in basement brothels.

Part of the reason for the new docility of Chinatowns was the end of their population growth. The fulminations of Dennis Kearney and other demagogues had led to a series of congressional moves to clamp down on Chinese immigration. The Chinese Exclusion Act of 1882 closed the door on the entry of Chinese laborers into the United States for 10 years. Chinese immigration plummeted from 39,000 people in 1882 to just 22 people three years later. Under the Exclusion Act, Chinese who were American citizens could still bring over wives from Asia. But even that privilege was removed by the Immigration Act of 1924. American Chinatowns became listless bachelor societies, the domain of lonely aging men cut off from their families overseas. From 1880 to 1940, the number of Chinese in the United States dropped from about 105,000 to 77,000. While the numbers increased after Congress repealed the worst of the Exclusion Acts in the 1940s, by 1960 there were only 53,000 Chinese in the San Francisco Bay area and only 36,000 in Greater New York. In some cities, Chinatowns disappeared altogether. Rose Hum Lee, a researcher at Roosevelt College in Illinois, noted that while this country had 28 Chinatowns just before the start of World War II, a dozen had vanished by 1955, including those in Butte, Montana; Boise, Idaho; and Denver, Colorado. She and other researchers wondered whether any Chinatowns would be left in a few years.[26]

These postwar Chinatowns, far from being the cauldrons of vice and murder that so aroused pubic indignation at the turn of the century, were seen as paragons of civic virtue. Right up until the 1960s, reported crime was rare. Young people who lived in Chinatowns almost never had run-ins with police. Authorities only recorded one arrest for serious crime in New York's Chinatown in 1964. As late as 1973, Boston's Chinatown spent the year without a single case of juvenile delinquency.[27] The once-feared *tongs* were no longer a threat. While some *tong* members continued to have involvement with gambling and other crimes, for the most part their societies were regarded as benign civic organizations, albeit with colorful histories. Betty Lee Sung, a Chinese-American writer, painted a sanguine portrait of the *tongs* in 1967. "The character of the tongs has changed," she wrote. ". . . Their activities take on the character of a fraternal lodge as the word *tong* intended it to be. They are becoming more socially conscious of the welfare of the Chinese community and are beginning to take an interest in philanthropic activities."[28]

As accurate as Sung's words may have been, she no doubt came to regret them. For the *tongs'* rehabilitation would not last, and neither would the image of Chinatowns as serene, crime-free communities. The mid-1960s saw the beginnings of explosive changes in American Chinatowns, some for the better and some for the worse. The catalyst for these changes was the Immigration and Naturalization Act of 1965, which allowed Chinese immigration at the same level as that of other preferred nations. Chinese immigration, which had been averaging a little more than 100 people a year, suddenly exceeded 20,000. New York's Chinatown, in particular, was flooded with newcomers. Long confined to blocks south of Canal Street and west of the Bowery, China-town expanded north into Little Italy and east into the tradition-ally Jewish neighborhoods of the Lower East Side. By the 1980s, the neighborhood had swelled to an estimated 150,000 people, far surpassing San Francisco as the nation's biggest Chinese en-clave.

Since the 19th century, American Chinatowns had been domi-nated by descendants of Kwangtung farmers, a clannish people who clung to old-world traditions of hard work, humility and re-spect for one's elders. But the vast majority of the newcomers were Hong Kong Chinese who had been exposed to Western val-ues in the British colony and did not observe the old traditions. They came from the slums of Hong Kong, Macao and Kowloon, where triad-linked street gangs were the law on the streets and the traditions of Chinese humility had become a memory.

In the Chinatowns of New York, San Francisco, Los Angeles and other cities, these Hong Kong Chinese found that getting started in the United States was not easy. The only jobs for peo-ple who couldn't speak English were sewing in garment sweat-shops or waiting on tables in restaurants for $1.50 an hour. The same overcrowded tenements that once held Jewish and Italian immigrants became the homes of Hong Kong Chinese. Apart-ments that were already too small to house a family were subdi-vided into illegal cubbyholes known as *gong si fong*. (With a new influx of immigrants from the Fujian province of southern China, the *gong si fong* are even more prevalent today. In 1991, New York city housing inspectors found 60 Chinese immigrants living in 6-by-9-foot cubicles in a Baxter Street tenement without heat or windows. Each cubicle was renting for $300 a month, and the immigrants thought they had a good deal.)[29]

For immigrant Chinese youth, life under these conditions was especially hard. Their inability to speak English made them poor students in big-city school systems, which had few bilingual pro-grams in the 1960s. Often teenagers were put in classes with children much younger than themselves. To make matters worse, they were ridiculed by American-born Chinese kids, or ABCs, who called the newcomers FOBs, meaning fresh off the boat. The most insecure and troubled of these youths coped with their problems by banding together into gangs.

Gangs had been in Chinatowns since the early 1960s, but they were relatively harmless cliques whose biggest crimes were occasional brawls with members of other ethnic groups. A gang called the Continentals was formed in 1961 by American-born Chinese seeking protection from Puerto Ricans and Italians at New York's Junior High School 65.[30] In San Francisco, American-born Chinese gangs like the Raiders, 895s and Leways rumbled with black gangs in the early 1960s at Samuel Gompers High School. On assignment for *Esquire* in 1969, writer Tom Wolfe described the origin of the San Francisco gangs: "The Chinatown gangs were sort of 1949 New York turf style, with the gang jackets, colors, pompadours, and the hard-bop gang girls with mini-skirts and beehive hairdos. One group of the Leways was heavy into the 1955 Southern California style of customized cars. They had a fleet of Chevrolets that were jacked up front and back, until they rose up about seven feet off the road and the grilles gaped over the street like they were about to roll over small cars and devour the mothers."[31]

But the new FOB gangs made Chinatown crime a more serious matter. San Francisco's first FOB gang, the Wah Ching (or Chinese Youth), was founded in 1964. The gang began improbably as a political movement aimed at convincing the neighborhood's American-born leaders to give jobs to immigrant youth. Members of the gang actually picketed City Hall demanding jobs and recreation facilities. "These kids tried, they really tried to get programs going, to find jobs," Alice Barkley, a community worker who tried to steer the gang into political activity, told a reporter in 1973.[32] But when its ranks swelled with disaffected immigrants after 1965, the Wah Ching gave up any pretense of being motivated by altruism. "All we want is money and girls and be with our friends," the gang's leader, Tom Tom, told Wolfe. "The Leways talk about Mao and the Little Red Book, but they crazy. We don't bother anybody unless they bother us. And then we beat the hell out of them." The gang's entreaties for jobs turned into demands for donations. By the late 1960s, the Wah Ching was hitting up business owners for monthly protection payments of up to $200.

The gang became a fearsome presence in the neighborhood. In January 1971, about 100 gang members went on a rampage to punish business owners who were not paying up. Among four movie theaters targeted was the newly remodeled Great Star Theatre. Marauders smashed its windows and hurled fireworks in the lobby. A Chevron station that refused to pay had its gas hoses severed 14 times in May and June of the same year.[33] Alarmed by the gang's growing influence, community leaders had met with Tom Tom and other leaders in the winter of 1968 and asked them to stop terrorizing the neighborhood. The Wah Ching said they were cut off from jobs and education. They wanted $4,000 from the Six Companies, they said, or they would riot in Chinatown. The community leaders didn't come up with the money and the trouble continued.

Meanwhile, the tongs, afraid the Wah Ching and other gangs would bring heat on their gambling operations, tried their own methods to stop the gang. First they took out advertisements in Chinatown newspapers threatening to kill gang leaders who shook down merchants.[34] When they didn't work, they put the gang on the payroll. The Wah Ching became affiliated with the Hop Sing tong, protecting the tong's gambling houses and providing muscle for its other criminal ventures.

In New York's Chinatown, gangs of Hong Kong-born youths were active within months of the 1965 immigration reform. A community hailed just two years earlier for its remarkably low crime rate suddenly had gangs of youths with ducktail haircuts and black leather jackets standing on corners. Gangs like the White Eagles, Kwon Ying, Hong Kong Refugees and International Brothers were formed to protect their members from American-born Chinese and other ethnic groups. They also picked up money by mugging people and breaking into parking meters, activities that would soon give way to more serious ventures, thanks in no small measure to the neighborhood's tongs. In contrast to San Francisco's tongs, New York's dark societies were behind the gangs from the beginning. As early as July 1965, *tongs* were criticized for encouraging the gangs to hang around in their meeting halls. Somewhere in the late 1960s, the On Leong *tong* formally adopted the White Eagles as its private army, giving the gang exclusive rights to shake down merchants on Mott Street.

But that did not stop the Eagles and other gangs from going to war with each other. Beginning in about 1970, newspapers began running small items about gang murders in Chinatown. James Yuen, a 17-year-old member of the Black Eagles gang, was stabbed in August 1970 in the yard of Junior High School 65 by a member of the rival Henry Street gang. Later that day, the wounded Yuen and another Black Eagle tracked down the assailant, a 14-year-old named William Wong, and stabbed him to death on the Bowery. In January 1972, 12-year-old John Cheung and a friend, David Chin, 15, were walking at Hester Street and the Bowery when a group of 10 to 15 youths spotted them and yelled "That's them!" The two youths, both recent immigrants, were robbed and stabbed to death.[35]

The once-peaceful community endured perhaps its greatest shock in the summer of 1972, when a community leader named Hung Moy was murdered. Moy was the leader of the 2,000-member Moy family association and the owner of several businesses. On July 8, 1972, he left his stationery store on Bayard Street at 2:35 A.M. with $2,000 in his pockets. He was heading for his car in a parking lot on Elizabeth Street, just across the street from the Fifth Precinct station house. But three youths accosted him and placed handcuffs on his wrists. After he resisted their plan to kidnap him, the youths stabbed him to death and fled with the money. Some 200 mourners marched through Chinatown a week later in a funeral procession festooned with black banners and a flower-framed portrait of the victim.[36]

If Chinatown was shocked by these killings, their feelings never made it into the American press. Most newspapers had only passing interest in Chinatown's gangs, and reporters who tried to report the trend found a community that was not interested in airing its dirty laundry in public. "Gangs? What gangs? You'll have to go to the Fifth Precinct," an official of the Chinese

Consolidated Benevolent Association told a reporter after William Wong's killing.[37] The community was not about to reach out to police or other city officials. And with the CCBA—the neighborhood's unofficial City Hall—dominated by the same *tongs* who were fostering the gang's growth, nobody in Chinatown was going to do anything about gang violence.

In the early 1970s, with Chinese gangs in their infancy, a solution to the problem was still possible. The merchants and Chinese community leaders in New York and San Francisco could have reached out to police and refused to give in to the gangs instead of turning their heads or exploiting the gangs for their own purposes. The police could have hired Chinese cops whom the neighborhood would learn to trust. Schools could have implemented bilingual programs and other efforts to help the Hong Kong immigrants adjust. Federal authorities could have brought their resources to bear on the growing problem of Chinese organized crime. "We tried like hell to get the Feds interested, but they ignored us. They didn't want to be bothered with gangs," said Neil Mauriello, who was a detective in New York's Jade Squad in the 1970s.[38] All these innovations would come in the 1980s, but they would arrive a decade too late. By then, Chinese gangs would be deeply entrenched in cities across the country. What had begun as an exotic juvenile-delinquency problem had been allowed to blossom into an insidious new form of organized crime.

6: Big Brothers

Nicky Louie told himself he had nothing to fear. The leader of New York's Ghost Shadows gang was playing *mah-jongg* with friends in the rear of a Mott Street barbershop. This was his turf. For years he had spent his days in its narrow confines, never even rounding the corner of Pell Street, where the rival Flying Dragons would be waiting to kill him. He didn't need Pell Street. On Mott Street, he was the big brother, the *dai lo*. He was a man of respect. Just about every business on Mott paid the Ghost Shadows. The only exceptions were a handful of stores with close ties to the On Leong, the Shadows' parent *tong*. Louie had killed members of the White Eagles to take this street four years before. He himself had taken a bullet to keep it. Mott Street was the only thing he had ever owned in his life, and he wasn't about to give it up to a bunch of young rebels in his gang. Gangsters had tried to kill him at least a dozen times before, but Nicky Louie had outfoxed them all. These little brothers would be no different. Relaxing with several older men on August 28, 1978, Nicky Louie was defiant. But he violated a simple rule that has guided New York gangsters since Five Points days. He sat with his back to the door.

Louie barely had time to notice the surprised looks on the other players' faces when the danger was upon him. Robert Hsu, a 17-year-old rebel Ghost Shadow known on the street as

"Potato," quietly walked into the barbershop and put a .38 to his head. He pulled the trigger, burying a bullet in Louie's cheek. Louie jumped from his chair and ran to the front of the barbershop, with Hsu running behind him firing. Three more bullets struck Louie as the two weaved in and out among the barber chairs. Finally, Hsu ran out of bullets and began hitting Louie on the head with the gun. (Louie would later tell a prosecutor: "At this point, I became very mad.") After wrestling with Hsu for a few moments, Louie staggered out the door and trailed blood three blocks to the Fifth Precinct station house on Elizabeth Street, where he collapsed on the floor.[1]

The gravely wounded Louie was finished as the Ghost Shadows' leader. But his legend still looms large on the streets of Chinatown. He was the neighborhood's first notorious crime boss since the *tong* wars had ended in the 1920s. Before Louie's reign, Chinatown's gangs were regarded as neighborhood pariahs who sold protection to merchants and mugged pedestrians. He was the first gang leader to give his criminal enterprise a cloak of legitimacy, the first to insinuate himself into the commerce and politics of Chinatown. He followed a path well worn by Irish, Jewish and Italian gangsters, that of the street ruffian who becomes a powerful figure in his community, as comfortable in legitimate circles as he is in the gang safe house. His Ghost Shadows were—and are—as influential in the center of Chinatown as any of the neighborhood's *tongs* or family associations. Their methods of controlling neighborhoods became not only a model for other New York gangs—the Flying Dragons, the Tung On, the Fuk Ching—but also for a host of other Chinese crime groups from Toronto and Boston to Chicago and New Orleans. Louie's era in New York—which roughly coincided with the emergence of the Wah Ching gang in San Francisco—was the first phase of Chinese organized crime in America. As we will see later in this chapter, Louie was not as sophisticated as the new breed of Chinese gangster that emerged in New York and various other cities in the 1980s. But he was the pioneer. The story of his rise and fall as a gang leader is essential to understanding the origins of Chinese organized crime in the United States.

He was born Yin Poy Louie in the slums of Kowloon, a section of Hong Kong, and came with his family to New York at age 15. The year was 1966, when Chinatown was in the middle of its first mass wave of Hong Kong immigration. Louie ended up living in a crowded tenement with his family. Both his parents were hard-working immigrants. His father ran a little restaurant on Hester Street. But instead of following his parents' example, Louie looked up to members of the Kwon Ying, one of the neighborhood's first gangs made up of Hong Kong Chinese. With the older members of the Kwon Ying as their mentors, Louie and another teenager named Philip Han formed a gang called the Sing Yee On around 1970. By choosing a name so close to that of the

Nicky Louie, founder of the Ghost Shadows gang, in a 1975 police mugshot. (AP/Wide World)

Sun Yee On, Hong Kong's notorious triad, Louie and his friends left little doubt as to their future plans.

By 1971, the gang had renamed itself the Ghost Shadows. Modeling its structure after the *tongs*, the gang created positions of chairman, treasurer, English secretary, and Chinese secretary. Louie was elected chairman, more because of his intelligence and charisma than his physical presence. Standing about five feet seven but weighing no more than 125 pounds, Louie never looked the part of the tough guy. He was boyish-looking and pale, with soft black hair and delicate features. He dressed casually, favoring Army-Navy wear over expensive suits. "Whatever type of clothes he wore one week, all the other kids on Mott Street would be wearing the next week," said John Feehan, a retired DEA agent who worked Chinatown for 25 years.[2]

Louie was renowned for his cunning. Rival gangsters would try to kill him more than a dozen times, but never succeed. Detectives also found him to be an elusive target. Whenever they had him pegged to an extortion or a shooting, witnesses would develop amnesia or he would have an unshakable alibi. His success at foiling the cops was legend in Chinatown. When a group of police officers entered a restaurant looking for him in the late 1970s, he slid into the kitchen, put on an apron and began tending a wok. The cops left without finding him. Another time he lowered himself out of a tenement window and into the apartment below. When the elderly couple who lived there looked up in alarm, he never said a word. He just placed his finger to his lips in a signal to be quiet. "Nicky is a smart guy and very charming," said Neil Mauriello, a retired detective who was Louie's chief nemesis for years. "You can always see the wheels turning in his head when you talk to him. If he had been raised in a different environment, he'd probably be a lawyer or a banker."[3]

In its early years, the Ghost Shadows had no set territory. Mott Street, the heart of Chinatown, was the property of the White Eagles and their powerful sponsor, the On Leong. So the gang's leaders busied themselves breaking open parking meters and committing other petty crimes on the dingy eastern outskirts of Chinatown. Louie's first attempt at serious crime ended in embarrassment. With his gang hard up for money, Louie pulled a gun on the owner of a Division Street dumpling house in 1972 and emptied his cash register. It turned out the restaurant owner was close to Wong Kee, a leader of the Kwon Ying, and Louie was forced to meet with the victim and, as a sign of respect, hand back the money in a traditional red envelope.[4]

By now known as the Ghost Shadows, Louie and Han planned another caper that was not much more successful—but a lot bloodier. With another Shadow named Kenneth Yuen, they attempted to rob the offices of the *United Journal*, a Chinatown newspaper. Louie stood at the door as a lookout, and Han and Yuen went inside with handguns. When Arthur Lai, the paper's 65-year-old manager, refused to turn over the money and swung a pipe at them, Han shot him in the chest with a .45-caliber bullet. Blood pouring from his chest, Lai was rushed to the hospital; he pulled through after days in critical condition. Louie and Han were indicted for the shooting after Yuen agreed to testify against them. On the day of trial, however, the Ghost Shadows abducted Yuen and held him in an apartment. Han wanted to kill him, but Louie came up with a smarter idea. He arranged for the On Leong to get Yuen out of town. With the star witness nowhere to be found, the charges against the two Ghost Shadows were dismissed.

The favor was the beginning of a long relationship between the Shadows and the On Leong. The *tong* was led by ruthless men, some of them former generals in the Kuomintang who had been part of the dreaded Green Gang.[5] In New York, they continued the dope-smuggling and gambling rackets that had been their mainstay, and they needed a reliable gang to use as muscle. Toward the mid-1970s, the White Eagles had been slipping out of the *tong*'s control. Many of its members were reckless dopeheads who often robbed patrons outside the gambling dens they were paid to protect. Louie had carefully positioned his gang to be friendly with both the Hip Sing and the On Leong, and was ready when the *tong* decided to dump the Eagles in 1974.

The Ghost Shadows and the White Eagles were already sworn enemies. Louie himself had been shot and wounded by the gang in his Sing Yee On days, and relished a chance for revenge. In March 1973, Louie and several other Ghost Shadows abducted an Eagle named Arthur Ha from Mott Street. Ha was known on the street as "The Joker," but he wasn't laughing when they stuck a gun in his ribs and pulled him into a hallway. A Shadow named Pak Chui got a car, and they drove Ha to a pier on the East River. With Louie directing, they bound his hands and feet with wire and threw him into the river to drown. Later, Louie told another Shadow who was not on the pier not to worry about the Joker. "He's floating," Louie said.[6]

It didn't take too many more killings to push the White Eagles off Mott Street once the On Leong gave the green light. A couple of White Eagles were picked off by Ghost Shadow snipers perched on Bayard Street rooftops, but the gang otherwise cut and ran. Victory over the Eagles brought Louie to the pinnacle of his power. He truly became the king of Mott Street, raking in money unmolested for the next several years. One police estimate in 1977, probably exaggerated, put the Ghost Shadows' annual earnings from extortion at $1 million. The gang also took in hundreds of thousands for protecting On Leong gambling houses from robberies. Hardly anyone in the Chinese press or the legitimate Chinatown Establishment would utter a word against Louie. And those who did paid dearly.

Man Bun Lee, a former chief of the Chinese Consolidated Benevolent Association and the unofficial "mayor" of Chinatown, learned that lesson first hand. Lee had tried to "westernize" Chinatown, to weaken the power of the tongs and open the community to the rest of New York. He urged merchants to call the police when gangs demanded lucky money. Late one evening in the summer of 1977, Lee was in the Kuo Wah restaurant on Mott Street when a quiet and respectful man approached him. "Uncle Man, may I speak to you for a moment?" the man said.[7] When Lee stepped with him into a hallway, the man pulled a six-inch blade from an envelope and drove it into his stomach. Lee lingered in critical condition for days before pulling through. But the message rang out loud and clear in Chinatown, and there was no doubting who had sent it. "Nicky was directly involved in ordering it," Detective Neil Mauriello said. "Even the assassin, when we talked to him, said Nicky put him up to it."[8]

The only people Louie couldn't silence in Chinatown were the leaders of other gangs. Throughout Louie's leadership of the Ghost Shadows in the 1970s, the gang was at constant war with the Flying Dragons and the Tung On, who were also at war with each other. Gangsters were cut down in restaurants, movie theaters, and bowling alleys. The murders took place in Manhattan, Queens and Brooklyn, and even in other cities.

On March 31, 1976, the violence took a horrifying turn. A month earlier, a Shadow named Richie Dong had been killed by the Flying Dragons on Pell Street. Bent on revenge, Louie had split his gang into three teams to hunt down rival gang members. On this night, they got word that Dragons were in the Co-Luck Restaurant at 42 Bowery, just south of Canal Street. Louie dispatched a team of three Ghost Shadows to assault the restaurant's dining room, not knowing how badly they would bungle the job. Confronted by a double set of glass doors, the gunmen opened one set but decided to fire through the other. With glass knocking the bullets off course, all but one of the Dragons ran to the rear of the restaurant and were unhurt. But innocent bystanders were not so lucky. A 39-year-old woman named Victoria Kwa, who was eating dinner with her husband and 10-year-old daughter, was shot in the head and killed. Five other bystanders and one Dragon were injured. When police arrived, the 10-year-old was standing over her mother's body crying, "Mommy, Mommy, Mommy!"[9]

The killing even got to be too much for the gangsters. Warned by *tong* leaders that the violence was hurting business, Louie called for a peace conference among leaders of the Ghost Shadows, Flying Dragons, White Eagles, and Black Eagles at the CCBA headquarters on Mott Street. The four gangs held an extraordinary news conference with the Chinese-language press on August 12, 1976, and announced that they were going to stop the killing. When a *New York Times* reporter showed up afterward, the gang members waved him off and refused to talk. Of course, the treaty did not last, largely because the Eagles were still consigned to the outskirts of Chinatown, but the real significance of the news conference is that it was held at all.[10]

By then, Louie had more to worry about than just other gangs. He was facing an insurrection in his own gang. Younger members like Peter Chin (better known as Kid Jai), Robert Hu (Taiwan), Shiu Ping Wu (Applehead) and others had been resentful of Louie for years. They accused him of keeping too much of the gang's extortion, loan-sharking and robbery money for himself. They also resented his recruitment of gang members from Chicago, Toronto and Boston, who they felt were sharing unfairly in the gang's spoils. Members of the rebel faction attempted to kill Louie several times, but never succeeded. It was Peter Chin who sent Potato to kill Louie in the Mott Street barbershop. After recovering from that shooting, Louie fled to Chicago, where he assembled some of his contacts there into a new gang.

But the troubles were not over for the legendary gang leader. A former Hong Kong police sergeant named Eddie Chan had taken over the On Leong in the late 1970s and had begun moving to control the rackets in Chinatown. He had a habit of sending Ghost Shadows to other cities when the *tong*'s affiliates ran into trouble. When Louie's new gang started disrupting the Chicago On Leong's gambling house in the summer of 1980, Chan paid Robert Hu—the Shadows' new leader—to send four of his gang members to take care of the problem.

Led by Lenny Chow, one of the gang's most reliable enforcers, the four Shadows planted themselves inside the Chicago On Leong's ornate headquarters on August 9, 1980, and waited for Louie's gang to show up. They weren't disappointed. Four gang members pulled in front of the *tong* building on Wentworth Avenue, but Louie was not among them. The four Shadows, positioned in various windows, opened fire on the car. Gang member William Chin was hit in the neck, chest and arm, and was immediately paralyzed from the neck down. Awaiting surgery in the hospital, he kept asking a nurse, "Am I die? Am I die?"[11]

Police who entered the *tong* headquarters after the shooting found a confusing labyrinth of corridors and locked rooms. They never found the one the Shadows were hiding in. The paraplegic Chin told police that "Lenny from New York" did the shooting and agreed to testify, but fate got in the way. Condemned to spend the rest of his life in a bed, Chin repeatedly tried to kill himself by pulling out his oxygen tube. He died in 1981 before the Shadows came to trial. And police investigators, relying on doctors' assurances that Chin would live, had never bothered to take an affidavit from him. Lenny Chow and the other Shadows walked.

Incredibly, Louie still had one trick up his sleeve. He had returned to New York before the Chin killing (when it took place, he was in Manhattan being prepared by Assistant District Attorney Nancy Ryan to testify against Potato for shooting him in the barbershop) to mount an attempt to regain power. He did this by taking control of the White Tigers, a Queens gang made up of other former Shadows who had been exiled from Mott Street. In late 1980, the Tigers began hanging around Mott Street in an effort to force a meeting with Robert Hu, the Shadows' new leader. On December 23, Hu agreed to meet them at 7 P.M. in the Mayflower Restaurant on Mott Street.

Hu and Louie sat down facing each other in a booth. Tension was thick in the air. Members of both gangs filled the other tables and booths in the restaurant. Louie, who was wearing a bullet-proof vest, had already given the Tigers orders to kill Hu if he didn't accede to their demands. The tension grew even thicker when two uniformed police officers walked in and sat in a booth. Their eyes almost popped out when they saw Louie back on Mott Street, and they ended up listening in on the conversation.

Louie said that his men were up and down Mott Street and that the Ghost Shadows needed a new leader. "Whatever was done in the past, it was not my fault," he said. Hu responded, "We all know what you did in the past. We know your way of doing things. It may be that once I get (outside), you'll gun me down. That's your way of doing things . . . If you want to fight, then we'll fight."[12]

Hu was right on the mark about Louie's methods. As soon as he got outside, a White Tiger named Billy Chin approached from across Mott Street. Tiger leader Peter Chan yelled out, "Shoot him!" but the gun jammed. He finally got off one or two shots that struck no one. All the Tigers were arrested. Chan and Chin were convicted, but Louie's incredible lucky streak was not yet over. He was acquitted after Hu changed his mind about testifying against him.

The attempt on Hu's life had been Louie's last stand. Hu himself was injured in a gun battle with another gang, and control over the Ghost Shadows passed to Peter Chin, a stone-cold killer who led the gang through what investigators see as its most violent period. More innocent people would be killed during Chin's reign than in all the other years of the gang's history combined.

Four years younger than Louie, Peter Chin was a fierce-looking character who had been raised in a troubled household. His father had been committed to a mental institution when Chin was a young boy, and he had been on the streets since his early teenage years. He had been seriously wounded in gang skirmishes at least twice before his 20th birthday.

Chin's hallmark as the Ghost Shadows' leader was violence. Out of paranoia, he ordered the murders of several former Ghost Shadows who had been Louie's allies but had left the gang. One of them, Pak Chui, the Shadow who had driven the Joker to his burial ground in the East River, had moved to Florida after Louie's shooting. When he came back to Chinatown a year later to visit his family on his birthday, Chin had him shot down as he walked toward his family's apartment complex.

In November 1979, Ghost Shadows abducted two men they believed to be Tung On members from the Pagoda Theatre and, on Chin's orders, executed them in the hallway of a tenement. But it turned out they had the wrong people; the victims weren't even gang members. An even more horrendous tragedy occurred on January 15, 1980, when the Shadows were at the height of their war with the White Tigers. Man Sze Wei, 24, and Kam Piu Lui, 19, were returning from a junket from Atlantic City and got off the bus in Chinatown. Both were students who worked part-time in a bakery and had no ties with any gang. But they made the mistake of walking into the territory of the paranoid Peter Chin.

The students were confronted by Ghost Shadows on Mott street, pulled into a doorway and interrogated about whether they were White Tigers. Terrified, the students said they were not. The Shadows believed them, but Chin said to kill them anyway to show other gangs what the Shadows were made of.

Under orders from Chin, gang members Daniel Lee, Steven Yau, Sam Kwang and Willie Chau forced the students into a black Cadillac and drove them across the Manhattan Bridge to a deserted spot in Brooklyn. The frightened students kept insisting that they weren't White Tigers, and Lee told them they then had nothing to worry about. Nancy Ryan, the assistant district attorney who was the Shadows' chief nemesis, says she is still haunted by what happened next. "When they took Man Sze Wei out of the car, he was so naive, he didn't even know what was going on," Ryan said. "He still had his hands in his coat pockets when they shot him in the back of the head. In the crime scene photo, his hands are still in his pockets and his schoolbooks are scattered all over the place." Kam Piu Lui was so terrified they had to pry him out of the car. He held so tightly to the leather door handle that he pulled it off. He tried to run, but Yau grabbed him and Kwang shot him dead.[13]

The Shadows were out of control. In July 1982, two of the gang's members met a 21-year-old Virginia tourist, Rita Nixon, in a Chinatown bar and took her back to an apartment for sex. When Kwang and several other Shadows showed up, the scene turned ugly. They took turns raping the woman. Then they played a children's game—rock-scissors-paper—to decide who would kill her. She pleaded for her life, telling them that she had a small child. But they were unmoved. It took four Shadows to hold the struggling woman while two others put an electrical cord around her neck and, with one holding each end, strangled her to death.[14]

By 1982, police had an informant in the gang named Raymond Wong. Wearing a wire, he recorded the Shadows discussing Nixon's murder, and all the participants were arrested. But that was only the start of the Ghost Shadows' troubles. With the informant's help, police detectives and Assistant District At-

torney Nancy Ryan amassed enough evidence to bring the Shadows into federal court to be charged under the RICO law. Ryan,
who had become known as the Dragon Lady in Chinatown for
prosecuting Chinese gangsters, was deputized as a special federal
prosecutor. On February 18, 1985, 25 top members of the Ghost
Shadows gang were named in a racketeering indictment that
cited crimes ranging from Louie's first armed robbery in 1972
and the wars with the White Eagles to the slayings of the innocent students in Brooklyn. It was the first federal racketeering
case against a Chinese gang, and it got Nicky Louie, Peter Chin,
Daniel Lee, Lenny Chow and most of the other major gang figures sent off to jail. Chin, the most vicious of the gangsters, was
sentenced to 60 years, the longest term of any of them. Louie
served nine years in prison and was recently released. In the
summer of 1994, he and Neil Mauriello were trying to interest
producers in a made-for-TV movie based loosely on Louie's life.

The RICO case did not destroy the Ghost Shadows. New leaders emerged after 1985, prodded by the On Leong, and the gang
split into Bayard Street and Mott Street factions. It remains the
dominant gang in the heart of Chinatown, and its members are
also active in Queens, Brooklyn and northern New Jersey. Apart
from several skirmishes with a Vietnamese gang called Born to
Kill around 1990, the gang appears to be operating without the
regular outbreaks of violence that helped bring down its earlier
leaders. But old habits die hard. In July 1991, several Ghost
Shadows exchanged gunfire during a dispute at the corner of Bayard and Mulberry Streets. None of the Shadows were injured.
But one of the stray shots hit and killed Rhona Lantin, a 26-year-
old University of Maryland graduate student. She had come to
Chinatown to have fun.

Nicky Louie laid the groundwork for the emergence of Chinese
organized crime. But a succeeding generation of gang leaders,
less ferocious and reckless than the *dai los* of the Ghost Shadows,
turned it into a reality. While the gang wars were raging in New
York in the late 1970s and early 1980s, more level-headed gangsters were forging ties across the country and plotting the emer-

gence of a national Chinese crime syndicate. It was their forays into international narcotics smuggling and a sophisticated array of white-collar crimes that captured the attention of federal authorities and led to congressional hearings on Asian organized crime. Some of the most insidious Chinese crime groups of the 1980s were not the violent New York gangs. In other cities, more sophisticated and businesslike Chinese gangsters helped to usher in a more profitable era for the Chinese Mafia. These gangsters were better at hiding behind legitimate businesses and more likely to exploit their ties with Hong Kong's criminal triads. They were also less prone to violence, recognizing—as had the Italian Mafia long before—that bloodshed only brings heat from the police.

One of those visionaries was Stephen Tse, founder of the Ping On gang in Boston. Tse, known on the street as "Skydragon," built one of the nation's largest and most prosperous Chinese gangs with little bloodshed and even without living off the earnings of Chinese merchants. With his ties to gangsters in Toronto, New York, San Francisco, Los Angeles and Hong Kong, Tse was a cunning international criminal who, were it not for a few missteps, would still be on top.

Born in Hong Kong, Tse came to Boston in the early 1970s after spending time in New York. Far from the bustle and prosperity of Mott Street, Boston's Chinatown for many years was a quiet and dingy 46 acres squeezed between the Massachusetts Turnpike extension and the Combat Zone, the city's raunchy red-light district. The post-1965 influx of Hong Kong-born Chinese breathed new life into the neighborhood, tripling its population to 5,200 by 1990.

A soft-spoken man and conservative dresser, Tse hardly stood out among the thousands of Hong Kong Chinese in Boston's Chinatown, and little is known of his criminal career in the early 1970s. His first brush with the law was his arrest for a 1974 home-invasion robbery. Tse admitted to slashing a Brookline, Massachusetts, woman with a knife as he robbed her of $2,000 in receipts from a Chinese restaurant. But he served only two years of a 10-year sentence because of a probation report that painted him as a law-abiding young man who had gone temporarily astray. "It was the most sanguine report I've ever seen," said an FBI agent who examined it years later. "It's kind of amusing in light of his subsequent behavior, but he fooled some social worker into thinking he was a model citizen."[15]

After his release from prison, Tse went to work in an On Leong gambling house on Beach Street. The On Leong had a monopoly on Chinatown's gambling in those days and was able to operate without any protection from gangs. Through most of the 1970s, the neighborhood had no local gangs, and the periodic forays of the Ghost Shadows and Flying Dragons into the district were always short-lived. That perhaps explains the On Leong's alarm when Tse began assembling some of the neighborhood's Hong Kong-born youth into a gang in the late 1970s.

In Boston, the plight of Chinese youth in the public schools was not much different than in New York. Indeed, it may have been worse. Racial tension in Boston was at an all-time high in the 1970s, and Chinese youth were thrown into the battleground of Charlestown High School, where teachers were too busy preventing wars between black and Irish kids to worry about the special needs of Asian immigrants. On the street, things were not much better. Any Chinese teenager who dropped out of school could look forward to a career waiting on tables in a Chinese restaurant. Ming Kwong, who became a top lieutenant in the Ping On gang, once told a neighborhood youth worker: "I didn't want to end up like this. You remember when I was out every day looking for a job and couldn't find anything."[16]

Stephen Tse reached out to these troubled sons of Chinatown. Some kids joined his gang with little prompting. Others were beaten by the new gang until they gave up and joined. And neighborhood residents learned not to stand in the Ping On's way. When an aging drug dealer named Sammy Chin confronted the gang about picking on the neighborhood's youth, he didn't live long to regret it. Chin was shot to death on November 5, 1980, by two gang members in Bob Lee's Islander restaurant on Tyler Street.[17]

Incidents like these so incensed the On Leong that they expelled Tse from the *tong*. But Tse had a new sponsor in Harry Mook, head of the local branch of the Chee Kung Tong, or Chinese Freemasons. Mook's father had once been a top civic leader in Chinatown, and his son had used the family name to develop impeccable connections both in Chinatown and elsewhere in Boston. Mook's restaurant on Tyler Street, the Four Seas, had an influential clientele that included everyone from politicians to Italian gangsters. "One Boston lawyer recalls walking into the restaurant in the late 1960s and seeing six state senators and staffers in one corner and a half-dozen North End gangsters in another," wrote Daniel Golden in the *Boston Globe Magazine*. "The groups were arguing about Robert Kennedy, who had recently been assassinated. The Italian mobsters hated Kennedy, while the Irish pols worshipped him."[18] Mook was widely reported to have sold numbers in Chinatown for the North End mob. And now, with Tse's muscle, he would have a chance to push the On Leong out of the way and develop some rackets of his own.

Tse incorporated his gang in state records as the Ping On Club in 1982 and made its headquarters the Freemasons' building at 6 Tyler Street. The gang had begun by shaking down black pimps who stationed their hookers in Chinatown late at night, but Tse quickly moved onto bigger things. The On Leong's prime gambling house was a building at 65 Beach Street (You could always tell when it was "open skin" because a sinister pair of eyes always watched the street through a small slot in the door.) Tse and a Freemason named Joe Bow Fong opened a competing house at 50A Beach Street. They also had gang members disrupt the gambling at 65 Beach and demand protection payments from the On Leong.[19]

The On Leong appealed to the New York chapter for help. Eddie Chan, the ruthless national president, sent Lenny Chow and three other Ghost Shadows to protect the gambling and deal with the Ping On. On March 18, 1982, Ping On members jumped the Shadows in broad daylight as they walked past 6 Tyler Street. Sui Keung Szeto, a 21-year-old Ping On member who had been forcibly recruited by the gang, got Chow in a headlock. But Chow, the Shadows' battle-tested enforcer, got the better of him. He pulled a knife out of his pocket and drove it into Szeto's neck, killing him. Though a jury later found that Chow had acted in self-defense, the Ghost Shadows' effort to scare off the Ping On had failed. The On Leong finally capitulated, and the neighborhood's most lucrative gambling house became an operation at 32 Oxford Street, operated by Tse and his second-in-command, Michael Kwong. Almost without firing a shot, the Ping On had taken over Boston's Chinatown.

Tse became a neighborhood big shot. With his wife, Angela, he opened his own restaurant on Tyler Street, the Kung Fu, and threw down $86,000 in cash to buy a house in suburban Quincy. His gambling houses alone were enough to make him a rich man, taking in up to $100,000 on a good night. What is more, they were protected from the police. Mook had seen to that, making payments to two police officers and a detective lieutenant. "Since the beginning of time, whoever's down here we take care of," Mook told a detective who was wearing a wire. "They go somewhere else, somebody else take care of them. They come back here, we take care of them."[20]

While Mook was taking care of things at home, Tse was forging ties with Chinese gangsters in other cities. He made regular trips to Toronto for meetings with that city's top Chinese mobster, Danny Mo, head of the local branch of the Kung Lok triad. They signified their alliance by performing an ancient triad ceremony called "burning the yellow paper."[21]

Together with Chinese mobsters from other cities, Tse set up a firm in 1981 called the Oriental Arts Promotional Corp. In Boston, the firm was incorporated at 6 Tyler Street, with Tse, Joe Bow Fong and Ming Kwong, Michael's brother, as its officers. In other cities, it was incorporated under other gangsters' names. The others were Danny Mo in Toronto; Peter Chin, the Ghost Shadows leader, in New York; Vincent Jew, leader of the Wah Ching in San Francisco; and Tong Young, Jew's lieutenant and leader of the Wah Ching in Los Angeles. The purpose of the corporation was to monopolize the booking of Chinese entertainers who came to the United States from Hong Kong, Taiwan or mainland China. It was a page taken right out of the triads' book, for the Hong Kong societies, especially the Sun Yee On, had long had their hands in entertainment. Indeed, three of the company's officers—Mo, Jew and Young—went to Hong Kong in 1983 to meet with Lau Wing Keung, then head of the colony's Kung Lok triad.[22]

Like Tse, Vincent Jew has been one of the nation's most cunning gang leaders. Before he fled to Asia around 1990, he headed the oldest and largest Chinese gang in the country. Until a recent challenge in the Bay Area by the Wo Hop To, a Hong Kong triad, the Wah Ching had monopolized Chinese rackets up and down the West Coast, from San Diego to Portland. At its peak, the Wah Ching was said to have 700 members, more than most of the nation's Mafia families. As of 1994, it was still the dominant Chinese crime group in Los Angeles and had interests around the country.

Jew was a veteran of the fierce gang wars that gripped San Francisco's Chinese underworld in the 1970s. The battle began around 1971, when two American-born brothers, Joe and Chung Way Fong, split off from the Wah Ching and formed a competing gang called the Chung Ching Yee. The new gang sought a piece of the Wah Ching's extortion rackets, but ended up being chased out of Chinatown. It began operating in the Richmond and Japantown districts of San Francisco while staging regular attempts to regain a foothold in Chinatown. The next two years were the bloodiest in Chinatown since the *tong* war days. Cruising the streets of Chinatown in hopped-up Firebirds and Chargers, rival gangsters with hip Fu Manchu mustaches and faded blue jeans shot at each other on sight. Eleven members of the two gangs were killed in 1972 and 1973 alone.

One of Joe Fong's older brothers was killed. His younger brother, Chung Way, then 15, was arrested for the murder of Wah Ching leader Anton Wong. Joe Fong himself received a life sentence for conspiracy to murder after a Wah Ching car was riddled with bullets in October 1972. "It was a really bloody battle," said Sergeant Dan Foley of the San Francisco police gang task force. "It always is when you have an internal split. You know who these people are and where they live. It's like getting pissed off at someone in your family."[23] Most of the original Chung Ching Yee rebels were dead or in jail by the mid-1970s, but the battle raged on. The gang became known as the Joe Boys, after its jailed leader, but the goal remained the same. For nearly a decade, the Joe Boys fought for a place in Chinatown.

The feud culminated in the Golden Dragon massacre. Michael (Hot Dog) Louie was high on the Joe Boys' hit list. At the time of the massacre, he was on probation for his part in the killing of a Joe Boy named Lincoln Louie three years earlier. He was also the prime suspect in the killing of Joe Boy member Felix Huie on July 4, 1977, at the Ping Yuen housing project on Pacific Avenue. Huie was killed in a dispute over fireworks sales. The Joe Boys had tried to kill Louie in 1976 in a shooting in Chinatown's Jade Palace restaurant, but the bullet had only struck his leg. Having had a year to practice for the Golden Dragon, their aim hadn't improved much.

After the Golden Dragon bloodbath, the Joe Boys leaders were arrested and the gang was all but finished. By 1980, the Wah Ching controlled the Chinese rackets in the Bay Area. Under its new leader, Vincent Jew, the gang expanded up and down the West Coast. Jew was a businessman who preferred profits to violence. "He was more of an intelligent person," an investigator told the *San Francisco Examiner* in 1990. "He was never a street fighter, never one of the guys on the street mixing it up. He was allegedly the brains of what was going on. But there was nothing on him that we could ever prove. If you met him, you would never think anything of him. He seems like a nice, easy-going person." Another investigator put it this way: "Jew is smooth, real smooth. He could talk his way out of anything. . . . Suave, handsome, very sophisticated. He has a nice suburban house, a wife, a luxury car, a nice watch, all the signs of a good young businessman."[24]

Jew sent one of his top lieutenants, Tony (Sweet Plum) Young, to Los Angeles, where he laid claim to Asian rackets in China-town and parts of the San Gabriel Valley. Jew stayed behind in San Francisco and built a sophisticated criminal enterprise. He made creative use of the Chinese mob's monopoly on entertainment, expanding it into Chinese video cassettes. Since the mid-1980s, demand for Chinese videos ranging from movies and soap operas to dubbed reruns of "Gunsmoke" has soared in American Chinatowns. The largest exporter of such videos had been a company called Hong Kong TV Broadcasts, headed by a businessman named Jack Soo. Jew leaned on Soo to make him a partner. First, Wah Ching members shattered Soo's office windows in San Francisco. Then Jew visited Soo's office and made veiled threats by commenting on the attractiveness of his wife and children. Soo relented and made Jew his marketing director—and he may have been glad he did. Says a 1988 U.S. Justice Department report: "Jew appears to have been extremely effective as marketing director. With few exceptions, competitors have gone out of business or accepted contracts as sublicensees. Uncooperative retailers have had their stores shot up and firebombed by suspected Wah Ching."[25]

In October 1990, federal agents raided Hong Kong TV's office on Bayshore Avenue in San Francisco and carted off 637 boxes of documents and $150,000 in checks as part of an investigation into money laundering and other crimes. Agents also searched the company's Jackson Street accounting firm, C&S Business Services. But they were far too late to get their hands on Vincent Jew. He had already named a young man named Danny Wong as his successor to the Wah Ching leadership and taken off for Asia. Reports have put him in Taiwan and Hong Kong, where he is allegedly associated with the powerful Sun Yee On triad.[26]

The growing influence of gangsters like Tse and Jew had not gone unnoticed by law enforcement. Even if the federal authorities were not yet interested, state and local investigators began having annual conferences on the Chinese mob in the late 1970s. Still, if average Americans knew anything at all about the Chinese mob, they viewed the problem as one of gun-toting juvenile delinquents. Few people used the term "organized crime" in connection with the Chinese before the President's Commission on Organized Crime held three days of hearings on the Asian underworld in October 1984. The commission convened in New

York's Foley Square, once home to the Five Points gangs and just a few blocks from present-day Chinatown. Among those issued subpoenas were Stephen Tse, Vincent Jew and several other Chinese mobsters. Jew was smart enough to be temporarily out of the country when the subpoena was issued. But Tse was caught flat-footed. After being offered immunity from prosecution, he was ordered imprisoned for 18 months for refusing to testify.

The commission can take credit for focusing public attention, however fleetingly, on the problem of Chinese organized crime. But it would be stretching the truth to say that the hearings galvanized federal law enforcement. If the Chinese underworld had stayed in the back alleys of America, shaking down immigrant merchants and gambling houses, the problem might have lingered on the back burner forever. What finally prompted federal authorities to act was the Chinese mob's headlong push into a racket that strikes at the heart of every community in America: dope smuggling.

During the years that Nicky Louie was building his legend on Mott Street, Michael Chen was his counterpart on Pell Street. He was the head of the Flying Dragons, a gang even deadlier than the fabled Ghost Shadows. Chen was Louie's opposite. If Louie could have passed as a college student, Chen looked the part of the gang leader. He was tall and always wore dark rumpled clothing. His hair was stringy and unkempt. Though quiet like Louie, Chen didn't have the same charisma. His control over the other Dragons was based on a simple formula. He was tougher and smarter than they were.

Chen always knew what other people were up to. He had spies in other gangs and moles in the Police Department. He could have license plates checked by a connection in the state motor vehicles division. Chen even had an official Police Department press badge that listed him as a reporter for a local Chinese radio station.

But the Hip Sing valued Chen for more than his espionage. He was also an able enforcer who kept a good watch on the *tong*'s gambling houses on Pell Street. With his boys on Pell, even the dreaded Ghost Shadows would never round the corner from Mott and venture into Hip Sing territory. He had led the Dragons through its years of combat with the Tung On, whose turf on Division Street and East Broadway lay just across the Bowery. "Michael was a tough kid and he knew how to follow orders," recalls John Feehan, the former DEA agent. "He almost killed every Tung On. It got to the point where there were only four or five Tung On kids left. One time he set a building on fire and he was going to shoot them as they came out."[27]

But Chen was not a gang leader for the 1980s. Chinatown's gambling houses were closing because of pressure from the police and competition from legalized gaming in Atlantic City. Many Chinese came to prefer hopping on a bus to the New Jersey resort to cramming into a filthy, smoke-filled basement. The gangs needed a racket to replace their lost gambling income, and by 1983 the heroin market was just waiting to be tapped. With the drug's popularity on the rise, Hong Kong triads were moving it into the country, and the Mafia was buying up the stuff. Anybody who acted as the middleman stood to make a fortune. One of Chen's underlings, Johnny Eng, was eager to jump into the business. But Chen wasn't interested. At 33, he was already old for a Chinese gang member. He was looking forward to raking in a couple more years' worth of extortion money and retiring. He had confided to friends that he wanted to get off the streets before he got killed.[28]

Johnny Eng wasn't the type to take no for an answer. Known as "Onionhead" to his friends, Eng was short, chunky and bespectacled. Known for his big mouth and fiery temper, Eng was fond of wearing expensive suits and waving around wads of cash. (Once, when he was planning to buy a Pell Street restaurant, he made a big show of it, telling everyone that he had $60,000 in a bag and was on his way to meet the seller's lawyer. When he got to the lawyer's office on Lafayette Street, two gunmen were waiting for him and stole the money.)[29] The pugnacious Eng told anyone who would listen that heroin was the biggest racket ever to hit Chinatown. He even confided to a federal agent that an Italian mobster from Mulberry Street had come into his restaurant and put a cash-filled briefcase on the counter. When you get the heroin, the mobster said, call me.[30] Only Chen stood in the way.

On March 13, 1983, an officer of the Hip Sing opened the door of the *tong*'s credit union at 15 Pell Street and found Chen's body inside. The gang leader had no shortage of enemies. Some of his own gang members had gripes against him for keeping too much of the gang's extortion money. But detectives zeroed in on Eng. "My personal belief is that Michael was killed because he didn't want to do dope," said retired police detective Neil Mauriello.[31]

Eng did plenty of dope, and so did lots of other Chinese gangsters. In the mid-1980s, Southeast Asian heroin controlled by the Hong Kong triads began flooding New York's ghettos, the nation's biggest market for the drug. The total amount of opium produced worldwide in 1985 was 1,458 metric tons. By 1989, production in Southeast Asia alone reached 3,054 metric tons, 72 percent of production worldwide. Suddenly, Chinatown's street-corner gangs, who had been confined to their own neighborhood for so many years, were in other parts of the city making drug deals with Italian, black and Hispanic gangsters. Gangsters like Stephen Tse and Vincent Jew were no longer just talking about entertainment on their trips to Hong Kong. They were talking about heroin. In one Hong Kong visit, Tse arranged to have heroin smuggled back in the bellies of frozen fish.[32]

Drugs were nothing new to Chinatown. *Tongs* had been smuggling opium into American Chinatowns since the 1800s. After Mao Zedong overthrew the Kuomintang in 1949, some of Chiang Kai-shek's crooked generals and fellow triad members took over New York's On Leong and brought their dope-smuggling rackets with them. The U.S. Bureau of Narcotics, the predecessor of the DEA, was in New York's Chinatown in the early 1960s trying to flush the dope smugglers out of the gambling dens.[33] But until the 1970s, Golden Triangle heroin was just a trickle compared to the poundage that the Mafia was smuggling out of southwestern Asia. The Turkey-Marseilles-New York pipeline—"the French Connection"—was the Feds' big problem.

The 1980s brought new opportunities for Chinese heroin

smugglers. Turkey had begun eradicating its heroin crop, and in the U.S. federal authorities dealt heavy blows to the Mafia's opium-smuggling apparatus. In the famed "Pizza Connection" case, the government convicted a former chief of the Sicilian Mafia, Gaetano Badalamenti, and 16 other American and Sicilian gangsters for operating a pipeline that dumped 1,650 pounds of heroin into this country over five years. American mob bosses across the country had their hands full with other federal indictments.

The market was wide open for the Chinese, and they had the means to take it over. Opium poppies are cultivated in the mountains of Thailand, Laos and Myanmar (formerly known as Burma) with little interference from their governments. The most famous of the opium producers is Khun Sa, a warlord who commands a 15,000-man army in the eastern hills of Myanmar's Shan state. Khun Sa is ostensibly a separatist fighting for Shan independence from the brutal government of Myanmar. But there are never any battles with the government forces. Khun Sa's real business is opium. He oversees the annual harvest of hundreds and sometimes thousands of tons of opium, up to 80 percent of the Golden Triangle's heroin production. His minions grow the opium and process it into heroin in jungle laboratories; then his army protects the mule caravans that transport the powder to the country's borders. Khun Sa's business is hardly a secret. The affable, sixtyish general meets with reporters in his jungle lair, dressed in his customary green fatigues. "We grow opium and deal in it so we can clothe ourselves and eat," he told one reporter. "If your only command is to stop opium, then you are killing us."[34] Attorney General Richard Thornburgh slapped the opium lord with a 10-count indictment for drug trafficking in 1990, but it was almost laughable. Khun Sa is as remote and unreachable as Colonel Kurtz, the out-of-control ivory trader in Joseph Conrad's *Heart of Darkness*.

After the heroin leaves the Golden Triangle, it becomes the property of the Hong Kong triads and their Chinese-American partners. Small parcels of heroin come to the United States on the bodies of couriers, or mules, who walk it through the airports, but bigger loads come in ship containers, often hidden among legitimate cargo. In one case, New York authorities seized more than 850 pounds of heroin hidden inside hollowed-out lawn-mower tires. The tires had been brought by ship from Hong Kong to Seattle, then transported East by rail. In September 1988, Boston authorities found 183 pounds of nearly pure heroin inside the steel roller of a machine made for washing bean sprouts.[35]

Chinese heroin smugglers have become the new international criminals, linking gangsters in Asia with their Chinese counterparts in Europe and the United States. Together with the Colombian cocaine cartels and the Sicilian and Russian Mafias, they have raised fears of the emergence of a global crime syndicate that could overwhelm any single country's criminal-justice system. "The prospect of a new 'super Mafia' of the nineties is a daunting one," U.S. Senator Joseph Biden said after a 1990 committee hearing on Asian heroin smuggling.[36]

The leaders of this super-Mafia would be people like Johnny Kon, a member of Hong Kong's Wo On Lok triad and the biggest Chinese heroin smuggler ever arrested by American authorities. A muscular man with wavy black hair, Kon started out as a legitimate Hong Kong furrier in his early 20s. In the 1960s, a friend working at U.S. military headquarters in Vietnam convinced him to go to Saigon. Kon set up business there, operating lucrative concessions on U.S. military bases and peddling furs to servicemen. He also arranged R&R tours for servicemen in Hong Kong, a business that gave him contacts with triad members who owned many of the colony's nightclubs. Kon was a rich man when he caught one of the last planes out of Saigon in 1975, but he made the mistake of pouring his money into Hong Kong real estate. The bottom fell out of that market after Britain started negotiating to return Hong Kong to China in 1997, and suddenly Kon was nearly $5 million in debt. So he opened a trading company in New York's fur district and began making regular trips back and forth from Hong Kong.[37]

At the time, the Big Circle Gang, made up of former Red

Guard militiamen who had been driven from China during Mao's Cultural Revolution, had been committing jewelry-store robberies in Hong Kong. Several of them approached Kon and convinced him to fence stolen goods through his international business contacts. But after only a few months of selling jewelry, Kon decided heroin would be more profitable. So he assembled several Big Circle members into a gang called the Flaming Eagles, which he intended to operate separately from the triads.

Between 1984 and 1989, Kon's gang smuggled more than 1,700 pounds of heroin into the United States. It shipped the powder in ice buckets, vases, picture frames and other containers. The profits were enormous. A kilo of heroin purchased for $7,000 in Bangkok would sell for $90,000 in New York. Kon invested the profits in real estate around the Western Hemisphere. He bought a million-dollar home in Panama City, Panama, commercial real estate in San Francisco, part of a shopping mall in Queens and a movie theater in New York's Chinatown. He also bought a $400,000 ranch house in Short Hills, New Jersey, for his wife.[38]

Authorities caught onto Kon's operation in 1984, when 126 pounds of his heroin were seized in a fishing trawler in Hong Kong harbor. But the Feds couldn't build a case until October 1986, when one of the Flaming Eagles was arrested and gave up his boss. Kon was arrested in 1988 as he stepped out the door of the New York Hilton. He had $32 in his pocket and a $25,000 diamond-studded Piaget watch on his wrist. "I smuggle gems, jewels and cigarettes, but not drugs," he told the arresting agents.[39]

The Flying Dragons, the Ghost Shadows and other gangs have become distribution arms for smugglers like Kon. A member of Stephen Tse's Ping On gang told an undercover agent that he could supply him with a pound of heroin a week, valued at $1 million on the street. Johnny Eng made so much money off heroin that he started smuggling it himself, dividing his time between New York and Hong Kong. Among the loads of heroin he shipped to the United States were the 163 pounds that Boston authorities seized in the bean-sprout-washing machine. Eng invested his money in New York restaurants and South American farms. But his luck ran out when he was indicted by a federal grand jury in Brooklyn and extradited from Hong Kong. In September 1993, he was sentenced to 24 years in prison. "You ruined the lives of many other families and many children," Judge Reena Raggi told Eng before she sent him off to jail.[40]

7: Four Seas, One Brother

On November 17, 1987, a U.S. Customs inspector stopped a red Toyota Celica that was crossing the border from Canada into Blaine, Washington. The inspector had no real reason to pick on this particular car. It was driven by a conservatively dressed Chinese man in his 40s who was calm and more than cooperative as he answered the inspector's questions and displayed documents showing that the Toyota was rented. But something, nothing more than a hunch really, told the inspector that this was a car he should look over more closely. When he opened the trunk, his suspicions were borne out. A Chinese illegal alien and alleged heroin courier named Lee Ying-yee was hiding in the trunk.

The Customs inspector could hardly have known it at the time, but he was lifting the lid on more than just a case of alien smuggling. The car's driver was Peter Chong, a high-ranking member of the Wo Hop To triad in Hong Kong, a man who personified the worst fears of law enforcement officials who monitor the international movements of Chinese gangsters. For nearly a decade, U.S. authorities have been wringing their hands over what will happen when Britain's 99-year lease of Hong Kong expires in 1997 and the colony reverts to the control of mainland China. Their worst fear is that triad bosses will flee the colony and set up operations in the United States, bringing with them a vast trove of criminal experience and millions of dollars to invest in illicit enterprises. Were this to happen, Hong Kong's underworld, older and wealthier than the Italian Mafia, would suddenly have a new home in this country, making our previous experience with Chinese gangsters pale in comparison.

The possibility of such a triad invasion is real, and we no longer have to speculate on what it would look like. After Chong walked away from the alien-smuggling charge without any jail time, he proceeded to plant the triad flag in the United States, taking over northern California's Asian underworld with an efficiency that even Meyer Lansky would admire.

The Wo Hop To—the name in Cantonese means "Harmoniously United Association"—is not one of Hong Kong's biggest triads. It is dwarfed by the 47,000-member Sun Yee On and is a relatively small player in the world heroin trade and Hong Kong's mobbed-up entertainment industry. But it makes money the old-fashioned way. In Hong Kong's Wanchai neighborhood, a red-light district famed for the dozens of all-night bars and brothels that once made it a popular destination for foreign sailors, the Wo Hop To collects protection money from some 200 businesses and controls prostitution, gambling, and loan-sharking.

The Wo Hop To triad made its U.S. debut in the person of Alfred Chu, a reputed enforcer and convicted felon who managed to hide his criminal past long enough to immigrate to San Francisco in the early 1980s. Chu wasted little time in establishing a Wo Hop To outpost in the Bay Area. First he infiltrated the loosely regulated "card clubs" that are a form of legalized gambling in California. He found work as manager of the Key Club in Emeryville, bolstering the club's already large Asian clientele by introducing the Chinese game *pai gow* and running shuttle buses there from Oakland's Chinatown. Soon Chu was running a loan-sharking business out of the Key Club and recruiting young thugs in Oakland to act as collectors, according to law enforcement officers. In late 1987, gang investigators in Oakland and San Francisco began to hear kids in their Chinatowns bragging that they were part of something called the Wo Hop To. "Just about that time, we had some kids in our interview room and when they left,

'WHT' was scratched into the table," said Sergeant Daniel Foley of the San Francisco Police Department's gang task force. "We didn't know much about the Wo Hop To then. All we knew was that it had something to do with Alfred Chu."[1]

Chu did not last long in San Francisco. A U.S. immigration investigation revealed in 1988 that he had lied on his residency application five years earlier, forgetting to mention that he had Hong Kong convictions for gambling, extortion and statutory rape dating back to 1966. Prior to his arrest by immigration officials, Chu had also been linked to a loan-sharking operation at the Sante Fe Club in Emeryville, where a police raid found documents tying him to known Bay Area gang members. Brushing aside Chu's complaints that "evil people" were setting him up, a federal judge sentenced the 41-year-old gangster to five years in prison for the immigration violation.[2]

After Chu's imprisonment, the Wo Hop To structure he had built in Oakland fell into the hands of Peter Chong. Chong had impeccable connections in the Wo Hop To. He was a close confi-

Sgt. Daniel Foley of the San Francisco Police Department tracked the Wo Hop To "invasion." (John O'Hara)

dant of Chan Ting-Hung, the Wo Hop To's elderly "dragon head," and had been romantically involved with his daughter. Respectable looking, well-dressed, fluent in English, the soft-spoken Chong was the perfect emissary for the triad. He pursued the syndicate's interests quietly, setting up gambling houses and other criminal operations without challenging existing crime groups or attracting the attention of police. San Francisco's Chinese rackets had been dominated by the Wah Ching since the late 1970s, and Chong did nothing to ruffle the gang's feathers. He treated the gang's leaders with respect, giving them a share of his profits like all of Chinatown's other gambling-house operators. None of them could have guessed that the smiling businessman with the cherub's face was planning nothing less than their extinction.

For while he was "giving face" to the Wah Ching, Chong had quietly begun to court independent Chinese gangsters around the Bay Area. Drawing on what seemed to be an endless supply of cash from Hong Kong, Chong won the allegiance of young hoodlums by offering them financing for gambling and loan-sharking operations. The most important of these new allies was a ruthless young gangster named Raymond (Shrimp Boy) Chow. Chow had been a member of the Hop Sing Boys, a gang allied with the Wah Ching during the Joe Boys war, and had a reputation for being wild and unpredictable. Back in 1978, Chow and two other armed gangsters had walked into the banquet of a Chinese engineers' society on Waverly Place and forced some 30 people to drop their cash and jewelry into a sack. The job got him a stint in prison, and when he got out in the early 1980s, his gang no longer existed in San Francisco. But Chow was an ambitious young gangster who was not about to genuflect before the Wah Ching. He started his own gang in Oakland's Chinatown and trained them to commit home-invasion robberies. In a matter of months he had shaped a ragtag group of thugs into a professional robbery crew. They would observe their victims for days, rent vans for the heists and burst into the homes carefully attired in masks and gloves. In one string of eight robberies in

San Francisco, the gang netted $450,000. But Chow's reckless-ness soon put him back behind bars. He became embroiled in a dispute with Wah Ching member David Quach in 1986 and burst into the Gold Key restaurant on Powell Street with a gun looking for him. His target was not in the restaurant, but he men-aced the other patrons enough to pick up two more years in prison.[3]

Back on the streets in 1988, Chow fell in with Peter Chong. The Wo Hop To leader gave Chow financing for a loan-sharking operation and helped him set up a brothel in Pacifica, a city just south of San Francisco. The two were as perfect a pair as Torrio and Capone. Chong supplied the financing and experience, and Chow supplied the muscle. It was a potent alliance that would soon be felt in Asian communities up and down the West Coast.

The Wo Hop To was also able to take advantage of a growing torpor within the Wah Ching. By the late 1980s, the gang was a legend in San Francisco. It had emerged as the Bay Area's domi-nant Chinese crime group after the Golden Dragon massacre, and its word was the law on the streets. Gambling-house opera-tors had to pay a tax to the Wah Ching before opening and then make regular weekly payments, or even take on a Wah Ching member as a partner. But with no other major gangs left in Chi-natown, this was all accomplished with little resort to violence. "The Wah Ching didn't have to send people to the gambling dens to threaten people or break up the place," said Foley of the gang task force. "It was just expected."[4]

Secure in their domination of Chinatown, the Wah Ching's leaders had grown soft. They were no longer the hungry young gangsters who had shot it out with the Joe Boys. Vincent Jew had moved to Hong Kong in 1984 and left the gang in the hands of his right-hand man, Danny (Pig Knuckles) Wong. Wong had been an able custodian of the Wah Ching's 25-year legacy as long there was no serious competition. He had made a fortune in gambling and extortion and he oversaw Jew's interests in the en-tertainment business. But he had no stomach for the kind of vio-lence that had convulsed Chinatown in the 1970s. He had a wife and children and a nice suburban home. When he ran into trouble with rival gangsters, his first reaction was to appease them rather than set off a gang war.

Danny Wong took just such an approach to a growing restlessness in the Wah Ching's ranks. One of the chief malcontents was Johnny Yee, a hot-headed gangster who had been in the Wah Ching since the 1960s. Yee was the *dai lo* of his own crew, a man who made a good living out of gambling and extortion. But he had never been cut in on the big money that he knew had been flowing into the pockets of Jew, Wong and other Wah Ching leaders. His dream was to follow Jew into the entertainment business, but he had neither the temperament nor the organizational skills to put it together. Yee had a reputation in Chinatown as a renegade. He would get drunk and wave his gun around or beat people up for no reason. Eventually his antics got to be too much for the Wah Ching's leaders. He had been stalling on repaying a gambling debt to gang member Tony Yan. Then one day in December 1989 he got drunk and, for no reason, tore up the Suey Sing *tong*'s gambling house on Jackson Street. Yan and another gang member, Johnny (Mun Jai) Ly, showed up at the scene and dragged Johnny Yee onto the sidewalk, beating him bloody in front of his wife and children.[5]

The dispute gave Peter Chong the opening he needed. He played the role of peacekeeper in the dispute, convincing Yee to approach Ly and request that they settle their differences. He even presided over a peace banquet in a Chinatown restaurant a few days after the beating. Chong spoke the language of peace and reconciliation, using the expression "Four Seas, One Brother" to describe the merits of cooperation between crime groups. By the end of the banquet, all sides were calling him *kow fu*, or "Uncle," a traditional term of respect. Through the next months he continued to cultivate his role as peacemaker—a man whose interests lay in preventing bloodshed on the streets of Chinatown. But what he was really doing was building up his own influence in the community and gathering more and more of Chinatown's factions into his orbit. When Yee felt he had lost face over the beating and moved to Portland, Oregon, Chong lent him $100,000 to open a gambling den there. Then, when Yee moved back to Chinatown and opened a *pai gow* house at 20 Beckett Alley, Chong gave Yee financing for a loan-sharking operation at the site. Yee, in essence, had defected from the Wah Ching and brought his people to Peter Chong's Wo Hop To, and Danny Wong hadn't done anything about it.[6]

Peter Chong slowly chipped away at the Wah Ching's power. Chong not only had Yee's faction under his control, but Raymond Chow was recruiting other disaffected Wah Ching members into the Hop Sing *tong*, which in turn had become affiliated with the Wo Hop To. (The Hop Sing had expelled its youth gang in the late 1970s after the Golden Dragon massacre had brought too much heat on its membership, but Chow bullied the *tong*'s leaders into accepting its return.) The Wo Hop To had also absorbed two Oakland gangs, the Hung Pho Vietnamese gang in San Jose, and a 60-member Vietnamese gang in Chinatown headed by Bobby Tsang, who had previously operated under the Wah Ching's auspices. The headquarters of this growing federation was the New Paradise nightclub in Oakland, whose name translates into Cantonese as "San Ying Kung," the same name as a famous massage parlor that the Wo Hop To owned in the Wanchai district of Hong Kong. The owners of this nightclub were Peter Chong, Raymond Chow, Johnny Yee and William Mui. Mui is the nephew of Hui Lui, a Hong Kong gangster who is the right-hand man of Chan Ting-Hung, the Wo Hop To's "dragon head." Mui's claim to fame in San Francisco was having been arrested in 1988 for smuggling heroin into the country inside condoms stuffed in the bellies of dead goldfish.

But even with all this new power behind him, Peter Chong was still careful about confronting the Wah Ching in Chinatown. When skirmishes between the two groups began cropping up in 1990, Chong would always say it was the fault of the reckless "little ones," that he was opposed to violence in the rackets. Violence, he would say, was bad for business. And yet with each shooting or beating the Wah Ching's power and respect dwindled and the balance of power shifted in Chong's favor.

The trouble started in July 1990, when Bobby Tsang and a

notorious Wah Ching enforcer named Danny Phat Vong got into a fight in a nightclub in San Francisco's North Beach section. Tsang was a wild Viet Ching (Vietnamese Chinese) gangster whose exploits in Chinatown were legendary. He once got into an argument with an off-duty California Highway Patrol officer in front of a San Francisco tavern and brutally karate-kicked the man in the head in front of his wife. When the man pulled out his service revolver and identified himself as a police officer, Tsang said, "Go ahead and shoot us," and fled with two others.[7] Tsang and Vong had a long-running feud over extortion collections in Chinatown, which no doubt played a part in their argument at the nightclub. Vong left Tsang beaten and bloodied, and word got out on the street that Tsang wanted revenge. It didn't take long to happen. On August 4, 1990, Vong had just left a nightclub called Cats, at Geary Boulevard and Gough Street, and was opening the trunk of his car when two men walked up and shot him to death. A month later, Vong's crew struck back. Bobby Tsang and some friends, as well as several gangsters from Johnny Yee's crew, were walking out of the Purple Onion nightclub on Columbus Avenue when gunmen opened fire on them. The bullets killed Michael Bit Wu, a 37-year-old Wo Hop To member, and injured six other people. Bobby Tsang was not hurt, but his brother John was gravely wounded.[8]

Always eager to be seen as the peacemaker, Peter Chong stepped in to arrange a truce between the Wah Ching and Bobby Tsang's crew. This time the banquet was at the Harbour Village Restaurant at Embarcadero Center, where Chong brought together leaders of the Wah Ching and the Wo Hop To; this was the last time the two gangs would sit together in the same room peacefully. Among the 14 people at the banquet were Wah Ching leader Danny Wong, Johnny Yee, Peter Chong, Raymond Chow, Bobby Tsang, Tom Tsang and Harry Dan-sin Vong, brother of the slain Wah Ching enforcer. Sitting at a round banquet table with a blood-red tablecloth, Wong explained that the Purple Onion shooting was the work of Danny Phat Vong's crew and was not sanctioned by the Wah Ching leadership. The Wah Ching would be willing to forget the two skirmishes, he said, and guarantee no trouble in Chinatown for six months. In return, Chong said he would take care of the living expenses of Tsang's gang members and keep them out of the Wah Ching's way.

But then Chong brought up the subject of Chinatown's rackets. He told the Wah Ching that all the competition between gangs threatened to bring back the bad old days of gang warfare in Chinatown. Violence only attracted the attention of police. What Chinatown needed, he said, was a single smooth-running syndicate with enough experience and financial backing to make money for everybody. Up until that time, the Wo Hop To continued to pay tribute to the Wah Ching for its gambling operations in Chinatown. But Chong proposed that the arrangement end, that the Wah Ching come under the triad's umbrella. Danny Wong listened with astonishment as Chong proposed that he surrender what the Wah Ching had spent more than 20 years in building: supremacy in Chinatown. He then politely rejected the plan. The meeting ended with smiles, but both sides knew that blood was about to be spilled in Chinatown.

The Wah Ching apparently made the first move. Though police never verified the incident, Peter Chong and Raymond Chow claim that gangsters from Johnny Ly's crew tried to kill them as they walked out of Jackson Pavilion in Chinatown a few days after the banquet, but were scared off by bicycle cops before they could fire. Not long after that incident, Chow and Chong ran into Ly at the grand opening of the Josephine of the Islands nightclub on San Francisco's Broadway. Chong's henchmen led Ly out of the nightclub at gunpoint and gave him a beating on the sidewalk. Chong then sent men to Ly's gambling joint on Jackson Street, where they chased out the gamblers and smashed the tables. Ly saw the writing on the wall and left town. So did what remained of Danny Phat Vong's crew.

Suddenly Danny Wong was just about all that remained of the once-mighty Wah Ching. But he was a stubborn man. He was not going to bow to the Wo Hop To's pressure and join the triad. Nor, since he had sought to distance himself from the dispute between Johnny Ly and Peter Chong, did he see any point in running and hiding. He followed his same routine in Chinatown and never even kept a bodyguard by his side. "He told us that he'd been out there since 1984 minding his own business and taking care of his family," said Sergeant Foley, "so no one was going to kill him. That's just the kind of person Danny was. He knew in his heart that they were going to kill him. But to leave Chinatown would have meant losing face."[9]

On April 19, 1991, Wong played his usual nightly game of *mah-jongg* in the basement of the Suey Sing *tong* on Jackson Street. At about 3 A.M., he walked to his car on Washington Street. Two men walked up, pulled the 35-year-old gang leader from his car and shot him to death. Both Raymond Chow and Peter Chong had convenient alibis. Chong was in Hong Kong and Chow was on a belated honeymoon in Hawaii. Both came back immediately after the killing and protested to the police that they had nothing to do with poor Danny's death. But nobody was fooled. The killing was a naked power play.

For about a month after that, the gambling houses in Chinatown did not have to pay tribute to anyone. But then Chong and Chow assigned Johnny Yee to take over the collections and split the proceeds between the Wo Hop To, the Hop Sing, and Yee's old Wah Ching faction. All of the gambling houses dutifully paid their new overlords. Yee designated a Vietnamese gangster named Sam Tran to make the actual collections. Two of Ly's uncles—Phu Phuoc-huu and his brother, Phu Tri-huu—shot and killed Sam Tran on July 11, 1991, as he was collecting a debt at the Greenleaf nightclub in San Francisco. But it was a meaningless rub-out. It didn't change the fact that the Wah Ching was finished in San Francisco.

Peter Chong became known as the *lo yan ka*—or elder—of Chinatown and Raymond Chow was acknowledged as his enforcer. Together, they became the lords of the Bay Area's Asian underworld. No longer consigned to sleepy Oakland, the two gangsters became fixtures in such Chinatown restaurants as the Jackson Café and Hong Kong Deluxe, always picking up the tab for their underlings in the Wo Hop To. They were frequently seen in

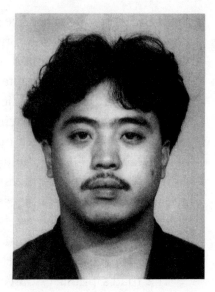

Wo Hop To leader Peter Chong, top left; his enforcer Raymond (Shrimp Boy) Chow, top right; Wah Ching defector Johnny Yee, bottom center. (San Francisco Police Department)

nightclubs wearing expensive suits and surrounded by large, dot-
ing entourages. Their authority as the new leaders of the Asian
underworld was recognized as far north as Portland and as far
south as San Jose. On September 15, 1991, Chow dispatched
about 30 Wo Hop To soldiers to Oakland's Chinatown to go
door to door and tell merchants they had to start paying the
triad. The gangsters fanned out over a seven-block area of downtown Oakland. "It was pretty incredible," said Sergeant Harry
Hu, an Oakland police investigator. "The merchants looked out
the windows and saw all these gangsters they had never seen before."[10] The plan backfired, because police showed up *en masse*
and arrested 12 of the extortionists. But the incident exemplified
the new audacity of the Wo Hop To.

The triad's primary source of income was protection money
from seven gambling houses in Chinatown, ranging from the Sun
Wah 13-card poker club at 759 Jackson Street to the Kiu On *pai
gow* and *fan tan* club at 22 Beckett Alley. At each location, one or
two Wo Hop To members would act as employees or sharehold-
ers and oversee the gambling operation. The triad also had plenty
of other criminal ventures. Chong became a wholesale loan shark
for the Asian underworld, lending money to street-level loan
sharks at 5 percent weekly interest. The street-level operators
would then lend the money out at 10 percent weekly interest.
Loan sharks haunted the illegal gambling joints in Chinatown
and the legalized card clubs in Emeryville and San Bruno. Raymond Chow became the city's leading street-level loan shark,
putting tens of thousands of dollars on the street at a time and
often beating up those who did not pay on time.

Peter Chong, Raymond Chow, William Mui and two other
gangsters also started a lucrative bookmaking enterprise that they
called the "Big Five" group, according to authorities. A network
of Chinese street bookies would collect bets on baseball games,
football games and other sports events and then call them into
Chong's central bookmaking office at 888 O'Farrell Street. But
none of the street bookies knew the address of the office or dealt
directly with Chong. Anyone who failed to make good on his

gambling debt would answer to Chow's underlings in the Hop Sing *tong*.

Raymond Chow was the front man for all of the Wo Hop To's dirty work. He was the man to be feared in Chinatown, the person whom unlucky gamblers begged for mercy when they were late on a gambling debt and whom gambling house owners met with to discuss tribute payments. Chow was a pitiless gangster. When one underling asked him what to do when prostitutes were overworked at his Pacifica brothel, he told him to buy more sponges. People who asked for time to make loan-shark payments were told to come up with the money—or else. Once a dealer in a Wo Hop To gambling house at 38 Wentworth Street fell behind on her $200-a-week interest payment on a $2,000 loan. Chow accepted no excuses but allowed the woman, Annie Chan, to help pay off the debt by taking a flight out of Hong Kong with heroin taped inside her girdle. The woman was arrested with the drugs in Hong Kong's Kai Tak Airport and went to prison.

For all of Peter Chong' pretensions, the Wo Hop To was hardly a genteel organization. It was not above engaging in brutal home invasions and commercial robberies, so long as the purse was big enough. Chien I. Chiang, a Wo Hop To member who was frequently seen traveling with Chong, was tied to a number of home invasions and robberies. He was charged in the January 1991 kidnapping of businessman David Lai from his suburban San Francisco home. Lai, half-owner of the Pelican Bar and Restaurant in Foster City, was surprised outside his home by four men, who forced him into a car at gunpoint. One of them said, "My boss wants to see you," as he shoved Lai into the car.[11] Lai was taken to a home in El Sobrante, where his eyes and mouth were taped over and he was lashed to a pole in the garage. The kidnappers told him to come up with $150,000 or be killed— and then released him to raise the money. Lai never called the police. Instead, he turned to a friend, the same Chien I. Chiang, who hung around his restaurant and was known to have underworld ties. Lai, not knowing that Chiang was involved in the kidnapping, asked if he could pull some strings in the syndicate and get the amount lowered. Chiang tried but told him apologetically that it was just not possible. The unfortunate restaurateur ended up paying the full $150,000. When Chiang was finally arrested for the crime in 1993, his relationship to the victim was not the only surprise. The arrest took place in the home of Marshall Wong, a San Francisco police officer who worked on the Asian-gang task force and whose wife, Vivian Lee, was one of Lai's business partners. Phone records showed that numerous calls had been made between Officer Wong's home and the El Sobrante address on the day of the kidnapping. Wong was transferred out of the gang task force but was not charged with a crime. His police colleagues felt he had been victimized by his wife's poor choice of friends.

Peter Chong built what one investigator called a "supermarket of crime," a Chinese syndicate more diverse and sophisticated than any that had come before it in the Bay Area. If the federal government had been complacent about the Wo Hop To, the triad might have become so deeply ensconced in San Francisco that it would have been as difficult to dislodge as a Mafia family. But this is one case where the federal government wasted no time in countering a new dynamic in the Asian underworld.

Indeed, the FBI's San Francisco office had made Chinatown the biggest priority of its organized-crime investigations as early as 1989. The office had recruited a number of Chinese agents who spoke the Cantonese dialect and were familiar with triad history and culture. One of the key investigators was Tony Lau, a Hong Kong native who had been a high-school teacher in San Francisco in the 1970s and who knew many people on both sides of the law in Chinatown. When the Asian team started out, its target was the Wah Ching, which was then the only crime group that mattered in Chinatown. So the agents were already wired into the community by the time the Wo Hop To emerged. "We were already taking a hard look at the Wah Ching, and we watched them get pushed right out of town," said Special Agent Thomas Carlon, who headed up the investigation.[12]

But the Feds were hardly disappointed. The Wo Hop To presented an even fatter target. In his efforts to bring all of the Bay Area's Asian crime groups under one well-structured hierarchy, Peter Chong had built an organization tailor-made for a RICO prosecution, and that became the goal of the FBI. The only problem was that Chong kept himself insulated, leaving the day-to-day operations of the Wo Hop To to Raymond Chow. The investigation would have to focus on the tough young Hop Sing Boys and then make some kind of link to Chong. In the Wah Ching probe, Lau had developed a number of sources in Chinatown; they gave him enough inside information about the triad's operation to convince the courts to approve wiretaps on telephones used by Chow and other gang members.

While the FBI was putting together the wiretaps, city police delivered the first blow against Chong, almost by accident. On January 2, 1992, San Francisco's vice squad swooped down on a high-stakes dice game being played right in front of tourists on a sidewalk in Chinatown's Portsmouth Square. To their surprise, police saw Chong himself run into the nearby Great Eastern Restaurant at 649 Jackson Street. They arrested him in the kitchen with $5,400 in his pocket. The same investigation linked him to a bookmaking operation in the city's Richmond district, adding up to some fairly serious charges against the crime boss.

In February 1992, the FBI's wiretaps began picking up cryptic telephone conversations between Raymond Chow in San Francisco and Wayne Kwong, a Boston restaurateur and On Leong member. The two used coded words—like "dentures" for drugs and "water source" for cash—but it was clear that they were discussing Chow's interest in buying significant amounts of heroin. Wayne Kwong was already well known to investigators of Asian organized crime as an ambitious young gangster in Boston and a longtime associate of Peter Chong. Boston's Asian rackets had been in disarray since Ping On leader Stephen Tse, facing police pressure and harassment from Vietnamese gangs, had moved to Hong Kong in 1991. Several groups were vying for supremacy in the city's Asian underworld, and Kwong had assembled a following of young thugs to help him come out on top. But first he had to get some rivals from the Ping On out of the way.

Wayne Kwong had a reputation for ruthlessness. In 1986, a businessman named Harry Yee threw Kwong and his brother off the board of directors of a Chinese restaurant in a Boston suburb. Two days later, two men surprised the restaurateur outside his home in Braintree. They tied and blindfolded him and then made the mistake of telling him why they were there. "How come you kick your partner out?" one of them asked. "Your partner gave me $30,000 to kill you."[13] One of the men dragged a knife across the 55-year-old victim's neck, sending blood gushing everywhere. Yee pretended to be dead, but survived to testify against his attackers, one of whom hanged himself in jail. Kwong was never charged in the crime.

Wayne Kwong was also widely suspected in the slaying of Stephen Tse's right-hand man, Michael Kwong (no relation to Wayne). The two gangsters had had a long-running feud, which in the summer of 1989 resulted in Michael Kwong hitting Wayne Kwong on the side of the head with a cellular phone in the middle of a Chinatown restaurant. On August 11, 1989, Michael Kwong was shot dead by a lone gunman who had walked into his restaurant in suburban Arlington.

Michael Kwong's murder was never avenged, which in Chinatown was considered a major loss of face for the Ping On. By 1992, Stephen Tse was out of the country and Wayne Kwong's biggest rival had become Bike Ming, a former Ping On member who had emerged as an important Vietnamese gang leader in Boston. Wayne Kwong and Ming had once been partners in a gambling house, but Ming had taken control of the establishment and the two had become bitter enemies. Kwong had been linked to the attempted murder of two of Ming's followers, Thong Vo and Phoung Nguyen, who were shot and wounded on August 6, 1991, outside the China Grill restaurant on Boston's Portland Street.[14] After the botched attempt to kill Harry Yee, Wayne Kwong went to San Francisco while the heat was on in Boston, staying as a guest in a home owned by Peter Chong. By February 1992, Kwong was back in Boston and about to become an important source of heroin for the Wo Hop To, making Bike Ming as big a problem for Raymond Chow and Peter Chong as he was for Kwong.

In March 1992, Chow came up with a solution to the Bike Ming problem. He sent three Hop Sing underlings—Brandon Casey, Wilson Phan and Sean Hiyagon—to Boston and told them to follow Kwong's instructions for killing Ming. On March 9, Kwong drove the three young hit men from his home in suburban Randolph, Massachusetts to another home in nearby Quincy, where they picked up three guns and were told that Ming was eating in the China Pearl restaurant on Tyler Street in Chinatown. Kwong told them that Ming wore a bulletproof vest so would have to be shot in the head. But the execution never took place. Ming's people spotted two of the gunmen as they walked toward the restaurant, and the hit team drove off. By then the FBI's Boston office, which had been tipped off by their counterparts in San Francisco, were leaning on Kwong to explain the visitors in Chinatown. Chow summoned his underlings back to San Francisco and Ming stayed alive.

The FBI was just waiting for its chance to bring down the hammer. That chance came in June 1992, when the first heroin was to change hands between Kwong's people and the Wo Hop To. Tony Young, the Wah Ching leader in Los Angeles and now an operative of the Wo Hop To, was arrested picking up five ounces of heroin from Kwong's people at the Atlantic City airport. The Feds then pulled in the nets. Chow was arrested in New York after arranging the transfer. Kwong was arrested in his home in Randolph. At the same time, an army of 80 federal and local authorities raided 23 homes, apartments and businesses in the San Francisco area and carted away reams of documents and other materials linked to the Wo Hop To.[15]

The next blow came in October 1992, when the San Francisco police and the district attorney's office charged Chow and 14 other members of the Wo Hop To's Hop Sing faction with a series of robberies and home invasions and the operation of Chow's whorehouse in Pacifica. One of the crimes cited in the indictment was the robbery of a Geary Boulevard restaurant in which

31 patrons were robbed by two bandits armed with an Uzi sub-machine gun and a meat cleaver. For the prostitution offense alone, Raymond Chow faced life in prison.

But the federal authorities have not had as much luck with Peter Chong. The wily triad figure was not implicated in either the heroin or the prostitution case. And by the time the government executed its *coup de grace* on October 12, 1994—a RICO indictment against Chong, Chow and 16 other Wo Hop To leaders—Chong had already slipped away to Hong Kong. He was arrested in the colony, but as of this writing U.S. authorities have failed in their efforts to have him extradited.

The Wo Hop To is a new phenomenon in the nation's Asian underworld. It is not a street gang fighting crude battles with its rivals over extortion territory. Nor is it a shadowy *tong* passing itself off as a fraternal organization while dabbling in gambling and narcotics. It is a criminal syndicate from top to bottom, an exact replica of the triads that have haunted Asia for centuries. No one has ever established whether Peter Chong took orders from the triad's Hong Kong "dragon head," Chan Ting-Hung, or whether Chong was establishing a beachhead for other high-ranking triad members who were planning to flee the Communist Chinese takeover in 1997. But his connections to Hong Kong were well documented, as was his access to a seemingly endless supply of financing for criminal ventures in San Francisco. As of this writing, the Wop Hop To is considered still active in San Francisco, though not with the power and influence that preceded the federal crackdown. It is not known whether Chong continues to direct its operations from Hong Kong or whether other emissaries have been dispatched to San Francisco. But one thing is clear. If Hong Kong's triads ever do successfully set up widespread operations in the United States, Peter Chong will be remembered as the pioneer.

The battered old freighter, its green paint badly faded and its hull pitted with rust, had braved tempestuous seas and a mutinous crew only to run aground in the moonlit darkness off the Rockaway Peninsula of Queens, New York. The cry of "Jump! Jump!"

cut through the night and hundreds of desperate Chinese immigrants poured over the sides. Many were weak from months at sea. Some were clad only in their underwear. But after being crammed into the ship's hold for what seemed a lifetime, this was their only chance at freedom. So they plunged blindly into the roiling 55-degree water. The swirling, pounding surf swept many of them into the jetties, smashing them like floating debris against the jagged rocks. Five bodies washed ashore even while the rescue crews were at work. Five more bodies would turn up over the next few days. The remaining passengers were rounded up by police, turned over to immigration authorities and herded into prison cells.

The *Golden Venture*, a smuggling ship that ran aground on June 6, 1993, with a cargo of nearly 300 Chinese illegal immigrants, stands as a symbol of the new "boat people," the tens of thousands of immigrants from the Fujian province of southern China who have flooded New York City in the last several years. Theirs is the third great migration to New York's Chinatown, and its impact on the neighborhood's economy and culture promises to be nearly as dramatic as that of the Hong Kong Chinese who crowded the district after 1965. Already Chinatown sidewalks are crowded with Fujianese peddling everything from firecrackers and fried rice to illegal pet turtles. Housing is in such short supply that tenement after tenement is being carved into the cubicles known as *gong si fong*.

And with this crush of humanity has come a new dynamic in the neighborhood's underworld—a new wave of immigrant gangsters that looms just as large in the future of Asian organized crime as the triads. New York's authorities don't have time to worry about people like Peter Chong importing preexisting triad societies from Hong Kong. They are too busy watching immigrant Fujianese gangsters build crime families the old-fashioned way—from the ground up. Fujianese gangs are every bit as aggressive as their Cantonese predecessors in staking out territories for gambling and extortion. They are just as eager to peddle heroin, commit home-invasion robberies and loan money at illegal interest rates. But they have one thing the Cantonese haven't—a growing

A fireman helps a Chinese immigrant ashore from the Golden Venture smuggling ship, which ran aground in June 1993 off Rockaway, Queens, with nearly 300 "illegals" on board. (Todd Maisel)

trade in human bondage. As enforcers for unscrupulous alien-smuggling syndicates, the Fujianese gangs subject thousands of immigrants to a medieval system of indentured labor until they pay off the price of their passage. Their method of collection has brought a new level of brutality to Chinatown—poor immigrants kidnapped from their homes in the dead of night and imprisoned and tortured until family members come up with tens of thousands of dollars to pay off the smugglers.

The vast majority of Chinese smuggled into the United States are from a single county in Fujian, a maritime province of some 28 million people on China's rugged southeastern coast. With its tea-growing estates and fertile copper and iron mines, Fujian is more prosperous than many of the provinces in China's interior. What makes it such a wellspring of emigration has more to do with its history and culture than with the relative poverty of its inhabitants. Fujian's western border is composed of vast mountain ranges that have kept the region isolated from the rest of China for centuries. Its inhabitants speak seven distinct Fujianese dialects that bear little resemblance to the national Mandarin language or the Cantonese spoken by most Chinese-Americans. For centuries, the Fujianese have been a seafaring people whose emigrants founded Chinese colonies throughout Southeast Asia. Thousands of Fujianese seamen assisted the U.S. Navy during World War II, and many of them settled on our Eastern seaboard after the war. Fujianese may not have a greater need than other Chinese to escape the poverty and repression of their nation, but through friends and relatives overseas, they have a greater opportunity to do so, and a greater awareness of the easier life that awaits them in other lands.

Although Fujian's cities may be more prosperous than those in China's southern interior, life in the province is anything but easy. Most of its inhabitants are poor. In 1992, the average yearly income of a Fujianese was 2,087 yuan, or about $209. Jobs are tough to find, especially outside the teeming provincial capital of Fuzhou. And the malevolent arm of the country's totalitarian government reaches into even the tiniest peasant villages. National population-control policies restrict families to one child and allow the state to sterilize men and force abortions on women if they try to exceed their quota. It is this limitation on the basic human right to bear children, as much as the desire to escape poverty, that drives many Fujianese to risk their lives on the journey to America.

The Fujianese who settled in New York City's Chinatown in the early 1980s, when the city was in the middle of an economic boom, sent back stories of overnight wealth that fired an entire generation with the desire to come to America. They heard tales of Fujianese who landed in New York with only a few hundred dollars and two years later owned shops and restaurants. Fujianese pioneered the little express-Chinese-food joints that sprouted like dandelions on city thoroughfares from the South Bronx to Staten Island. With men who had once been poor farmers hitting it big in New York, young people huddled on the sidewalks of Fuzhou spoke of little else but Chinatown. All of them had the same question on their lips: "How can I arrange passage to America?"

Human nature being what it is, Fujianese criminals were quick to exploit this passion. Alien smugglers known as "snake-heads" slithered through the streets of Fuzhou and surrounding Changle County, offering passage to America for $25,000 to $35,000 a head. Such an amount might as well have been a million dollars for the average Fujian peasant, but the snake-heads told them not to worry. Only a small percentage of the money had to be given up front. The rest could be paid off after the immigrant arrived in the United States and began working. It would prove to be a Faustian bargain, but one that tens of thousands of Fujianese found too good to refuse.

One of the first notorious alien smugglers in New York was Cheng Chui Ping, a Fuzhou native who was 34 years old when she herself was smuggled into New York around 1983. An internal memorandum of the U.S. Immigration and Naturalization Service stated in 1985 that Ping and her husband, Cheng Yick Tak, were running an alien-smuggling operation out of the Tak Shun variety store at 145B Hester Street in Chinatown. The couple would smuggle Fujianese to the city by way of Hong Kong, Central America and Mexico, with Ping herself acting as the chief guide. Ping usually moved no more than a dozen at a time, but by the time she was arrested for smuggling three Chinese across the Canadian border in 1990, she had smuggled thousands of people and made an estimated $30 million. Ping served only four months in jail and soon resumed her business at the Yung Sun variety store on East Broadway, in a building she purchased for $3 million in cash.[16]

Though she may seem like evil incarnate to immigration officials, Ping is regarded as a folk hero in Fuzhou. She is known as "Big Sister Ping," the woman who rescues peasants from the hardships of Fujian province and gives them a chance for a better life. Her concern for the well-being of her charges is legendary, if a bit exaggerated. "If anyone dies on the trip, she compensates the victim's family," said one Fujianese immigrant in New York. "If anybody gets deported, she will make sure they are first on the waiting list (to be smuggled back in)."[17] Ping also offers a valuable service to the people she smuggles across the border—the illegal transfer of money back to Fujian. She reportedly can get money to a Fuzhou home in three days, while it takes the Bank of China up to three weeks.[18]

As the orderly procession of immigrants turned into a stampede in the late 1980s, criminals less scrupulous than Big Sister Ping moved into the smuggling trade. Hong Kong's triads and Fujian's homegrown syndicates teamed up and turned immigrant smuggling into big business. Whereas Ping and other entrepreneurs would smuggle Fujianese in manageable groups, the new breed of snake-head packs them into the holds of freighters by the hundreds, making their trip to America a journey through hell. Immigrants spend months at sea, surviving on at best one meal a day, usually a small bowl of rice. They are forced to share one bathroom with hundreds of others. Women are routinely reduced to "sex slaves" along the way, raped not only by other immigrants but often by the ship's crew as well.

In the summer of 1993, U.S. authorities were overwhelmed by the number of smuggling ships arriving around the country. At the time the *Golden Venture* ran aground, U.S. immigration officials had intelligence that 24 more ships were on their way to the United States, each packed with illegal Fujianese.[19] In the previous 22 months, authorities had intercepted 14 such ships around the country, and no one could even estimate how many might have gotten through undetected. Four days before the *Golden Venture* arrived, the Coast Guard seized two fishing trawlers with 200 illegals aboard as they landed 60 miles apart on the northern coast of California. The previous month, a freighter dropped 200 illegal immigrants at the foot of San Francisco's Golden Gate Bridge. Of these, 125 were seized by authorities, but 75 escaped into the darkness.[20]

That many of the ships were succeeding in getting through the Coast Guard's net was obvious. Fujianese immigrants were easy

Smuggled immigrants from Fujian province aboard a fishing trawler that was nabbed by U.S. authorities as it entered Half Moon Bay in California in 1993. (AP/Wide World)

to spot on the streets of New York's Chinatown, where most of them ended up. They lined up for jobs at Chinatown employment agencies and milled about in front of the Fukien American Association, a Fujianese *tong* with an office at 125 East Broadway. Their influx was also evidenced by the alarming number of cases in which police discovered gang members holding immigrants prisoner in warehouses and cramped basements. After the *Golden Venture* fiasco, New York City police came across three such makeshift prisons in the month of June 1993 alone; they freed 43 captives and arrested 14 gang members. The week before the *Golden Venture* wreck, authorities in Jersey City, New Jersey, discovered 57 immigrants in a locked warehouse. They were guarded by four armed thugs who loaded their prisoners into vans every morning to be driven to low-paying restaurant jobs. The same vans brought them back to the warehouse at night. "The scariest part is that this place was locked," said Lawrence Perlaki, owner of the company that managed the building. "If God forbid there had been a fire, there would have been 60 body bags."[21]

This indentured servitude is perhaps the ugliest aspect of the alien-smuggling trade. Snakeheads often begin harassing families for repayment of the money as soon as the immigrant arrives, ignoring the terms that were agreed upon before the trip. The immigrants are routinely kidnapped and held in confinement by armed gangs until the money is paid; in the meantime, they are forced into slave labor in restaurant kitchens and garment factories. The prettiest of the women are frequently forced into prostitution, laboring long hours in the barbershops that act as fronts for massage parlors throughout northeast Chinatown. The victims dare not complain to police, who they figure are in the pockets of the criminals, just as they were in southern China. Besides, even if they come to trust American justice to protect them from criminals in New York, who will protect their families from retaliation back in Fujian province?

For all this sacrifice, many of the more recent Fujianese immigrants are not finding the easy road to riches that they had expected. Less educated and without the family ties that greeted many Fujianese immigrants in the 1980s, the newcomers are finding New York in the recessionary 1990s to be an inhospitable place. So many illegal immigrants are competing for jobs in restaurant kitchens and garment factories that openings are scarce and wages have fallen through the floor. Often the only jobs available are in dangerous neighborhoods where the newest Fujianese entrepreneurs have opened express takeouts as they struggle to find a niche in a city saturated with Chinese restaurants. Many of the new immigrants live in overcrowded *gong si fong*, trying to save up enough money to open a small business or send something to their families in China. Food and merchandise vendors crowd almost every inch of sidewalk on the Bowery,

Canal Street and other Chinatown streets, all competing for a fi-
nite number of tourists. Fujianese women scour Manhattan's
downtown in search of empty soda and beer containers that can
be redeemed for five cents each. The author saw one Fujianese
immigrant standing on the corner of Center and Worth Streets
clutching four cheap Bic pens that he was selling for 10 cents
apiece.

The Fuk Ching is the most notorious of the gangs that have attached themselves like leeches to the struggling Fujianese, both
in alien smuggling and Chinatown street rackets. Founded by
young men who were already hardened criminals back in
Fuzhou, the Fuk Ching emerged in the mid-1980s in an area
north of Canal Street and east of the Bowery that had become the
heart of the Fujianese ghetto. Although that territory had never
before been claimed by a gang, over the years merchants had
made sporadic payments to the Ghost Shadows, the Flying Dragons, and the Tung On. When the Fuk Ching also demanded payoffs, the merchants took a step almost unheard of in Chinatown—they called the police. "We must have made 60 arrests for
extortion," said James McVeety, who at the time of the arrests
headed the Jade Squad. "The merchants had put up with the
older gangs for so long, they didn't want to start giving to this
gang, too."[22]

The crackdown plunged the young gang into disarray and led
to bitter feuds among its leaders. One of the original leaders, Kin
Fei (Foochow Paul) Wong, split off in 1986 and formed the
Green Dragons, a ruthless gang that terrorized Chinese neighborhoods in Queens for several years. Another Fuk Ching leader, Kin
Tai Chan, tried to have Wong murdered, but the job was
botched. Wong was shot and wounded in January 1989 as he
was leaving a friend's house in Flushing, Queens. After recovering, Foochow Paul fled to China, but retained control of the
Green Dragons gang from overseas. One of the jobs he reportedly
assigned to them was the murder of Kin Tai Chan, which was carried out on August 23, 1989, at 142-20 84th Avenue in Queens.

After Chan's murder, the leadership of the Fuk Ching fell to a

23-year-old Fujianese named Kwok Ling Kay, who also goes by the name Guo Liang Qi but is best known by his nickname, Ah Kay. Ah Kay had been brought to New York as a teenager and put to work as an enforcer and debt collector by the Fukien American Association. He was a charter member of the Fuk Ching and eventually distinguished himself as one of its most ruthless enforcers. He was arrested for extortion in 1985 after a store owner said Ah Kay has threatened to kill him and his family and blow up his restaurant if he didn't pay $36,000. The young gangster served two and a half years for the crime and was deported in 1988. But he had sneaked back into the country within a matter of months.

After Chan's murder, Ah Kay took control of the gang and relished his new role as crime boss. The slightly built gangster with his trademark pompadour made the rounds of northeast Chinatown in a black Saab with tinted windows. He impressed no one with his casual, almost sloppy dress, but he won respect through fear. Though he was always accompanied by two bodyguards, he personally attended to the beatings of store owners who resisted paying extortion money. "He beat up a lot of people that we know of," said Sergeant Douglas Lee of the Police Department's Major Case Squad. "People were scared to death of him."[23]

The Fuk Ching's new stronghold became a small strip of Eldridge Street in a dingy overcrowded neighborhood beneath the Manhattan Bridge. It is one of the newest parts of Chinatown, and most if its residents are illegal Fujianese crowding into the four-story brick tenements that have been housing Lower East Side immigrants for more than a century. He exacted tribute from merchants and from the numerous massage parlors that had sprung up in the neighborhood to service Fujianese men who had left their wives back in China—a throwback to the days of bachelor-society Chinatown. Gambling was one of Ah Kay's most lucrative activities. While many of the Cantonese gamblers now prefer Atlantic City casinos to the *mah-jongg* parlors of Mott and Pell Streets, the Fujianese do most of their gambling in Chinatown. They work long hours in restaurants and have a natural timidity about leaving Chinatown and hopping a bus to Atlantic

City. So, in the late 1980s, they began patronizing the Fuk Ching's chief gambling parlors at 13 Eldridge Street and in the basement of the Fukien American Association at 125 East Broadway. The association—which sponsors the Fuk Ching in much the same way as Cantonese *tongs* sponsor their gangs—is headed by Alan Lau, who once gave $6,500 to former Mayor David Dinkins' reelection campaign.[24]

In 1989, Ah Kay discovered the huge potential of alien smuggling. Under the leadership of Foochow Paul Wong and others, the gang had for years been smuggling heroin from the Far East, turning it over to Dominican distributors on the Lower East Side. But Ah Kay realized that he could make the same amount of money in alien smuggling with a fraction of the risk. Someone caught smuggling aliens typically spends only a few months in jail, compared with anywhere from 25 years to life for a major heroin-smuggling conspiracy.

Working with his father and brothers, Ah Kay began in the smuggling business by using the traditional land and air routes that had been the staple of Big Sister Ping and other pioneering snakeheads. By 1991, he had joined the rest of the smuggling underworld in packing hundreds of immigrants into the hulls of ships. One Fuk Ching ship after another arrived in ports ranging from Hawaii and California to North Carolina and Massachusetts. With so many ships arriving, the number of smuggling accounts the gang had to keep track of grew exponentially. And so did the numbers of cases in which the Fuk Ching resorted to terror to collect the debts. People were routinely kidnapped and tortured until they came up with the money. One technique that proved particularly effective was allowing family members to hear the screams of the victims over the telephone so they would waste no time in putting together the payment. In one typical case, Fuk Ching members kidnapped two men from the front of 176 Rivington Street in November 1990 and demanded the $25,000 that each of them owed for passage. They took them to an apartment and beat them with guns and sticks, allowing their family members to listen over the phone. Gang members then took them to a basement on 58th Street in Queens and intensified the torture over the next several days, burning them with cigarettes, beating them with an exercise bar and pulling plastic bags over their heads. By the time police raided the apartment and freed them, the two had suffered severe burns and broken ribs. Police later said that several of the calls to relatives had come from the Fukien American Association at 125 East Broadway.[25]

In January 1991, 13 Fuk Ching members were arrested in the kidnapping of an illegal alien whom police had rescued from an apartment in the East Tremont section of the Bronx after he had been held hostage for 12 hours, beaten with a claw hammer and threatened with death. The victim, Kin Wah Fong, had gained entry into the country with a fake passport provided by a Hong Kong smuggling operation for $20,000. The gang members had been hired to collect the original amount plus a late fee of $10,000. Police who raided the apartment found Fong hand-cuffed to a bed, where he had pleaded for his life and begged family members over the phone to come up with the money.[26]

In many cases, the Fuk Ching held smuggled aliens in servitude for months until they paid off their passage. Only two days after the *Golden Venture* fiasco, police raided an apartment in Brooklyn's Sunset Park neighborhood and arrested two Fuk Ching members who were holding 13 frightened Fujianese in a cramped basement. The only time the aliens were allowed out of the basement was when they boarded minivans that drove them to restaurant jobs as far away as Maryland and Pennsylvania. Often they did not return to the apartment until midnight, only to get up again at dawn.[27]

While busy with this international smuggling conspiracy, the Fuk Ching also had the more mundane task of looking after its turf on Eldridge Street. Although the Fuk Ching's territory is well removed from that of the Ghost Shadows and Flyings Dragons, Ah Kay trained his underlings to be ever vigilant in protecting the gang's turf from incursions by the rival Tung On, whose turf lay just to the southwest. On some occasions, they were too vigilant. Among their innocent victims was Cho Yee Yeung, a young man who on July 4, 1992, was walking on Eldridge Street with two friends on his way to play basketball. The Fuk Ching mistook

Fuk Ching leader Kwok Ling Kay, better known as Ah Kay, in custody after he was arrested in Hong Kong in 1994. (Joseph DeMaria)

him for a rival gang member and beat him with a baseball bat and a machete, slicing open his knee. A similar incident occurred on April 17, 1993, only this time the attackers knew they weren't dealing with rival gang members. Three high-school students offended the Fuk Ching by using toy guns to film a fake Chinese gangster shootout on Eldridge Street for a school project. Fuk Ching goons descended on them, smashed the movie camera and led them at gunpoint into a tenement at 19 Eldridge Street. The oldest of the three was taken into a rear room and stomped and pistol-whipped, while listening to his friends getting the same treatment in another room. One of his tormentors held up a gun and said, "Do you see this? This is the real thing," before hitting him again.[28]

Like any good *dai lo*, Ah Kay fed and clothed his gang members, provided them shelter in safe houses and paid them healthy salaries. But the gang leader was making such obscene profits from alien smuggling that some of his lieutenants began complaining that they were not getting a big enough share. One of his top men, Dan Lin Xin, broke away from the Fuk Ching in late 1992 and attempted to start his own gang, taking along two others, Liu Xiao Dong and Xiu Chu Chin. To allow this secession would have meant a loss of face for Ah Kay. He told them never to show their face in Chinatown again and ordered his men to kill them if they did. But the three rebels ignored him. On January 8, 1993, Ah Kay received a telephone call from Fuk Ching member You Lin Song, who told him that Dan Lin Xin and Liu Xiao Dong were in Chinatown. "*Dai lo*, those two are down there . . . Do it?" he asked Ah Kay. The gang leader responded, "You say do it, so do it. Do a clean job." You Lin Song answered, "*Dai lo*, don't worry."[29]

As it turned out, the job was anything but clean. When You Lin Song caught up with the two gangsters in a cellular-phone and beeper store at 2 Allen Street, he was surprised to find that Xiu Chu Chin was with them. He fired at Dan Lin Xin and missed, but then shot and killed Liu Xiao Dong. When he turned to take another shot at Xin, Chin wrestled with him. The gun went off and killed Chin.

Ah Kay had started a war within the Fuk Ching, but he didn't stay around to see it through. He went to China to oversee his smuggling empire and live the life of an international playboy while leaving his brothers behind to deal with the rebels. According to prosecutors, Dan Lin Xin actually followed Ah Kay to Asia, planning to track him down and kill him. When that didn't work out, he returned to the United States with an alternative plan. First he became an FBI informer and provided information about the Allen Street shootings. Then, on May 24, 1993, he allegedly assembled a group of Fuk Ching renegades and headed for a safe house that Ah Kay's two brothers and other loyalists maintained on Somerset Road in suburban Teaneck, New Jersey. Five 10-year-olds were playing on a neighbor's lawn when the four gangsters arrived in the placid middle-class neighborhood at about 7:30 P.M., but that didn't deter them. They forced their way through the door with guns drawn and exacted their revenge. Police arrived to find the body of one of Ah Kay's brothers shot and stabbed inside the front door. Another brother, Guo Liang Wang, 25, was found lying with several gunshot wounds on nearby Waverly Place. He died later in the hospital. Two other men were found bound, gagged and executed in the basement. Xin and the four other rebels were arrested by Fort Lee police as they attempted to cross the George Washington Bridge. All five were drenched in blood.[30]

Ah Kay was having the time of his life in the Far East. He lived in a walled mansion on the edge of Fuzhou and constantly slipped over the border into Hong Kong for visits to nightclubs, expensive restaurants and gambling casinos, where he would spend up to $30,000 in a night. But after the killings, the fun came to a halt. He was so enraged that he began making arrangements to slip back into the States to deal with Dan Lin Xin personally.

By then, the FBI was wrapping up a two-year investigation of the Fuk Ching and had gathered some damning evidence against the gang leader. Agents had recruited one of Ah Kay's key associates to call him in China on a tapped line and trick him into discussing his role in the Allen Street shootings. Ah Kay talked of his regret that "Gui"—the nickname for Xiu Chu Chin—had been in the beeper store. "If I had known that Gui was there . . . I would have sent more than one person down, at least three weapons, four guys," Ah Kay said. "We would charge in, get them all down on the floor. We would tell Gui, 'This has nothing to do with you.' We would push the foolish Gui out after we searched him and we would say 'get out' . . . But, fuck, only because the caller didn't mention Gui, we were now in such an awkward position."[31]

Ah Kay was arrested by Hong Kong police on August 28, 1993, as he and several bodyguards walked away from a food stall in a crowded outdoor market. The next day, federal authorities swept through northeast Chinatown, raiding a series of gang safe houses and arresting 14 of the gang's members on racketeer-ing charges. Ah Kay waived extradition from Hong Kong amid widespread reports that he was cooperating with authorities. If he was indeed cooperating, an intriguing question is why author-ities would give a break to the boss of the gang. Such deals are usually offered to underlings who deliver the bosses to authori-ties. The answer could only be that authorities were trying to build a case against someone higher up in the alien-smuggling business, perhaps the masterminds of the *Golden Venture* fiasco.

Ah Kay ended up in a prison cell, but the Fujianese epoch in Chinese organized crime is just beginning. The number of Fu-jianese gangsters in New York increases by the day. In many cases, youths smuggled into New York are forced into gangs to pay their passage, creating a vicious cycle of criminality. After the *Golden Venture* debacle produced an international crackdown on alien smuggling, Fujianese gangsters dealt with the shortfall of cash by unleashing a wave of kidnappings in Chinatown, Queens and Brooklyn. Only these crimes weren't aimed at former smug-gling clients. They were outright demands for ransom from suc-cessful immigrant families—the most predatory of crimes. One of the most brutal examples of these kidnappings took place on August 22, 1995, when Chinese immigrant Gao Liquin, 39, was abducted as she walked home from her job as a garment factory worker in Corona, Queens. Gao was taken to a basement apart-ment in Borough Park, Brooklyn, where she was beaten and tor-tured over several days while the kidnappers tried to get $28,800 in ransom from her family in China. When they were only able to get $5,000 out of the family, the gang members put a plastic bag over Gao's head, smashed her skull with a television set, and then strangled her with a telephone cord. They left behind a note that read: "Those who don't pay off their kidnapping debts are bound to die. The police can't get to us. If you want to know who we are, just look for your clue among a deck of playing cards." They signed the note, "The Devils That Are Flouting You," and scrawled a picture of a King of Clubs. In Chinese, the word for clubs, "mei," is the name of a village in Fujian. Five men who were arrested in the kidnapping were reputedly members of the

Fujianese Flying Dragons, a renegade cell of the Chinatown gang by the same name. The gang had been linked to several other violent kidnappings.[32]

Other Fujianese criminals have begun exploring other ways to make money. In September 1994, federal authorities arrested more than 60 Fujianese immigrants for alledgely operating the biggest food-stamp-fraud ring ever uncovered in New York City. The defendants were obtaining hundreds of thousands of dollars in food stamps on the black market, where they can be purchased for cash at 50 percent of their face value. They would then get the full value of the stamps by redeeming them with the government in the names of businesses where no real food-stamp purchases were made. In some cases, the businesses were just empty storefronts.

As long as Chinese immigrants arrive in this country poor and defenseless, gangs will be there to prey on them like a wolf pack on a herd of sheep. While it may frustrate law enforcement, many immigrants accept their oppressors as a fact of life. They have been the underside of Chinese culture for hundreds of years. The author, with the help of a Fujianese interpreter, once brought up the topic of the Fuk Ching to the owner of a cramped little noodle house on Eldridge Street. A short, stocky man with a silver tooth, the owner just shrugged his shoulders. He had purchased his business from a Fuk Ching gang member, he said, and was spared extortion payments as part of the deal. But many of the younger Fuk Ching members weren't aware of the arrangement. So they would come in and try to shake him down. The owner pointed to slits in the orange vinyl cushions on each of the chairs. Those, he said, were made by the knives of young Fuk Ching members. Still, he said, having the neighborhood controlled by one gang is preferable to being plundered by every crook in Chinatown. "To be honest with you," he said. "It's probably safer to have them around."[33]

8: Born to Kill

The funeral of Vinh Vu, second in command of Born to Kill, a feared Vietnamese gang in New York City's Chinatown, was an audacious affair. His fellow gang members paraded through the streets of Chinatown on July 27, 1990, like people who had lost a great leader, carrying large banners bearing the gang's name. Vuu's killers had been trying to send a message to the maverick BTK, a gang that had broken the rules in Chinatown by robbing gambling dens and shaking down restaurants in other gangs' territories. But the message wasn't getting through. The BTK members were neither contrite nor discreet in their mourning. They marched young Vu's coffin up Mulberry Street, right through the middle of Ghost Shadows-On Leong territory, sending a message of their own—that the BTK would not be tamed. BTK thugs even had the audacity to strong-arm Canal Street shop owners for money so that their *dai lo* could be buried in style the next day.

At Rosedale Cemetery in Linden, New Jersey, a 20-minute drive from Lower Manhattan, dozens of Vietnamese men and women wearing black pants and black jackets over white shirts—the BTK's unofficial uniform—stood around a casket wrapped in a red banner emblazoned with the gang's logo, a yellow coffin with three candles on top. The casket was draped with a red-and-black flag bearing the words "Stand by the BTK" and "Canal Boys," another name for the BTK. David Thai, the gang's suave

David Thai, founder of the Born to Kill gang, attending the burial of Vinh Vu in a New Jersey cemetery. This photo was taken by Thai's own followers moments before rival gangsters opened fire on the gathering. (ATF)

and handsome leader, stood somberly holding a white carnation as the casket was lowered into the flower-bedecked grave.

At around 2:40 P.M., gang members had begun burning the deceased's personal belongings—an old Vietnamese custom—when three men approached the grave from across a cemetery roadway. They attracted little notice at first. They were dressed in black like the other mourners and carried flowers at their breasts. One mourner looked into the face of one of the strangers and was mouthing the words "Hey, I know him," when the trio dropped their flowers, revealing machine pistols, and begun firing over the tops of cars parked on the roadway. Bedlam erupted in the cemetery. Some of the mourners pulled out their own weapons and returned the fire. Others dove into the grave for cover or fled across the lawn and scaled a fence into a nearby factory yard. Bullets chipped gravestones on both sides of the roadway and tore into several fleeing mourners.

Miraculously, no one was killed in the gunfight, though seven people were shot and six suffered minor injuries while fleeing. David Thai was unharmed. When a police car arrived at the scene, its driver radioed to headquarters that about 25 Asians were clawing at his car and trying to get inside, shouting that someone was trying to kill them. Police managed to round up about 100 mourners, but as many as 100 more fled across Linden's industrial landscape and were never picked up. The killers were believed to have escaped in a small foreign automobile and have never been caught. Police who rounded up the mourners for questioning found several weapons and a lot of close-mouthed people. One woman had $23,000 stuffed in her pocketbook.[1]

The most telling thing about the incident is that so many people hated the BTK that police didn't know who to consider the prime suspects. The gang of young Vietnamese waifs, ranging in age from 13 to 35, had been stepping on toes in Chinatown since 1986, when its members broke away from the Flying Dragons and Ghost Shadows and formed the BTK. Instantly recognizable with their black clothing and their hair tied into tiny ponytails, the gang members claimed a stretch of Canal Street on the western edge of Chinatown. But they made regular forays into central Chinatown to commit robberies, extortions, murders and other crimes. In a neighborhood where young thugs usually paid homage to Chinese *tongs*, the BTK tangled with anyone in their path. "They even try to rob auxiliary police officers," said Chiu Kuen Wong, himself an auxiliary cop in Chinatown's Fifth Precinct. "They say, 'So what, cops have to pay us, too.'"[2]

The story of the Born to Kill gang is just a small part of a terrifying new phenomenon in organized crime. Vietnamese gangs are as ruthless and enterprising as any crime group in the country, but their lack of strong roots in any community and their almost constant mobility make them a unique threat to society. Born to Kill was putatively based in New York's Chinatown, but its members spent much of their time on the road, committing robberies and shakedowns as far away as Alabama and Rochester, New York. Other Vietnamese gangs are even less rooted. They make up highly disciplined robbery and extortion gangs that circulate among Asian communities around the country, spending a couple of days here and there at gang safe houses that exist in Vietnamese communities from Texas and California to Virginia and Massachusetts.

Since they emerged in the 1970s, Vietnamese gangs have been most infamous for home-invasion robberies, a crime that was rare in this country until the Vietnamese popularized it among Asian gangs. Indeed, Chinese gangs did not appear to favor home invasions until after the Vietnamese made it their trademark. Gang members force their way into the homes of Asian businessmen and steal the cash and jewelry that many immigrant families keep at home to avoid paying taxes. And they rarely just take the valuables and leave. Part of the scheme is usually to leave the family so terrified that they will not report the crime to police, lest they risk another visit from the gang. Some of the cases that have made it to the attention of police have been brutal. In one case in Orange County, California, bandits held a two-year-old's head in a toilet bowl until her mother came up with $500 in hidden cash. Vietnamese robbers stabbed a 13-year-old girl in Malden, Massachusetts, and poured boiling water on an elderly woman's leg in Stockton, California, to force her husband to come up with some money.[3]

Having cut their teeth on these brutal robberies in the 1970s, Vietnamese gangs have slowly become more involved in organized crime. Some gangs have moved into computer chip theft, auto theft, Medicaid fraud, credit-card fraud, loan-sharking, and bookmaking. Others, usually those comprising Vietnamese of Chinese descent, have attached themselves to Chinese syndicates. For years, Chinese gangs kept the Viet Ching—as the ethnically mixed gangsters are called—in the most subservient roles, using them as hit men and money collectors. Stephen Tse, head of Boston's Ping On gang, was fond of hiring Vietnamese to rob gambling dens that weren't paying him tribute. But in recent years Vietnamese have risen to the top of many Chinese gangs. More ruthless than their Chinese employers, they have actually taken over in some cities. Both Tse and his friend Danny Mo, head of Toronto's Kung Lok, were deposed by Vietnamese, who now control rackets in the Chinatowns of Boston and Toronto.

These ruthless gangs are a direct legacy of the Vietnam War. Indeed, the Born to Kill gang took its name from the slogan that U.S. servicemen used to scrawl on their helmets. Two decades after the last of our soldiers came home, as the national trauma of our failed war begins to heal, the gangs move stealthily along our interstates like some hidden and malevolent virus brought back from the jungles of Asia, a stubborn reminder—like Agent Orange and posttraumatic stress syndrome—that we can never completely escape the horror of Vietnam.

Vietnamese gangs emerged in California in the mid-1970s, having immigrated with 130,000 other refugees after the fall of Saigon in 1975. The first wave of refugees was made up largely of families who had been part of the merchant and professional class in South Vietnam. Despite a lack of acceptance by Americans and difficulty in adjusting to Western society, many of the newcomers made an impressive start in this country. They opened restaurants and other businesses. Their children developed a reputation for academic excellence, winning spelling bees and science awards and in some cases becoming class valedictorians only two or three years after learning English.

The "orderly departure" program that the Ford administration set up to accept the South Vietnamese refugees had envisioned spreading them around the country so as not to burden any one community. But the plan did not take human nature into account. Most of the refugees were processed at Camp Pendleton in Southern California. Having experienced the region's warm climate and seen its prosperous Chinese communities, many Vietnamese were not anxious to start their new life in the snows of Minnesota or Massachusetts. So the Vietnamese migrated back to California, settling by the tens of thousands in the working-class Orange County communities of Westminster, Garden Grove, and Santa Ana. Some 150,000 Vietnamese were living in Orange County by the time of the 1990 census.

Their impact on the three communities has been enormous. South Vietnam's ruling class smuggled millions of dollars in gold out of the war-torn nation, and invested much of it in shopping centers and other real estate in Orange County. Bolsa Avenue, once a sleepy little strip in Westminster, became a bustling commercial center known as Little Saigon—a mile and a half of glittering new shopping malls, restaurants and office buildings that caters almost exclusively to Vietnamese. The best known of the shopping centers, the Asian Gardens Mall, is a sprawling two-level complex that is crowded day and night. Glittering boutiques and jewelry stores line its hallways. Vietnamese men and boys gather around tables in the cafés playing chess and sipping *cafe su da*, a French-Vietnamese iced coffee similar to espresso.

From the very beginning, organized crime has been part of this outwardly pleasant and prosperous community. The old Saigon regime and the South Vietnamese Army had been brutal and corrupt, and many of their foulest denizens were part of the Vietnamese exodus. Former SVA personnel in various American cities set up anti-communist brigades that were ostensibly intended to fund and arm rebels in the jungles of Vietnam who were fighting to overthrow the communist rulers in Saigon. Merchants were pressured to give money to this patriotic cause or risk being branded as communists.

In reality, these anti-communist groups were little more than extortion gangs. Former military leaders who had spent their entire careers plundering their countrymen in Saigon saw little reason not to pursue their vocation in the Little Saigons of America. This reality was hardly lost on the Vietnamese community, but few dared to question the perquisites of Saigon's old elite. Some who did paid with their lives. Since 1980, nine Vietnamese journalists have been attacked or murdered for criticizing the wrong people. Nguyen Dam Thong, 48, the editor of a Vietnamese-language newspaper in Houston, was shot to death outside his home on August 24, 1982. Three weeks earlier, Thong's 30,000-circulation paper had run an article branding the anti-Communist groups as fronts for gangsters and extortionists. Next to his body, police found a "hit list" with the names of Thong and four other journalists who were to be murdered, signed by a group calling itself the Vietnamese Party to Exterminate the Communists and Restore the Nation. The same group took responsibility for the August 9, 1987, slaying of Tap Van Pham, 48, the editor and publisher of *Mai*, a popular Vietnamese-language entertainment magazine, who was killed when arsonists set fire to his office in Garden Grove. A month before his death, Pham had complained to his friends about being victimized by extortionists. He had even confronted gang members in a Garden Grove restaurant, saying, "Leave us [journalists] alone. We are just doing this for fun. Go somewhere else—they have more money."[4]

Sadly, federal authorities have been lax in their investigations of these slayings, never even questioning Thong's widow. No individual has ever been definitively tied to these killings or to the extortion of money in the name of anti-communism. But testimony before the President's Commission on Organized Crime in 1984 shed some light on the matter. A witness who was hidden behind a screen to shield his identity testified that he belonged to a Vietnamese anti-communist group that had chapters around the country. Within that group, he said, was a shadowy society known as the Dark Side, which was responsible for committing robberies and extortions to send money to rebels in Vietnam. He said the leader of the Dark Side was Nguyen Cao Ky, the former South Vietnamese prime minister and military leader, and that several other top members were former SVA generals. The witness said the Dark Side sponsored four gangs: the Black Eagles in San Francisco, the Fishermen in Houston, the Eagle Seven in Chicago, and the Frogmen in Orange County.[5] The witness' testimony was not the first report linking Ky to a criminal network. Two years earlier, syndicated columnist Jack Anderson had reported that Ky was a crime boss and said he had fled Vietnam with $8 million in gold, diamonds and currency. Anderson said he based his report on a confidential report by the Arizona Narcotics Strike Force and interviews with police in 15 cities.[6]

An air vice marshal in charge of the South Vietnamese Air Force during the early part of the war, Ky was a clownish character who wore purple jumpsuits and carried two pearl-handled revolvers. When he became prime minister in a June 1965 military coup that also installed General Nguyen Van Thieu as head of state, William Bundy, the assistant U.S. secretary of defense, called the combination "the bottom of the barrel, absolutely the bottom of the barrel."[7] Ky was brutal and autocratic. He once put down a rebellion in the SVA by ordering an assault that killed more than a hundred civilians in Danang.

For many years Ky had played a key role in the smuggling of raw opium into Saigon from the Golden Triangle. He started out in the drug trade as head of the First Transport Group, a division of the South Vietnamese Air Force that in the early 1960s was flying intelligence missions into Laos for the CIA. Ngo Dinh Nhu, brother of South Vietnamese President Ngo Dinh Diem, thought it would be a great idea if the planes returned from Laos loaded with opium. When Ky became prime minister, he maintained his role in the opium traffic but also assigned his chief aide, General Nguyen Ngoc Loan (who would become known worldwide in 1968 when he was photographed summarily executed a Vietcong suspect) to collect payoffs from Saigon's vice rackets.[8]

After both Anderson's report and the commission testimony, Ky strongly denied any criminal activity in this country. And some police officials expressed doubts about the reports. Ky, after all, had opened a modest liquor store in Garden Grove after fleeing Vietnam and tended the counter himself, not the usual behavior of a man with $8 million stashed away. He also declared bankruptcy in November 1983 and put his $250,000 house up for sale. "If he's a godfather, he's the poorest godfather in America," said Jon Elder, chief of police in Monterey Park, California.[9]

Either that, or he's the smartest godfather in America. He wouldn't have been the first person to file a phony bankruptcy petition, and the liquor store may have just been a convenient front. But whatever his involvement, there is ample evidence that former SVA personnel, be they generals or lowly infantrymen, played a role in the initial wave of terror in Vietnamese-American communities. Much of the gang violence in the early 1980s bore the stamp of experienced military personnel. On October 11,

1981, a woman was killed and eight others were injured when two gunmen wearing military fatigue ponchos opened fire in a Garden Grove restaurant in a botched attempt to kill a gang leader. What is more, the existence of a gang called the Frogmen, supposedly made up of former SVA underwater-demolition experts, was well documented. The gang made a bid to take over San Jose's Vietnamese extortion rackets in January 1982, walking into the Anh Dao restaurant one day at lunchtime and opening fire on a table of eight Vietnamese men, killing one and paralyzing another. Gary Palmer, a former Marine interrogator in Vietnam who used his language skills to investigate gangs for the Monterey Park police, ran into former military personnel in a number of cases. "The leaders of the Vietnamese gangs are people in their 30s and 40s who went into the military when they were teenagers," he told a reporter. "They're the guys who floated up rivers into North Vietnam to assassinate people. To blow away a guy is nothing to them. They have a total disregard for prescribed ethics. Their attitude is, 'If you're my enemy, I've got to kill you before you kill me.'"[10]

A new breed of Vietnamese gangster emerged in the 1980s, part of what has been called the "lost generation." They sprang from a far less prosperous class of people than South Vietnam's old elite, and they didn't have the luxury of being airlifted out of Saigon in 1975. These were the tragic "boat people," impoverished peasants from the Vietnamese countryside who made their way to Hong Kong in rickety homemade vessels. Desperate to escape the repression of communist Vietnam, they met even greater horrors on the South China Sea. Thai pirates robbed and murdered many of them. Others drowned when their flimsy boats capsized or slowly took on water. Many more—estimates out them in the thousands—died from starvation or lack of water.

And for those who made it to Hong Kong, life was not much better. They were forced to live for as long as five years in squalid resettlement camps where overcrowding and boredom bred mental illness, juvenile delinquency, and riots. The Kai Tak camp, a grim collection of concrete blocks and corrugated shacks in one of Hong Kong's poorest and most crowded districts, housed 14,000 refugees when it opened in 1979. Two academics, Kwok Chan and David Loveridge, spent time in Kai Tak in the early 1980s and found the conditions intolerable. "The bunks are stacked three high from floor to ceiling, with narrow, dark passages dividing the interiors," they wrote. "Old blankets, sheets and hardboard have been cobbled up around the bed spaces to give some semblance of privacy. There are, draped throughout the blocks of huts, streams of illicit electrical wires leading to televisions, refrigerators and, most importantly, fans. Even so, in summer the metal huts in particular are stifling hot."[11]

Many of the people housed in these camps were ethnic Chinese who had long faced official repression by the communist authorities in North Vietnam and who were forced out of the country after a military clash between China and Vietnam in 1979. Others were Amerasian children—the offspring of U.S. servicemen and Vietnamese women—who were outcasts in Vietnam. With little else to do, many of the young refugees formed gangs and terrorized their already beleaguered countrymen. Often there were brutal clashes between North Vietnamese and South Vietnamese gangs. In February 1992, just a few months before the 17-year Vietnamese exodus finally drew to close, a clash between two such gangs fighting with homemade spears, knives and sticks set off a bloody riot in Hong Kong's Shek Kong camp. Screaming "Kill! Kill!" southerners attacked a hut where 230 northerners had barricaded themselves and set it on fire. The mob dunked one northerner in a cauldron of boiling hot water before tossing him in the burning hut, where he died with 23 others.[12]

Chan and Loveridge found that more than half of the refugees in the Kai Tak camp in 1984 were under age 16. Many of these youths had been put on boats without their parents, who could not afford the trip themselves but wanted better lives for their children or wanted to spare their sons service with the Vietnamese armed forces, which had invaded Cambodia in 1979. Often parents had given the children no warning that they were being sent away from their families, for fear they would tell friends and word would get to the authorities. Youths were pulled from their beds in the middle of the night and put on a boat without even having a real chance to say goodbye to their parents.

Reared amid the horrors of warfare in their own country, cut off from their families, witness to murder and starvation on the South China Sea, treated like human garbage in Hong Kong refugee camps, these youngsters arrived in the United States in need of help. What they found instead was the hostility of American communities that viewed them as ugly reminders of the war we had "lost." They faced the taunts of schoolchildren who laughed at their customs and their inability to understand teachers. Many of them carried around heavy emotional baggage: the sense that they had been abandoned by their parents, the guilt of living in America while their families suffered in Vietnam, the recurring images of violence from their pasts. "Many of these kids have witnessed atrocities that you or I could not even imagine," said Leland Yee, director of Asian-Americans for Community Involvement, an organization in San Jose that works with Vietnamese youth. "We have one boy whose boat capsized in a rough sea. To this day, he has nightmares of his parents calling out to him and him not being able to do anything to save them."[13]

Many of the youths ended up staying with foster families or in the homes of friends and relatives who were so preoccupied with their own family's struggle for survival that they had little time left to nurture someone else's troubled child. Countless Vietnamese youths dropped out of school and ran away from such homes, left to their own devices on the uncaring streets of America. Adopting gangs as their families, they slept in hotels or gang crash pads while traveling the country in search of extortion and home-invasion victims, whom they treated with the same pitiless brutality that they had known their whole lives. They turned their parents' dreams for the future into an American nightmare.

Detective Mark Nye is part of an Asian gang unit in the Westminster Police Department. A young man in his 30s, Nye spends his days focusing on crimes on the lowest rung of the Vietnamese underworld: the street gangs, or "gang bangers," as he calls them. It is an almost impossible task. Nye is often on his own in keeping track of a growing gang problem. Westminster is a suburban community with a 100-person police force that cannot afford a well-staffed intelligence unit or a big Asian gang squad. A city of some 75,000 people, it is home to about 13 Asian gangs with names like the Natoma Boys, the Oriental Killers and the Cheap Boys. From these, Nye targets about 75 hard-core gang members whose crimes he considers a top priority. But for every hard-core gang member who operates in Westminster, there are several others who occasionally come through town. As the nation's largest Vietnamese community, Orange County is a magnet for traveling bands of Vietnamese robbers and shakedown artists. Nye communicates regularly with police investigators from around the country who know that sooner or later their Vietnamese perpetrators will end up in Little Saigon.

One night in April 1993, Nye and his partner took the author along on one of their nightly cruises through the streets of Little Saigon. On many nights, the two find themselves responding to the drive-by shootings that have become common among Vietnamese gangs in the city—a tactic they have learned from their Mexican and black counterparts. "What we're seeing is a real strong emulation of Hispanic gangs," Nye says as he drives among the blocks of drab two-story, cinder-block apartment buildings that house the Vietnamese and Mexican poor. "It grew out of the Vietnamese kids' experiences in the correctional system. They are starting to tattoo themselves and give themselves gang nicknames. They throw hand signs like the black and Hispanic gangs, and they are starting to scrawl their names on walls."

There are no shootings on this night, so Nye pulls his car into the parking lot of one of the city's Vietnamese cafés. He knows there are gang members inside from the cars in the parking lot— old Datsun 280Zs with fur covering the seats. Inside the restaurant, the suspected "gang bangers" look like innocent teenagers. They are all neatly dressed in polo shirts and calf-length baggy shorts. But they act like people with something to hide. When the two cops enter the room, the conversation stops and they stare straight ahead at their tables without looking up. Even the

employees avoid the glances of the two investigators as Nye surveys the crowd and pokes his head into a couple of back closets.
No one in the café has any outstanding arrest warrants, so the
two cops move on.

"A lot of these bangers live each day as it comes," Nye says as
he gets back into the car. "When they run out of money, they go
out and do a robbery and they share the loot with the other gang
members. The other gang members are their family and they
treat each other well. If they do a robbery and they get $5,000 in
cash, they are going to rent a motel, maybe a high-class motel,
rent a car, take everyone out to dinner and go to nightclubs."

Nye says not to be fooled by their benign appearances. They
may look a lot like the Vietnamese kids who win science contests
and play on tennis teams, but there is a world of difference.
"Some of them have no respect for human life," he says. "If you
question them about someone they just killed or injured in a
home-invasion robbery, they'll say, 'It's not my fault the guy's
dead.' They don't blame themselves for what happened. 'It was
fate. It was his time to die. God dealt him the cards.' They have
no remorse. I have yet to see one of these guys cry. You catch
them in a very serious crime and they don't even blink an eye. I
think some of it has to do with growing up in that country."

The kind of crimes Nye is talking about have often shocked
suburban Orange County. One of the most horrendous took
place in Santa Ana in 1986. It involved Trung Ngo and Huyen
Thi Hoang, a couple who had fled their country after the fall of
Saigon. The journey to the West had been typically harrowing.
Their extended family of 22 people had crammed aboard a rickety boat and paddled for five days before the vessel capsized off
Malaysia. They were in the water for hours before a boat rescued
them. By 1986, life was still a struggle for the couple and their 12
children. They had a modest house in Santa Ana, but Ngo was
unemployed and at 59 years of age was looking for work. His
wife, then 46, stayed home and cared for the children. "She was
a housewife," said her daughter, Kim Huong Ngo, 19 years old at
the time. "All she did was cook and clean and take care of the
children."

On May 5, 1986, Kim was returning from night school at 10:15 P.M. when a youth with a scarf over his face walked up to her car in the driveway. At first she thought it was a joke. But then the youth grabbed her keys and was joined by four others, also with their faces covered. They herded the family members into the living room and demanded money. One of the gunmen began walking through hallways and checking bedrooms. In one room, he found Hoang kneeling next to her bed praying. The other family members heard her yell "Oh, my God!" and the sound of a gunshot. Hoang had been killed because she had no money to give the robber. The killer was allegedly a 14-year-old from Garden Grove. One of the other robbers was 12 years old.[14]

"There is no question that the Vietnamese gangs are violent," says Nye. "Between us and Garden Grove, there is a shooting every other night involving Asian gangs. Hispanic gangs are violent. They do the drive-bys. But with the Vietnamese, we're talking about sophisticated weaponry. We have found fully automatic weapons, pipe bombs, hand grenades. They are supposedly getting the stuff from the Wah Ching and the Mexican Mafia. Wherever they get it, we know where they end up using it. Right here in Westminster."

The kinds of gangs Nye investigates are only the finishing schools for more sophisticated Vietnamese crime groups. Vietnamese organized crime is an elusive phenomenon that has rarely been successfully penetrated by federal law enforcement, largely because the gangs often lack the pyramidal structure that has made Chinese and Italian crime groups such easy targets. Operating without gang names and with constantly shifting membership, these groups augment their lucrative home invasions or commercial robberies with a mind-numbing array of other crimes. In San Jose, whose 75,000 Vietnamese form the largest concentration in any one U.S. city, police have seen Vietnamese gangsters involved in everything from bookmaking and loan-sharking to insurance scams and Medicaid fraud. "They leave no criminal stone unturned," says San Jose police sergeant Douglas Zwemke. "With most ethnic groups, you will have a guy who is a burglar, but he isn't macho enough to do robberies. Or you will have a guy who does robberies, and he won't commit burglaries. An auto thief is an auto thief. But when you put a Vietnamese robber in prison, you have also put away a burglar, an extortionist, a car thief and an insurance fraud artist. They are doing it all, and that's what separates them from mainstream crooks."[15]

San Jose realized it had a Vietnamese gang problem when the Frogmen shot up the Anh Dao restaurant in 1982. The police department has since been fighting an aggressive but ultimately losing battle to keep pace with the Vietnamese criminals. Home-invasion robberies in San Jose were running at about 15 a month in the early 1990s, commonly ending in severe injuries or murders. So the San Jose police countered the problem with an innovative sting operation. Investigators induced Vietnamese informants to put the word out on the street that they knew good targets for home-invasion robberies. After someone took the bait, the informants would show them a location. Gang members would then discuss and plan the crimes in hideouts that police had equipped with video monitors, and the crooks would be arrested en route to the robberies. Police once rounded up 15 home invaders in a single operation, and the rate of such robberies dropped to less than one a month.[16]

But temporarily solving the home-invasion problem did little to deter the Vietnamese gangs from committing other crimes. One of their favorites is auto theft, which they have turned into a science. Not only do Vietnamese account for 60 percent of San Jose's stolen automobiles, they have come up with a way to get the city to help them. Thieves will completely strip a car, place all of its parts in carefully marked bins and then leave the shell on a San Jose street. The car body is towed away and eventually auctioned off by the city. The thieves show up, take legal title to the body for a couple of hundred dollars and then reattach all the stolen parts and sell the stolen car legally.[17]

Vietnamese criminals in San Jose are also deeply involved in credit-card, welfare and Medicaid fraud. In February 1984 San Jose police and California authorities arrested 52 Vietnamese doctors and pharmacists who had conspired with gangs to steal millions from the state's Medi-Cal health-insurance program. Physicians were building entire medical files for people who didn't even exist. But the biggest surprise came when investigators began checking into the backgrounds of some of the doctors. "We found out that some of them were not doctors at all," Zwemke said. "They had some medical training in Vietnam, but they had shills go to the testing center and take the certification test. They had one ringer who took the test for a bunch of them."

Another big moneymaker for Vietnamese gangs both in San Jose and in Orange County is the theft of computer chips, especially in northern California's Silicon Valley. The gangs gravitated toward the chip thefts in the late 1980s because so many of the employees at all levels of the Silicon Valley companies are Vietnamese. Of those, a small percentage are crooks with contacts in the underworld. Chips are either stolen outright by employees or gangs steal them in burglaries or brazen armed robberies. Between October 1988 and the same date the following year, there were 12 armed robberies of computer chips in Orange County and the San Jose area.[18] Typical of these was the August 1989 robbery of Express Manufacturing Inc., an electronics firm in Santa Ana. Owner Chauk Chin was leaving the company for the night when two Vietnamese men forced him back into his office at gunpoint and let three accomplices in through a back door. The gang's leader was barefoot and wore black pajamas. He referred to the other robbers by number and ordered them around like a military commander. Robbers used duct tape to tie up employees and then ordered them to lie on the floor. Chin was taken at gunpoint to the company's storage room, where the thieves helped themselves to $500,000 worth of chips.[19]

Computer chips, which are used in everything from F-16 jet fighters to microwave ovens, range in price from about $15 to $500. One of the chips most coveted by the thieves, for example, is the Intel 486-dx-66, a computer "brain" that retails for about $460. The chips are tiny, have no serial numbers, and can be stolen by the thousands. One computer giant, Western Digital

Corporation in Irvine, California, estimated that it had lost $7 million in chip theft during the first nine months of 1989. After their theft, chips sometimes change hands a dozen times before they end up being sold in small electronics stores or shipped to Pacific Rim countries, where they are in great demand. Some criminals get rich off this scheme alone. One Vietnamese gangster from Santa Ana was extradited from Vietnam in the summer of 1993 after being charged with stealing $3.7 million in chips. He had purchased two hotels in Ho Chi Minh City, where he was seen flitting from nightclub to nightclub in a BMW.[20]

The Born to Kill gang was a different animal from the gangs that terrorize Orange County and San Jose. It was made up not of pure ethnic Vietnamese but of "Viet Ching," the term for Vietnamese who are of Chinese ethnicity. As we have seen, Viet Ching for years have worked for long-established Chinese gangs in New York, San Francisco, Boston, Toronto, Los Angeles and other cities. The Chinese gangs valued the Viet Ching for their ruthlessness, using them as killers and leg breakers. But for a long time they were loath to give the Vietnamese positions of real authority in the gang. The Vietnamese were good enough to murder and maim for the *dai los*, but not to share in their riches. It was a pecking order that the tougher, hungrier Vietnamese would not long tolerate.

One of the most cunning and ambitious Viet Ching gangsters in New York was David Thai, the Born to Kill leader targeted in the cemetery shooting. If one is to believe David Thai's own story of his beginnings in the city, he started out as little more than a waif. He ran away from an Indiana foster home in the 1970s and arrived in New York City with only $150 in his pockets. After two nights of sleeping in the Port Authority Bus Terminal, he managed to find work washing dishes at a nursing home in Farmington, Long Island. The next few years brought a succession of restaurant jobs, a year of college at New York University, and an ultimately failed marriage.[21] What Thai leaves out of his version is that in the early 1980s he was recruited by the Flying

Dragons in Chinatown. The gang was assembling a Vietnamese faction to handle the gang's enforcement, and the handsome, charismatic Thai became an adept recruiter.

But Thai wouldn't waste his talent on the Dragons for very long. In 1988, he broke off from the Flying Dragons and formed the Canal Boys, a gang made up of Vietnamese he recruited from both the Dragons and the Ghost Shadows. The new gang claimed a strip of Canal Street west of central Chinatown and began demanding protection payments from business owners in an Asian minimall at 271 Canal and from the dozens of cheap clothing and jewelry vendors that line the bustling street.[22]

Thai was playing a dangerous game by breaking off from the Flying Dragons without permission from Benny Ong, a game that had ended disastrously for Herbert Liu and his Freemasons in 1982. Thai even refused a "sit-down" with the aging Hip Sing leader, the ultimate sign of disrespect. But the neighborhood *tongs* apparently made a decision to tolerate Thai for a time. He operated on Canal Street unmolested by the other gangs, perhaps because they were reluctant to ignite a full-scale gang war between Chinese and Vietnamese.

Thai was like a Fagin to the hungry young street urchins who made up his gang. He fed them and bought them clothes. They lived in gang safe houses in Manhattan, Brooklyn, the Bronx and Jersey City, where *dai los* taught them the finer points of pickpocketing, robbery and extortion. The gang gave these wayward youths, many of them with no real families, an identity and a sense of belonging. Thai once gathered a huge group of them for a late-night initiation ceremony in a midtown Manhattan restaurant, where he impressed upon each of them that they belonged to something important. Sitting under a flag emblazoned with the trademark coffin-and-candles logo, each of the gang members swore allegiance to Born to Kill and signed a paper that pledged them never to talk to police or hurt another member. "We were proud to belong to it. Nobody thought of leaving," a former gang member said. "If you were no longer in BTK, that meant you left New York or you were dead."[23]

David Thai was like God to the gang members. He also commanded fierce loyalty from his lieutenants, some of whom were experienced and vicious criminals in their own right. One of Thai's top aides was Lan Ngoc Tran, a homicidal 30-year-old who bragged to federal agents after his arrest that he used to tail Communist Party officials to their homes after the fall of Saigon and rob and murder them.[24] The agents dubbed the stocky five-feet-two-inch gangster the "Poet of Death" because of the verse he wrote to celebrate his murderous exploits. While Tran had access to Thai, many of the gang's rank-and-file members had little contact with him. Their orders were relayed through *dai los* who oversaw the various safe houses. When they did find themselves in his presence, the gang members were afraid even to talk to him. One gang member recalled being introduced to Thai in a mall on Canal Street. "I was so nervous, I looked down, I couldn't talk to him. I knew that if you didn't listen to him, you got killed. Everyone was scared of him."[25]

Thai didn't look the part of a tough guy. He was handsome and well-dressed and spoke in a soft, almost effeminate voice. When federal agents first heard his voice on a wiretap, they thought they were listening to a woman. Peg Tyre, a *Newsday* reporter who interviewed Thai in the Manhattan Correctional Center in 1991, was surprised by his charm and prep-school manners. "He is a very, very handsome guy. He looked like a person who ate well and worked out regularly. He looks right into your eyes when he talks to you. He put his hand on my knee when we were talking and even broke out crying once." But Tyre also saw Thai's menacing side. The gang leader became angry that *Newsday*'s Asian photographer was shooting so many pictures, and he told him to watch his step. "He was being Mr. Smarmy Nice Guy and suddenly his whole face changed when he looked at the photographer. You could tell then that he was a mean son of a bitch."[26]

Thai drove around Chinatown in a Jaguar and lived in a big house in suburban Melville, Long Island. Besides earning a living from Born to Kill's operations, Thai also had some enterprises of his own. He had turned the basement of his Melville home into a workshop for making phony Rolex watches, which vendors then sold on Canal Street as the real thing. Thai once bragged that he had made a million dollars on the watch scam.

But for all Thai's sophistication, his gang members developed a reputation for being the most reckless in Chinatown. They would hang out on street corners with their BTK tattoos and pompadour haircuts and terrorize Canal Street. Whereas Chinese gang members would be very subtle in their requests for protection money, the Born to Kill thugs would beat merchants in broad daylight. They also angered other gangs by shaking down stores and robbing gambling dens in their territory.

Many of the gang's crimes were committed outside New York. Like other Vietnamese gangs, Born to Kill was highly mobile, often committing robberies and home invasions hundreds of miles from its base. On November 26, 1990, six members of the Born to Kill gang walked into a Cambodian-owned jewelry store in Doraville, Georgia, and said they needed a necklace repaired. Odum Lim, the store's owner, described what happened next: "My wife repaired it . . . and asked for the money. They did not give the money, and one of them turned to the others and said 'Are you ready?' Six of them suddenly jumped behind the counter. One of them grabbed my wife's neck, and two of them jumped toward me. I saw the gun and tried to grab it out of his hand, but I didn't make it because another one stabbed my right arm." Lim was stabbed 12 times and left lying in a pool of blood, though he eventually recovered. The gangsters made off with cash, rings, a necklace and jewels.[27]

The gang was no less ruthless in New York. Its battles with other gangs in 1991 brought more violence to Chinatown than it had seen since the gang wars of the late 1970s and early 1980s. In February 1990, BTK members burst into Winnie's Bar on Bayard Street and murdered two members of the Ghost Shadows in cold blood. (The most prevalent theory holds that the murder of Vinh Vu and the cemetery shooting were the Ghost Shadows' retaliation for those bar slayings.) Six months later, the gang accidentally shot and killed one of its own members as they were robbing a vegetable warehouse on Broome

Street. Three months after that, three Born to Kill members were found shot to death in a parking lot across the street from a bar on Reade Street.

But the most sensational incident came after Born to Kill members robbed a jewelry store at 302 Canal Street in early 1991. When the store's owner, Sen Von Ta, 29, went to the Fifth Precinct to complain, detectives convinced him to be a witness against four Born to Kill members. Over the next few weeks, BTK members continually harassed the witness to prevent him from testifying, visiting his store and once mailing him broken glass wrapped inside a newspaper article about the robbery. But the witness refused to back down. Finally, Thai ordered his killing in a meeting with other gang members in Old Bethpage, Long Island. Thai was going to give the contract to a relatively inexperienced lieutenant. But Lan Ngoc Tran, Thai's chief enforcer, protested that he should be the one to handle the job. The Poet of Death walked up to Sen Von Ta in broad daylight outside a

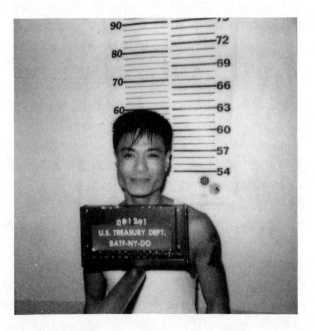

Lan Ngoc Tran, the Born to Kill enforcer who federal agents dubbed the "Poet of Death." (ATF)

store where his wife worked and shot him twice in the head in front of her and the couple's 12-year-old nephew.[28]

That killing of a police witness in the middle of Chinatown was Thai's gravest mistake. It only made investigators more determined to put the Born to Kill boss behind bars. With rival gangs also gunning for Thai by this time, it became a question of who would get Thai first—the police or the underworld. By this time, a team of investigators from the Police Department's Major Case Squad and the U.S. Bureau of Alcohol, Tobacco and Firearms had a secret weapon: one of Thai's closest advisers was an informant. When he first began cooperating with police, Tinh Ngo had just been another gang underling, with little access to Thai and other top leaders. But he rose quickly through the ranks and, after Vu's murder in July 1990, he became Thai's second in command.[29]

In the opening months of 1991, Ngo was telling authorities about Thai's every move in advance. Since the investigators were not ready to arrest the gang leader, they were forced to go through a series of subterfuges to stop crimes from happening without blowing their informant's cover and putting his life in jeopardy. When the informant told them of the gang's plan to rob a jewelry store in Rochester, New York, the investigators teamed up with the state police and pulled the BTKs over on an expressway, telling them they fit the description of some drug dealers. They searched their car and confiscated their weapons. But rather than arrest the BTKs and blow the investigation, they told them that the courts were closed on Father's Day and that they would be getting summonses in the mail. "They didn't suspect anything," said ATF Agent Daniel Kumor. "The informant told us later that they laughed at us. They thought we were assholes."[30]

But these "tap dances," as one agent called them, became progressively more complicated. On August 5, 1991, Thai showed up at the Brooklyn safe house with an assignment for Tinh Ngo, the informant. He told him to find two BTK members who were new to Chinatown and drive them to the Pho Bang Chinese restaurant at 117 Mott Street. He then handed the informant a bag. Inside was a homemade antipersonnel bomb—a package of nails, screws and glass wrapped up in duct tape and hooked to a detonator. Thai, who was being paid $10,000 by a rival restaurant to blow up the Pho Bang, had sent another lieutenant, Minh Do, to handle the job two weeks earlier, but Do made a mistake and blew up another restaurant, at 113 Mott, instead. Luckily, the restaurant was empty and no one was hurt. Thai was enraged and ordered Do brutally beaten and then ostracized. This time, he told Ngo, he wanted it done right. He didn't care that the Pho Bang was a popular restaurant and would be crowded at that hour.

Ngo called Kumor to tell him of the plot, and the two agreed that he would call back when the gang members were about to move. But the call never came. Ngo was pressured by the other gang members to get moving and never had a chance to call. The three were on the road and heading for the Pho Bang while Kumor was still pacing around his office. After an hour of waiting, Kumor decided to take no chances. He headed for Chinatown with ATF Agent Don Tisdale and members of the police Major Case Squad.

Chinatown's streets were crowded when the gang members parked their car on Centre Street just north of Canal at about 11 P.M. The two BTK members stepped out of the car with the bomb still in the bag and set off on their deadly mission. Kumor and Tisdale arrived at the corner of Centre and Hester Streets several minutes later. Kumor peered down Centre Street and saw the two gang members just as they rounded the corner of Canal, heading east toward Mott. His only chance to make the arrest without compromising the informant was to make it look like he was a passing police officer mistaking one of them for a wanted criminal. So Kumor sprinted down Hester Street toward Mott, heading for the Pho Bang by a different route than the gang members. On the way, all kinds of wild thoughts ran through his head. What if he got there too late? What if he walked in the door of the Pho Bang just as the bomb was going off? When he rounded the corner of Mott Street, he poked his head in the front door and saw that the restaurant was full. He scanned the floor for a bomb but saw nothing. As he walked out the door, he found himself face to face with the two gang members only a few feet away. They had already lit the cigarette they were going to use to ignite the fuse. Kumor told them he was a police officer and that one of them looked like a wanted criminal. He opened the bag and there was the bomb.[31]

After such a close call, the investigators decided to round up Thai and the other BTK leaders on whatever charges would stick and worry about a broader racketeering case later. Police crashed down the door of Thai's house at 12 Davis Street in Melville and found him standing in his bedroom wearing only a pair of magenta undershorts.[32] He quietly allowed them to slap on the handcuffs. In the house they found a 9-mm pistol, a Mac-10 with a silencer, a .38-caliber revolver and 169 rounds of ammunition. But the real treat was in the basement. There investigators found the workshop, with piles of internal mechanisms for watches and presses for turning them into phony Rolexes. And they found materials that they later determined were used to make the bomb intended for the Pho Bang.

The initial charges they brought against Thai were for three robberies. But a month later, federal authorities slapped Thai, Lan Ngoc Tran and several other lieutenants with a 20-count RICO indictment that included murder, robbery, extortion, bombing and racketeering charges. On October 23, 1992, Thai was sentenced to life in prison. BTK members still operate in Jersey City, Boston and Toronto but have been eliminated for the time being as a presence in New York's Chinatown.

The Vietnamese rebellion had failed in New York's Chinatown. But things would turn out differently in Boston and Toronto, where Chinese gang leaders had grown accustomed to running things with little violence and had a tougher time dealing with the aggressive Viet Ching gangsters.

Like other Chinese crime bosses, Ping On leader Stephen Tse had used Vietnamese thugs as enforcers since the early 1980s. When black pimps and drug dealers strayed into Boston's Chinatown from a nearby red-light district known as the Combat Zone, it was Vietnamese thugs, not Chinese, who attacked them and drove them out of the neighborhood. Tse also unleashed Vietnamese robbery gangs on gambling dens that failed to pay him tribute. Gradually, some of the Vietnamese gained influential positions in the Ping On. One of them, Van Huy Huynh, became a top heroin dealer for Tse in the mid-1980s, though he was only 22 years old.[33] Tse trained other Vietnamese gangsters to run gambling and other rackets in their own communities, but he kept a tight rein on them in Chinatown, even preventing Vietnamese businesses from opening in central Chinatown. To this day, Vietnamese restaurants are located to the west of Chinatown, cheek-by-jowl with the Combat Zone.

But Tse began losing control of the Viet Ching while he was in the Essex County House of Detention serving an 18-month prison term for refusing to testify before the presidential commission in 1984. He made the mistake of not designating a strong figure to watch over Chinatown while he was inside, and the hungry young Vietnamese took advantage of the Ping On's disarray. Renegade Vietnamese gangs began robbing the Ping On's gambling joints and shaking down businesses in Chinatown. The incidents kept up even after Tse finished his 18-month prison sentence. In the early summer of 1986, there were six robberies of gambling dens in the space of a month. Typically, the robbers would pistol-whip patrons, taking both the gambling proceeds and their personal jewelry and watches. In one incident, one of the gamblers shot the fleeing Vietnamese. The wounded man made it to the getaway car, but his compatriots pushed him out of the car as they sped through the Brighton section of Boston. Passersby found him bloodied and mortally wounded at the corner of Commonwealth Avenue and Harvard Street with a wad of cash clutched in his hands.[34] The terror, of course, was not limited to Chinatown. The owner of a television shop in the Allston section of Boston was beaten with a hammer by Vietnamese gang members who wanted extortion money. The wife of a Lowell, Massachusetts, jewelry store owner had her skull fractured from being pistol-whipped during a robbery.[35]

Police identified one of the ringleaders of this terror as Mai

Song, a 23-year-old Vietnamese who had between 30 and 50 ex-tortionists and robbers under his command. Police briefly put Song behind bars in December 1986 after he robbed a Viet-namese market on Tremont Street in Boston's Chinatown. The owner, a 53-year-old Vietnamese named Ven Do, identified Song as the robber and agreed to testify against him. But he soon had second thoughts. Several gang members came to his store and told him they had killed people in Texas and California and would not hesitate to do the same to him. "You may know us, but you won't know the people who come in to get you," they said. Detectives didn't blame the witness, but they were angry at the Chinatown community leaders who had been pressing them to do something about the Vietnamese gangs. None of them came forward to support Ven Do, and Song walked out of jail a free man.[36]

Stephen Tse was deeply disturbed by the challenge to his rule. Police picked up intelligence that Tse had arranged a meeting with Danny Mo, the Kung Lok leader in Toronto who was also having troubles with the Vietnamese, to talk about how to han-dle the problem.[37] In December 1986, Son Van Vu, a 33-year-old Vietnamese gang leader believed to be behind many of the gam-bling house robberies, was found shot to death in a Hollywood, California, motel room. Vu, who had lived in Boston and was once a close associate of Tse, was a heavy gambler who hung around card clubs in Emeryville and Gardena. He could have been killed over a gambling debt. But detectives considered it more likely that his murder was connected to unrest in Boston's Chinatown.[38]

Vietnamese eventually gained the upper hand over the Ping On. Tse, facing mounting pressure from police and the rival gangs, moved back to Hong Kong in 1989. (He would be ar-rested there in 1994 and extradited to the United States to face racketeering charges). His second-in-command, Michael Kwong, was murdered in his restaurant in suburban Arlington, Massa-chusetts, in August 1989. When the Ping On failed to retaliate for Kwong's murder, the gang was all but finished on the street.

By the early 1990s, three Vietnamese gangs—one of them

dominated by former members of a Los Angeles group that called itself the Viet Ching—were feuding for control over Chinatown, bringing the neighborhood a level of violence that it had never seen when Tse was in control. Two Vietnamese men were gunned down in front of a transit station in Boston's Dorchester section in October 1991. A month earlier, a Vietnamese gangster was machine-gunned to death in a Chinatown parking lot. But the bloodiest incident in this story was the killing of five men in a gambling club in January 1991. Among the three Vietnamese sought in that case was Hun Suk, a gang leader whose group had come to control Washington Street in Chinatown. By the time of those killings, the name Ping On was rarely heard anymore on the streets of Chinatown. The Vietnamese had taken over.

The struggles between Chinese and Vietnamese gangs came earlier to Toronto than they did in Boston or New York. Rackets in Toronto's main Chinatown, a bustling community surrounding Dundas Street and Spadina Avenue, had traditionally been controlled by the Kung Lok, a Chinese gang with links to a major triad in Hong Kong. The gang, whose name means "Mutual Happiness," was founded in 1974 by a Kung Lok triad figure named Lau Wing Kui, who had moved to Toronto to expand the triad's reach to North America. He ran the gang until he was deported in 1980.

His successor was Danny Mo, who had long been an enforcer in the gang but by the early 1980s was more renowned for his skills as a businessman. As we have seen, Mo forged the links with Chinese gang leaders in other cities and established control over the booking of Asian entertainers in the Toronto area. Mo more or less co-existed peacefully with a Toronto faction of the Ghost Shadows headed by Eddie Louie, brother of the legendary Nicky Louie. Eddie Louie and many of his Canadian Shadows were inducted into Hong Kong's 14K triad in the early 1980s, giving them even more legitimacy in Toronto's Chinatown.

The Vietnamese gangs that began preying on Toronto's Chinatown in the early 1980s could not have cared less about triad connections. Many of them thumbed their noses at both the

Kung Lok and the 14K, robbing their gambling dens and extorting money from restaurants in Chinatown. Like Stephen Tse and New York's gang leaders, Danny Mo was able to keep the renegades under control for a time, employing many of them in his operation. But Mo would not be on the streets long enough to keep the Vietnamese in check. He was convicted in 1985 of stealing $13,000 in tickets in order to derail a Vancouver promoter's attempt to book a Chinese concert at Toronto's O'Keefe Centre.[39]

By 1987, Vietnamese gangsters were even shaking down restaurants owned by 14K and Kung Lok triad members. Rather than face down the ruthless Vietnamese, some of the triads moved their operations to growing Chinese communities in the Toronto suburbs. Chinatown's street-level rackets were essentially handed over to Vietnamese gangs, who would not coexist as peacefully as the Kung Lok and the 14K.

The new crime boss of Chinatown became Asau Tran, a Viet Ching who had come to the city in his early 20s during the first wave of boat people in the mid-1970s. At 5 feet 9, Tran was tall for a Vietnamese. He had a lean, muscular body, wavy black hair, a delicate nose and mouth, and dark pencil-thin eyebrows. One Chinatown bar owner called him "a tall, dark, handsome man with many, many girlfriends."[40] Some of the girlfriends might also have been intrigued by Tran's fearsome reputation. He had started out in the rackets as an enforcer for the Kung Lok in the 1970s and had developed a reputation for being quick on the trigger. In September 1983, the 30-year-old Tran became angry when people laughed at him for not winning a dance contest at a Toronto community center. Tran and a friend pulled out weapons, shot and killed a 19-year-old and wounded two others. The pair were arrested two days later hundreds of miles away in Sault Ste. Marie, Ontario. But they were acquitted of the killing after police could not find a reliable witness to come forward.[41]

After his release, Tran founded his own gang in late 1983, calling it Asau's Boys. In less than a decade, he became the premier rackets boss in Chinatown, with control over street-level extortion and gambling and strong connections with the Chinese triads. It was a position of power that no other Vietnamese gangster

The scene of Asau Tran's slaying in Toronto's Chinatown. The Pot of Gold restaurant is in the building at the left. (Toronto Star)

had achieved in a major North American city—and it brought some measure of stability to Chinatown's underworld.

That period of calm ended when Trung Chi Truong showed up in Toronto in 1990. Truong had spent much of the 1980s as a member of the Ping On gang, but he was ejected by Stephen Tse for being too wild.[42] He and some followers had been robbing stores throughout metropolitan Boston, often injuring the victims and drawing heat from police. In 1987 he was arrested for his part in the jewelry store robbery in Lowell, in which the Cambodian owner's wife was pistol-whipped. At the same time, he was being questioned by detectives investigating the murder of Son Van Vu in Hollywood. While being held in the Lowell robbery, Truong escaped and spent a couple of years in hiding before showing up in Toronto newly baptized as a Born to Kill member. His plan was to trade on the New York gang's fearsome reputation and grab a piece of Toronto's extortion territory.

By then, Asau Tran was 37 years old and more interested in making money than fighting a gang war. But when Truong's people began wreaking havoc in Chinatown, he had to deal with the renegades or lose face. So he hired a gunman named Danny Tran to take care of Truong. Tran was perfect for the job. He already hated Truong from the days when they were rival gang members in Boston, and he had a reputation as a brazen hit man. Working for the Ghost Shadows in New York, Danny Tran was suspected of being the one who had murdered Born to Kill lieutenant Vinh Vu on Canal Street. He was also believed to have been one of the attackers at the Linden funeral. Tran was in Toronto hiding from the BTK, so he had his own selfish reasons for not wanting to see a chapter started in the Canadian city.

The only problem was that someone got wind that Danny Tran was gunning for Truong and decided not to wait around for it to happen. On December 27, 1990, the 31-year-old Tran had just sat down to a plate of noodles in the Kim Bo restaurant on Dundas Street when two men walked in with guns. "So you want to fool with big brother," one of them said as he pumped five bullets into Tran's chest.[43]

The killing ignited a gang war between Asau's Boys and Born to Kill that was the bloodiest in the long history of Toronto's underworld. Eleven people would die over the next nine months, an almost unheard-of streak of violence in a city that only gets a few dozen murders a year. A Born to Kill member named Le Mo was shot to death in front of a Dundas Street restaurant in January 1991. One of Asau's men died in a hail of bullets less than two weeks later on the same street. The violence took a turn for the worse on March 3. Three of Asau's acquaintances, not even gang members, were eating in the A Dong restaurant on College Street when teenaged members of the Born to Kill started an argument with them from another table. The gangsters left and then returned with their guns and killed all three of them.[44]

Asau Tran was losing the war, and everyone in Chinatown expected him to be next. But the cocky gang leader showed no outward fear. In midsummer of 1991, Tran met with police investigators and had the audacity to promise them an end to robberies and extortions in Chinatown if they would lay off his gambling dens. He even threatened them, saying he could not promise the safety of police officers if they did not agree to the arrangement. But the police talked tough right back, and reminded Tran that he was being hunted at that very moment by rival gangs. Tran shrugged it off. "If I die, I die," he said.[45]

Tran's reputation on the street had diminished. Having successfully avoided U.S. authorities, Truong was arrested by Toronto police as an accessory to the A Dong massacre and extradited to Massachusetts. Rumors spread in Chinatown that Tran had told authorities where Truong was hiding. He was being called a stool pigeon behind his back. Other gangsters were also angry that Tran had presumed to speak for them in his offer to the police. They had no intention of giving up their extortion income just so Tran could get protection for his gambling houses. Suddenly Tran had more than just the maverick Truong to worry about.

The end came on August 16, 1991. At 3:20 A.M., Tran was leaving the Pot of Gold karaoke club on Dundas Street with a business associate, Shaun-Keung Pun, 33, and a 28-year-old waitress named Tin Wah Lui. Two men dressed in suits stepped from the shadows and cut down all three of them with automatic weapons.[46] Asau Tran dropped to the sidewalk with four bullet holes to his head. The king was dead. And at least for the moment, the war for Toronto's Chinatown was over.

9: "Get Down or Lay Down"

The Broadway is a clothing store in what used to be Detroit's fashion district. Most of the other clothiers in the district have long since packed up and moved to the suburbs, leaving behind empty and boarded-up stores. The most conspicuous of these eyesores is the monstrous Hudson's department store on Woodward Avenue, which left a gaping wound in the middle of downtown when it closed in the mid-1980s. But The Broadway stayed behind and adjusted its inventory to meet the tastes of the city's growing black gentry. Everyone from former Mayor Coleman Young to professional athletes can be seen inside the white brick building at 1247 Broadway, browsing through racks of brightly-colored Italian and German suits that rarely sell for less than $500.

The floor was busy with customers and employees at midday on September 14, 1990, when a tall, thin man in his early 30s walked in and began looking through a display of expensive men's socks. Dressed in a well-tailored gray suit and black Italian shoes, he could have been one of Detroit's successful black businessmen or a lawyer leaving the nearby District Court building. But he was nothing so respectable.

With his back to the front of the store, Demetrius Holloway, 32, one of the city's biggest cocaine kingpins, did not notice the nondescript dark automobile that pulled up in front and discharged a tall, disheveled-looking man wearing dirty black clothing. Looking unhurried, the man walked into the store and nodded a greeting to one of the employees in the front of the store. He then walked up behind the elegantly dressed kingpin and, without blinking, yanked a handgun from his waistband and shot him twice in the back of the head. Holloway tumbled into a rack, splattering blood on the fine European suits, as his assailant strolled calmly from the store as if he had just bought a pair of socks.[1]

Holloway died a gangster's death—a fate he had cheated more than once over the five years his rivals had been gunning for him. They had already gotten his childhood pal, Richard (Maserati Rick) Carter, who was shot to death in a Detroit hospital bed in September 1988 as he was recovering from an earlier attempt on his life. But Holloway was cagier than most of Detroit's drug heavies. He once staged his own abduction at gunpoint from a local hamburger stand so that lawmen and drug hit men would assume he was dead. It was that same caginess that helped him build an empire that controlled an estimated 80 percent of Detroit's cocaine trade, affording him a lifestyle that included five homes, several apartment buildings, and all the expensive suits a man could want. Police searching his body after the shooting found $14,000 in cash and a .32-caliber handgun in his pockets.

Detroit's Mafia family, which once ruled the region's rackets with an iron fist, is rarely heard from these days, unless you count a few bookmaking indictments and gambling raids that never implicate family boss Jack Tocco. Tocco's gang hasn't killed anybody in years, but the city's black gangsters kill dozens and perhaps even hundreds of people every year. Holloway is believed to have been killed by a notorious murder-for-hire gang that had carried out more than 50 contracts on Detroit drug dealers before being rounded up by federal authorities. With muscle like that on the streets, Detroit's Mafia long ago ceded the city's numbers racket to black operators and stayed out of the local drug wars. "It used to be a Mafia guy would come into a black neighborhood and everybody would shake," said retired Michigan state police lieutenant John Fonger. "Now they tell the mob to go fuck themselves. They're badder than the mob."[2]

Frank Matthews and Nicky Barnes may have been ruthless, but even they would shudder at the mindless brutality and nihilism of today's black underworld. Both of those early heroin kingpins had been schooled by their Mafia predecessors. They understood that cooperation between crime groups was preferable to violence, because violence only drew the attention of police. They had rarely murdered competition to take over neighborhoods; indeed, Barnes even considered it useful to have other heroin dealers operating in the same neighborhood so his troops would not stand out. But Demetrius Holloway and the other black godfathers of the 1990s live in a different world. They operate in ghettos bristling with weapons, full of teenagers willing to use them. If Don Corleone had been the model for an earlier generation of black mobsters, Tony Montana—the murderous Cuban drug lord in Brian DePalma's *Scarface*—was the inspiration for the new drug gangs. They resort to murder rather than conciliation in dealing with competitors.

But even if black organized-crime groups are "badder" than everyone else, they have never lived up to predictions that they would one day replace the Mafia as a dominant national crime syndicate. If anything, black crime groups have become less organized since those predictions were first made 25 years ago. They remain imprisoned in the pathology of the American ghetto, their ranks filled with reckless young drug gangsters who live wildly and extravagantly for a few years and then self-destruct, ending up with long stints in prison or a plot in the graveyard. With a few notable exceptions, black crime groups have rarely been around long enough to build a criminal legacy like those of the Italians, the Chinese, the Cubans and others.

The ethnic-succession theorists who predicted a new Black Mafia in the mid-1970s were impressed by the wealth and sophistication of the drug organizations they saw forming in New York, Philadelphia and elsewhere. And since then, the number of highly profitable black drug gangs has only multiplied. Many of the black gangs that have operated in Detroit, Philadelphia,

Newark, New York, and other cities over the last decade have shown enormous sophistication, operating with military-like efficiency and discipline as they took over drug peddling in entire sections of major cities. They are as dangerous as any Mafia family while they last. But they have never taken the next step and formed a durable black syndicate. After two or three years of riding high, they self-destruct. Their growth is accompanied by so much violence and publicity that police mobilize and bring cases against the leaders. And once the leaders are behind bars, the gang invariably falls into disarray.

Ethnic-succession theorists overlooked several trends that conspired to stifle the growth of black organized crime beginning in the late 1970s. First, Chinese and Colombian crime groups—not blacks—eclipsed Italians as the chief smugglers of narcotics. And in New York City, the nation's primary drug market, the Colombians have chosen to deal almost exclusively with Dominican wholesalers, limiting blacks to smaller-volume deals and cutting them off from the large shipments of cocaine they would need to become bigger players in the drug business.

Second, the emergence of crack cocaine in the mid-1980s democratized drug dealing at the retail level. Crack intensified the cocaine high and made street packages available for as little as $10, making the drug tempting and affordable for the masses. Suddenly, any ghetto youth with a few hundred dollars could cook up some crack and post a few people on street corners to hawk the "rocks" in little plastic vials. These packs of young crack gangsters diluted the power of the large drug organizations that once controlled retail distribution in places like Harlem and Detroit's East Side, slowing the advance of black organized crime.

Third, and perhaps most important, life in the American ghetto took a sharp turn for the worse in the 1970s and 1980s. The middle-class and working-class African-American families that had been a stabilizing influence in the ghetto, the backbone of its churches and neighborhood organizations, took advantage of new opportunities yielded by the civil rights movement and relocated to cleaner, safer neighborhoods. Those left behind in the ghetto were the most desperate of the black poor, a segment of society known in the jargon of sociologists as the "underclass." It is a class with far higher rates of unemployment, welfare dependency, fatherless households, drug addiction, and infant mortality than the generations that preceded it in the ghetto. Experts disagree about the cause of this alarming trend in ghetto life. Conservatives blame the social-welfare spending generated by the 1960s Great Society programs. Liberals cite the continuing effects of racism and job discrimination. Both sides attribute some of the problems to the decline of heavy industries like steel, automobiles, and rubber—once the chief sources of jobs for many inner-city blacks—and their replacement by technology-based and professional service industries, which require an educated work force and usually build their plants in the suburbs. Whatever the cause, American ghettos descended into a shocking state of violence and nihilism in the 1980s, with so many wild gun-slinging teenagers on the streets that it became hard for any single crime group to bring control to the street-level distribution of narcotics. Those gangs that have captured drug sales over a large area of a major city have been able to do so only with a level of violence that ultimately brought about the downfall of their leaders. All these factors have conspired to keep black organized crime from fulfilling its deadly potential. So far, the black underworld has not had a Lucky Luciano, Meyer Lansky, or Johnny Torrio to overcome these obstacles and weld all of its constituent parts into an effective national machine.

And yet even with all these factors working against black organized crime, the possibility that some kind of national syndicate will eventually emerge remains frighteningly real. For the black underworld never goes away. When one drug gang is broken up by authorities, another moves into the neighborhood almost overnight. The grim tide of hopelessness that has overtaken the nation's black ghettos—the unemployment, out-of-wedlock births, child abuse, drug addiction and slum housing—has created a more fertile breeding ground for gangsters than anything the nation has ever seen. It hardly matters that black gang leaders may only control a single block, that the leaders change year by year, that there is no black John Gotti or Al Capone. In the worst neighborhoods, there is a little Al Capone on almost every block. The allure of gang life in the black ghetto is mirrored in popular music. "Gangsta rap" is replete with references to young men emulating Al Capone or the Mafia. Even black talk-show host Arsenio Hall calls his orchestra "my posse"—using a popular term that originated in the Jamaican drug posses that terrorized ghetto neighborhoods in the 1980s. The sheer numbers of young and hungry black criminals clawing up through the ranks of the drug underworld, even if most end up dead or in prison, suggest a prominent place for blacks in the future of organized crime. A 1992 study by the Los Angeles County District Attorney's Office found that an astounding 47 percent of the county's black males aged 21 to 24 had been linked to gangs.[3] Studies would no doubt show that comparable percentages of black youths are involved in Chicago gangs or are players, at least at low levels, in Detroit's drug underworld. The organized-crime potential of such criminal multitudes is blunted by their constant bloodletting, but if a visionary were to come along and knit all of these warring parties into a unified force—and some have already tried—black gangsters would form history's most formidable criminal syndicate. More worrisome, the foundation for such a national syndicate is already in place. Itinerant drug gangs from New York, Chicago, Detroit and Los Angeles have spread like a virus across the nation, setting up crude enterprises in smaller cities from Omaha to Buffalo. Black organized crime may have unstable leadership and a reckless propensity for violence; it may be fluid and ever-changing. But its sheer size and relentless mobility make it impossible for serious students of the underworld to ignore.

Milton (Butch) Jones was one of the new breed. He was the genius behind Young Boys Inc., a Detroit outfit that was the first legendary drug gang of the 1980s. Young Boys pioneered many techniques that later became standard for drugs gangs around the country: the use of young teenagers, who cannot get jail time, to transport narcotics; the use of brand names on the drug packets; the use of violence to capture street-level distribution in neighborhood after neighborhood until a wide area of the city was under the gang's control.

Jones was only 22 years old when he started building his organization on Detroit's near West Side. Stockily built, with a thick beard and a wide bulbous nose, he did not fit the part of the sleek young drug gangster. The brooding young drug dealer didn't drink, use drugs or hang around in nightclubs. But he was smart and tough—he had already served time in prison for assault—and he had the respect of teenagers in the Monterey-Dexter neighborhood. When he told them he was going to make them rich, they listened.[4]

Through Sylvester (Seal) Murray, a major heroin wholesaler in Detroit, Jones already had the ability to obtain large amounts of heroin on consignment. All he needed was a plan to put it on the streets, so he built an efficient, businesslike organization that would leave police shaking their heads in disbelief. Taking the name Young Boys Inc. from a smaller outfit that had gone out of business, Jones used a mixture of violence and smart marketing techniques to take over street-level heroin dealing around the city. He assembled an army of 300 people to sell drugs on street corners, inside houses, and in the hallways of public housing projects.[5]

Young Boys worked like a well-oiled machine. Butch Jones or a lieutenant would get heroin in bulk from Murray or another source. It would then go to a "hook-up" house, where about six people would stand at a long table for several hours cutting the heroin with lactose or quinine and pouring it into coin envelopes for sale on the street. The envelopes would already have been stamped with brand names like "Renegade," "Murder One," or "Rolls-Royce."

By 9:30 A.M. each day, trusted "hook-up crews" would deliver the bundles around the city to heroin runners, identifiable by their blue jogging suits. If a runner was not on time to receive the heroin, that would be his last day on the job. Throughout the day, money runners clad in red jogging suits would visit the sites and pick up the proceeds. Each drug-dealing site also had a "top dog" to oversee the various heroin runners.[6]

Young Boys lieutenants recruited employees by driving down streets in cars equipped with loudspeakers. And there was no shortage of volunteers. Base pay for the members was not fantastic, ranging from $300 a week for heroin runners to $700 a day for top dogs. But they earned sales commissions, and Jones regularly handed out bonuses when the employees gathered in a Detroit warehouse every Sunday to pick up their pay. Among the most frequent bonuses were Max Julian leather jackets with fur collars. The jackets became so closely identified with Young Boys Inc. that they became a symbol of prestige for teenagers and sold by the dozens at local malls. One store in Northland Shopping Mall just outside Detroit claimed to have sold several hundred. Eventually, students were shot over their jackets and they were banned from several high schools.[7]

Young Boys Inc. was not as violent as some of the gangs that succeeded it in Detroit. But several murders and beatings were tied to the gang, usually carried out by an elite unit of Young Boys enforcers known as the Wrecking Crew. One of the crew's victims was a 17-year-old amateur boxer named Gregory Browder. Browder and two friends had been pressured by a YBI recruiter in January 1983. The recruiter had driven them to several dope houses and showed them bags of money, expensive jewelry, and fur coats as an inducement to join. But all three said they wanted no part of it. Browder came under the gang's suspicion when one of the dope houses he had been shown was raided by police shortly afterward. A week later, the promising young boxer was walking through the parking lot of a West Side Detroit supermarket when a gold Pontiac pulled up beside him and someone pumped two bullets into his head.[8]

Butch Jones and 40 other YBI members were indicted in 1983 and ended up being sentenced to long prison terms. But their legacy continues to haunt the city. Certainly drugs and crime would have infested Detroit with or without Jones' enterprising nature. But the gang's influence on succeeding drug gangs was so strong that its leader cannot escape some of the blame for the sickening epidemic of drugs and violence that overtook the city in the late 1980s. By 1987, Detroit had an estimated 500 crack houses, one for every 2,000 people in the city. With the auto industry in steep decline, drugs became the leading sector of Detroit's inner-city economy. The profits were so enormous that even some otherwise dutiful public officials fell victim to temptation. Detroit Police Chief William Hart and other officials were linked to drug-related corruption scandals—a system of graft that was all the more shameful when one considers the toll that the drug trade took on young people's lives. Gunfire claimed so many young victims that the two Detroit newspapers began keeping running tallies of the number of juveniles killed each year. Between 1986 and 1993, the *Detroit Free Press* counted 2,393 youths under age 16 who were shot. Of these, 293 died immediately and many others eventually succumbed to their wounds.

The merchants of this grim tally were a generation of Detroit drug gangs that were even bigger and more deadly than Young Boys Inc. Four brothers from the small, impoverished hamlet of Mariana, Arkansas, started a crack-distribution organization in Detroit shortly after the Young Boys were taken off the street in 1983, and far surpassed the accomplishments of Butch Jones. The Chambers Brothers controlled about 200 crack houses and supplied cocaine to about 50 more, pulling in about $1 million every week. The gang was just as disciplined as the Young Boys but less forgiving when employees fell down on the job. A witness who testified at the Chambers Brothers' trial in 1988 said she had watched Larry Chambers discipline two teenage runners for selling soap powder to a customer instead of cocaine. He beat one of them with a chair leg and threw the other out of a second-story window. On another occasion, she said, she watched gang member Eric (Fats) Wilkins holding a bloody baseball bat and laughing after he had punished another runner whose money came up short. On still another occasion, she saw Wilkins and another man carry a body out of an apartment building and put it in a trash bin.[9]

More than a hundred of the Chambers Brothers' recruits were teenagers from their hometown. Everyone back in tiny Mariana knew that Larry, Billy Joe and Willie Chambers were drug dealers making big money in Detroit. But they didn't know how big until the family showed up for the high-school graduation of brother Otis in 1986 in three chauffeured limousines. With unemployment for teenagers hovering at about 50 percent in Mariana, teenagers were easily lured to Detroit by tales of easy money and fast life in the big city. Some came back in expensive automobiles with tales of glamour and high living. Others came back like James Ray Farris, with seven bullet holes in his body and a collection of wreaths around his coffin. "James Ray said he had friends in Detroit who could get him a job," said his foster father, the Reverend Lee Eggerson. "The next thing I know we have to talk to a coroner in Detroit."[10]

Detroit was not the only city whose drug trade came under the control of violent new black gangs in the 1980s. Philadelphia saw the rise of the Junior Black Mafia, which modeled itself after the infamous gang of the 1970s. Indeed, one of the old Black Mafia runners, James Cole, helped organize the new gang to protect local drug dealers from incursions by Jamaican drug posses. The JBMs, as they became widely known, were perhaps singular in the history of violent drug gangs in that several of their leaders were anything but ghetto kids. The gang's leader, Aaron Jones, was from a middle-class family in West Philadelphia. His father worked at the Philadelphia naval base and sent all of his kids to Catholic schools. Jones graduated from high school and even spent two years at Temple University before he embarked on a life of crime.[11]

The JBMs started out in 1985 selling cocaine and marijuana in the neighborhoods lining 52nd Street in West Philadelphia. But they would not be content for long with a single neighborhood. Aaron Jones and two of his lieutenants, Leonard Patterson and Mark Casey, were planning nothing less than a black syndicate modeled on the Mafia. They watched *Scarface* and *The Godfather* over and over again, memorizing the lines and mimicking the gangsters' style. "Jones was obsessed with the movie," said a former associate. "He saw himself as the Godfather and Leonard Patterson as Sonny. They focused on drugs because loan-sharking and numbers were not big moneymakers. Extortion was ruled out because people didn't go along with that anymore."[12]

Aaron Jones recruited some of the toughest young criminals in West Philadelphia and began plowing like a Panzer division through other drug dealers' territories, warning them to "Get down or lay down"—join the gang or be killed. And it was not an idle threat. More than a dozen murders were tied to the JBMs in their drive to take over the city's drug trade. One of Jones' enforcers, Anthony (Tone) Reid, had one of the itchiest trigger fingers in the city. He shot a 16-year-old to death in March 1989 simply for throwing a snowball at his car.[13] The JBMs developed a fearsome reputation and spread their operation with little trouble into North Philadelphia and the impoverished Germantown and Mount Airy sections of the city.

The JBMs were expanding across Philadelphia for about two years before police even knew they existed. But they weren't exactly keeping a low profile. JBM members would ride around Philadelphia's ghettos in dark-colored Jeeps and wear diamond-encrusted rings engraved with the initials JBM. Some people were charged a $1,000 initiation fee to join. Others had such large drug operations of their own that they were welcomed into the organization—or forced to join. Mark Casey, a drug dealer who controlled large sections of Germantown and Mount Airy, was absorbed by the JBM and quickly rose to a top position. "Mark Casey became the brains of the JBM," said Jones' former associate. "Casey was the one who came up with the ideas and knew how to put things together. Leonard Patterson was most likely the person who came up with the name JBM and the idea for the rings."[14]

But Aaron Jones was the undisputed leader. He was handsome, educated, and well-spoken, and had a knack for winning his followers' loyalty by showering them with gifts and praise. "He treated them like kings," said an investigator who traced the gang for years. "He made sure that they had the best clothes. They went to fights all the time in Atlantic City and Las Vegas.

They stayed at the best hotels. He gave them clothes, money and respect, and they went all over the country, first class."[15]

Aaron was also the one with the drug connections. James Cole had moved to California not long after the gang's formation. He and another Philadelphian who had moved West acted as middlemen between the JBM and Mexican drug dealers in California who were closely linked with Colombia's Cali cartel. Jones would get hundreds of kilos at a time on consignment from the Mexicans. But the arrangement didn't always run smoothly. Jones was constantly in debt to the Mexicans, at one time getting $2.5 million behind in the payments. They also complained that he didn't handle their deals like a professional. Cash shipped back to California would be bundled so poorly that it had to be repackaged, once delaying the takeoff of a Colombian-bound plane for two days. The Mexicans even came to Philadelphia to show JBM members how to package the cash. During the meeting, a defiant Jones emptied a garbage bag full of cash on the floor and said, "OK, you show me how you want it wrapped."[16]

The JBM unleashed a reign of terror on Philadelphia ghettos. Its murder victims were independent drug dealers, disloyal members of the organization itself, and even innocent bystanders. One of the victims, a North Philadelphia drug dealer named Dwight Reid, was killed on December 12, 1989, because he refused to pay a street tax to the JBM. His body was found in some weeds off Chamounix Drive—near Philadelphia's historic Ridgeland mansion—with 13 bullet holes, including 10 in the head. Most of the shots had been discharged at close range after he was already on the ground.[17]

JBM enforcers did most of the killing, with Jones accused of pulling the trigger himself on only one occasion. That was when a convicted North Philadelphia drug dealer named Richard Isaac refused to "get down" with the Junior Black Mafia. On February 21, 1989, Jones and two of his associates allegedly accosted Isaac at the corner of 23rd and Turner Streets in North Philadelphia. Isaac tried to flee but was felled by a bullet to the hip. "They stood over top of me shooting and shooting," Isaac later told a grand jury. "As I was laying on the ground, I was laying face down on my stomach and as the shots kept ringing out, I see my arm jumping and then Aaron came over, knelt beside me, picked up my head and put the gun to my head. I put up my hand . . . and the bullet went in right here and came out on the side (of the right hand). Then I heard him say, 'I don't have no more bullets. Come on, let's go,' and they ran."[18]

Isaac, who was shot 10 times in the arm, hip, chest and face, was left paralyzed and confined to a wheelchair. He agreed to give testimony in the secrecy of a grand jury, but he was terrified about facing Jones and the two other JBM members in open court. When he took the stand at Jones' trial in late June 1989, he was horrified to see JBM enforcer Ronald (Rock) Mason sitting in the second row of the crowded courtroom with a loaded 9-millimeter handgun tucked in his waistband. Police noticed the gun as Mason was leaving the courtroom and arrested him. But the damage was already done. Isaac froze on the witness stand and suddenly could not remember who had shot him. Jones and his two associates were acquitted of the shooting.[19]

In late 1988, the JBM went to war with a large South Philadelphia drug organization run by John Craig Haynes, who had refused to "get down" with Aaron Jones. The clash started when the two gangs were both expanding into the Mount Airy section and pushed up against each other's territories. But the conflict degenerated into a bitter personal feud between Haynes and Jones, one that cost several innocent bystanders their lives. Unlike Jones, Haynes was no middle-class kid. He was raised in a poor family in South Philadelphia. But he was more low-key than Jones. He just wanted to operate his $5 million-a-year drug operation quietly without any trouble. The word on the street was that he only acted the part of the murderous drug lord after the JBM's numerous attempts to kill him. Once Haynes was shot and wounded as he sat in a car outside a Germantown nightclub. Another time a passerby found a bleeding Haynes lying in the roadway near 20th and Pierce Streets in South Philadelphia. He had bullet wounds in his chest and hand. Still another time JBM members tried to kill him as he walked to a court hearing in Philadelphia's Center City. The attack turned into a wild shootout right in front of City Hall that left pedestrians scurrying for cover.

But the final indignity for Haynes did not even occur in Philadelphia. Haynes and several members of his gang were in Las Vegas for a Sugar Ray Leonard–Roberto Duran fight when they bumped into Aaron Jones and other JBMs in the lobby of Caesar's Palace. Haynes' followers didn't have their guns, so they stood by helplessly as the JBM thugs beat Haynes and, in front of a crowd of horrified onlookers, threw him through the plate-glass window of a gift shop. It took 20 stitches to close the wounds in his face. When the hotel managers rushed into the lobby, Jones threw a pile of cash on the floor to cover the damage. Humiliated, Haynes' people went to the nearest restaurant, ordered steaks, and stole the steak knives in case they were attacked again. But there were no more clashes that weekend.[20]

Haynes flew back to Philadelphia in a deep depression. His defense lawyers would argue later that he became so obsessed with killing Jones that it added up to temporary insanity. This obsession led to the ugliest episode of the war. Haynes had gotten a tip on August 10, 1989, that Aaron Jones was eating in Tobin's Inn, a restaurant in the West Oak Lane section of Philadelphia. Haynes and gang members Curtis Perry and Patrick Coleman burst into the restaurant, not knowing that Jones had already left. Unable to make out faces in the darkened dining room, they shot and killed Donald Branch, a computer software expert from suburban Montgomery County who slightly resembled the JBM leader.[21] The shooting of the innocent victim, together with two other instances in which Haynes and his gang had mistakenly killed innocent bystanders, led to an 18-month investigation by a combined federal-state task force that wiped out Haynes' gang in April 1991.

By then, the JBM also had its share of troubles. In February 1991 Jones had been sentenced to 10 to 20 years in state prison for stabbing an inmate at the Philadelphia Industrial Correctional Center while he was being held there in the Isaac shooting. But the bigger blow came in October 1991, when Jones and 25 other members of the JBM were swept up in a massive federal racketeering indictment that accused them of distributing more than 2,200 pounds of cocaine on Philadelphia's streets. Jones was given life imprisonment under the federal "drug kingpin" statute. He and two other JBM leaders were forced to surrender $12 million in drug profits to federal forfeiture. Jones, who was just 30 years old, showed no emotion at his sentencing. He just slowly bowed his head.

Similar fates awaited virtually every other major black kingpin in the 1980s. Rayful Edmond III, a 24-year-old drug kingpin in Washington, D.C., came from an extended family that had operated numbers and sold heroin in the District as far back as the 1950s. But when young Edmond tried to turn the family business into a drug empire in 1985, authorities had him behind bars within four years. Edmond had it all while he was riding high. He wore expensive jewelry and bought a Jaguar, a Porsche and a Range Rover. He ran up bills of thousands of dollars in expensive hotels and paid them in cash. He was smart enough to field an army of 150 drug dealers and take over up to 50 percent of the District's cocaine sales. But he succumbed to the same recklessness that is ultimately the downfall of most major black drug gangs. The 30 murders that his organization is alleged to have committed in its drive for underworld supremacy outraged the community. The police crackdown was only a matter of time.[22]

Young Boys Inc., the Junior Black Mafia, the Edmond organization—they all were among the dominant crime groups in their cities while they lasted. But such huge and well-organized drug gangs are becoming a rarity in the black ghetto. Their successors in the later 1980s and early 1990s have been more reckless and less organized. Detroit, Philadelphia, New York, Washington and other cities have seen fewer major black groups succeed in taking control over enormous drug-dealing territories. Instead, dozens of smaller gangs carry out murderous campaigns to control miniempires that may only cover a few blocks.

One of the big reasons for this shift has been the emergence of crack, which brought a wild new breed of gangster into the drug business. Powdered cocaine was a rich man's drug. Anyone who wanted to make big money selling cocaine, even at the retail level, needed to invest tens of thousands of dollars and then had to supply a steady base of customers willing to shell out $100 for a gram or $50 for a half-gram. Less than a half-gram wouldn't get a serious cocaine user through one night. But the development of crack, a crystallized, smokeable form of cocaine, made the high more powerful and immediate. For as little as $10, a user could buy a couple of rocks that would make for a pretty good party, if not an entire evening. It opened up cocaine to masses of new consumers and masses of new suppliers. Drug dealers now needed to buy only about $1,000 worth of cocaine to cook up enough crack to yield $6,000 in profits.

This easy entrance into the drug underworld meant new competition for large drug organizations, and it unleashed the murderous young crack gangster on American cities. The trend was already in place in New York by the mid-1980s. The same upper Manhattan drug market that was once Nicky Barnes' exclusive domain became a patchwork of territories for American black, Dominican and Jamaican gangs. Dozens of gangs competed for crack sales in the 80-block area between southern Harlem and the northern end of Washington Heights. New York City police estimated that the gangs were responsible for up to 520 murders in upper Manhattan between 1982 and 1988. Crack gangs were blamed in large measure for a 15 percent increase in the city's yearly murder rate from 1985 to 1987.[23]

In Queens, the yearly number of murders climbed from 187 in 1985 to 232 the following year, a 25-percent increase that police blamed on the crack trade. Middle-class neighborhoods in southeast Queens, near the border of Nassau County on Long Island, were once a quiet haven for black families who had saved enough to move away from the tough streets of Harlem and the South Bronx. But proximity to Nassau County also made Southeast Queens convenient for suburban crack-heads. Crack gangs began flourishing in the area. Queens neighborhoods like Jamaica, St. Albans, Laurelton and Cambria Heights turned into a battleground for crack gangsters armed with machine pistols and bullet-proof vests. "The violence was just endless," a former Queens crack dealer told a reporter. "It was no big deal getting rid of a body—you put it in a trunk and leave it at the airport. Or you bury it. Or you burn it."[24]

The new gangsters played by different rules from the large smooth-running heroin organizations that used to run things in southeast Queens. Howard (Pappy) Mason, a jailed drug dealer in the South Jamaica section of Queens, did something that would have been unthinkable for more careful crime groups. He tried to counter police pressure by ordering a hit on a police officer. On February 26, 1988, a 22-year-old police officer named Edward Byrne was sitting in his car at 107th Avenue and Inwood Street, guarding the fire-bombed home of a man who had complained to police about crack dealers. Two young gangsters walked up to his car and put five bullets in his head. The killings shocked a city that is all but inured to violence. A prosecutor at the killers' trial called them "five shots that were felt across America." If nothing else, it drove home the point to New Yorkers that it was amateur hour for the city's drug business. "With $20,000 and a gun anybody can play," said Thomas Reppetto, president of New York's Citizens' Crime Commission. "If there had been some grand council and a hit like that had to be submitted, it would have been turned down."[25]

In other cities, the drug trade took longer to dissolve into anarchy, but the trend is unmistakable. Often the biggest black gangs these days are little more than bands of predators that feed off the drug underworld rather than organizing it. After the Chambers Brothers were locked up in Detroit, the city's drug trade was reduced to chaos. Demetrius Holloway and Maserati Rick Carter made a play for supremacy, but neither lived long. Big Ed Hanserd, another major drug dealer on the city's east side, was packed off to prison. Much of the drug trade then fell into the hands of mere bands of killers and rip-off artists.

Best Friends was a murder-for-hire gang formed by Carter and East Side drug lord Richard (White Boy Rick) Wershe to protect their sprawling drug operations. But with Carter dead and Wershe in prison, the gang made its own move for control over the drug trade, launching a homicide spree that added up to an estimated 80 to 100 bodies. Best Friends' leader, Reginald (Rockin' Reggie) Brown, was the worst of the bunch. Fearing that a former drug dealer named Alfred Austin was going to testify against him in May 1992, Brown walked up to Austin's front porch on Detroit's East Side in front of several witnesses and opened fire. The bullets killed not only Austin but also two others, including a 3-year-old girl.[26]

Just as ruthless was the Clifford Jones organization, a Detroit murder-for-hire gang that carried out more than 50 contracts between 1984 and 1993. Jones, the gang's leader, was so feared on the streets of Detroit that federal informers who were otherwise cooperative would deny even knowing who he was. He was once a lieutenant in Holloway's gang and is believed to have been responsible for his murder. Jones' gang was known for its military-like efficiency and well-rehearsed murders, but it was anything but a responsible business enterprise. It was not uncommon for Jones to carry out a contract for a drug dealer, get paid for the work, then kill the drug dealer and steal his drugs. When Jones and his gang were rounded up in February 1993, Detroit community activist John George, head of the Motor City Blight Busters, put it best: "When you have these vigilante, machine-gun-toting gangsters roaming the streets, it makes it hard for citizens and neighborhood groups to say, 'OK, let's go out and plant flowers to keep up our area.'"[27]

With the drug trade in such chaos in the nation's major cities, it would be easy to dismiss the new black crime groups as common street thugs who should not be of concern to students of organized crime. But their potential for organizing into a national syndicate remains awesome. When one pulls down a map of the United States and looks at who is controlling the drug trade in the hundreds of small and medium-sized cities across the country, the insidious threat of "itinerant" black drug gangs is hard to miss. Drug gangs from a handful of the nation's largest cities are literally all over the map.

The most prolific of these itinerant drug dealers have been the two infamous Los Angeles street gangs, the Bloods and the Crips.

These two organizations have an almost mind-boggling presence in the ghettos of Los Angeles and the surrounding county. It is a misnomer to call them gangs. They are really federations, made up of dozens of independent gangs that each claim at the most a few blocks of territory. In Los Angeles County, there are more than 220 Crips gangs and more than 80 Blood gangs.[28] (When you throw in Hispanic, Asian and white gangs, the county's total climbs to a mind-numbing 1,030 gangs, according to one often-cited count.) Estimates of the number of people who belong to the two federations vary, but they are always in the tens of thousands. Incredibly, 47 percent of the county's black males aged 21 to 24 were identified as gang members in 1992 in the databases of either the city police or the Los Angeles County Sheriff's Department.[29]

Identifying which federation a gang belongs to is not hard. Since the gangs emerged in the aftermath of the bloody Watts riot in 1965, the Crips have traditionally worn blue colors and the Bloods have worn red. Blood gangs can go under any name, but Crips gangs usually carry the name of their federation in their title—such as the Eight Tray Crips, the Rolling 60s Crips or the Compton Crips. Though a Crip is always a Crip and a Blood always a Blood, that doesn't make it any easier to know which gangs are allied. Blood gangs almost never battle each other, but Crips gangs are constantly at war. Crips kill Crips far more frequently than they kill Bloods. Together, the two groups account for hundreds of killings in Los Angeles County every year.

But unlike the drug gangs in eastern cities, the Bloods and the Crips don't kill each other over drugs. Says Sergeant Wes McBride, a gang expert with the Los Angeles County Sheriff's Department: "They don't kill each in Los Angeles over narcotics. They kill each other over hate. Our turfs are so well established, Gang A knows better than to go to into Gang B's areas and sell dope. It would be suicide. Now those baggers and taggers come out of the homicide unit and they see they got a dead Crip. He's got a pocket full of rock. They say, 'Well, it's a dope murder.' Well, it's not a dope murder. These guys have to present themselves as targets to sell crack. They have to make themselves available to their customers, to be out in the open. A guy maybe used to stay behind cover, but he steps out on the street to sell crack, and it's the wrong gang or the wrong homeboy and he gets blown away. It don't make it a drug-related killing."[30]

In that sense, the black underworld in Los Angeles is even more anarchic and less organized than elsewhere. No Crip or Blood stands out as a boss of the federation. Leaders of the member gangs are killed so fast that none of the gangs develops a lasting command structure. If the gangs stayed within Los Angeles County, they could be safely dismissed as run-of-the-mill street thugs.

But they are not limited to Los Angeles County. In the early 1980s, the Bloods and the Crips began spreading across the country. Hundreds of Bloods and Crips invaded Denver, Portland, Seattle, and St. Louis, taking over the local drug trade and bringing drive-by shootings and other L.A.-style violence to these cities for the first time. But the gangs didn't stop there. McBride has a map of the United States in his office with little red and blue flags pinned to the cities where Bloods and Crips have established a presence. There are hundreds of them. He's got flags pinned on Shreveport, Louisiana, and Huntsville, Alabama; Corpus Christi, Texas, and Tulsa, Oklahoma; Omaha, Nebraska, and Little Rock, Arkansas; York, Pennsylvania, and Anchorage, Alaska. In many cities, the plague may start with only one or two Los Angeles gang members. They then recruit locals and move in on the territories of local drug dealers, terrorizing them with drive-by shootings. "You end up with some bad-ass Bloods and Crips who have never even been to Los Angeles," says McBride. "We got a call from St. Louis about a guy from the Rolling 60s Crips. He had 'RSC' tattooed all over his neck and back. But we couldn't find him in our files. It turns out he was born and raised in Tulsa and was running dope back and forth between Tulsa and St. Louis." The new Crip and Blood chapters often have at best a loose affiliation with the mother gangs in Los Angeles. In many cases, the itinerant gangsters set up more sophisticated drug enterprises than the gangs in Los Angeles, where the first order of

business is always mindless turf battles. But the migrating gangsters do retain drug suppliers and other contacts in Los Angeles,
and the potential for greater syndication is always there.

The Jamaican posses were the pioneers of this migration of violent drug gangs into the nation's heartland. Beginning around
1985, the posses moved out of their bases in Brooklyn and
Miami and blanketed the nation, introducing crack to many
smaller cities for the first time. Their appearance in Kansas City
in 1985 was especially dramatic. Just about the time federal prosecutors were toasting the apparent demise of the city's Mafia
family, Jamaican posses showed up and began opening crack
houses and murdering local drug dealers. Kansas City's annual
homicide rate soared, jumping from 91 in 1985 to 131 two years
later.

More than 450 possemen moved into the city in a matter of
months in 1985 and set up dozens of crack houses. They were
credited with singlehandedly introducing crack to Kansas City,
leaving police to marvel at their marketing skills. "The Jamaicans
brought in a much better quality of cocaine—that's what made
them catch on real well," Kansas City Police Captain David Bar-
ton said in 1989. "They weren't cutting the dope like everybody
else, and they were giving bigger pieces for the money. They just
flooded the market."[31]

A similar blend of marketing and murder brought the posses
to cities around the country, where they left a trail of bodies that
was unprecedented in the history of organized crime. In 1988,
the U.S. Justice Department blamed the posses for 1,400 drug-
related murders since 1985, including more than 700 in a single
year. One of the groups, the Shower posse, executed five people
in a crack house in Miami in 1984, including a pregnant woman
who police found in a praying position, as if she had been beg-
ging for her life. Federal authorities estimated in the late 1980s
that there were 10,000 posse members in the United States split
up among 40 gangs that controlled 40 percent of the nation's
street-level cocaine sales.[32]

The posses, named after the vigilante groups in spaghetti westerns that are still popular in Jamaica, grew out of the island nation's fratricidal politics. They emerged in Central Kingston, a section of the capital that had once been a bustling waterfront district catering to American sailors and English tourist, but that by the 1970s had degenerated into a horrendous slum. It was a world of shanty towns, garbage-strewn gullies and street corner gangs that acted as brokers between the "sufferers"—Jamaican patois for ghetto dwellers—and the country's two main political clans, the People's National Party and the Jamaican Labor Party. In a district where government largesse was one of the only sources of income, the gangs were important conduits for patronage jobs and public contracts. The gang chieftains, known as "community leaders," were seen as champions of the poor who pressured the parties to dole out relief to the sufferers.[33]

But that image was tarnished in the 1976 election, which came amid a campaign by the Central Intelligence Agency to destabilize the government of P.N.P. Prime Minister Michael Manley, a socialist who was friendly with Fidel Castro. The gangs were used as hired thugs by the P.N.P. and the J.L.P.'s Edward Seaga, who unsuccessfully challenged Manley in the election. Seaga's stronghold, a Central Kingston neighborhood known as Southside, was flush with gang members who exported cocaine and marijuana to the United States to buy guns for the political warfare. In the 1980 campaign—a rematch between Manley and Seaga—the political struggle grew even uglier. Hundreds of Jamaicans died as gang members toting M-16s fired on party clubhouses, political rallies and even police stations.

Seaga won the election—and immediately took steps to rein in the monster he had created. The new prime minister unleashed the brutal Jamaican police on maverick gang members, who had served their purpose but were now a nuisance for the J.L.P. By 1984, many of the gang members had fled to New York City and Miami, where their organizational skills and penchant for violence gave them a leg up on local drug dealers.

One of the exiles, Delroy (Uzi) Edwards, who acquired his nickname because he was fond of hiding the weapon under a

trench coat, founded the Renkers posse, credited with introducing crack to Brooklyn's Bedford-Stuyvesant section. Edwards told
an interviewer that he got his start in crime as a $10-a-week
henchman for the J.L.P. in Kingston.[34] In the United States, he hit
the big-time. His operation expanded from Brooklyn to Philadelphia and Washington, and by 1987 was said to be taking in
$100,000 a week in crack sales. Described by one prosecutor as
a "cold-hearted, brutal, vicious killer," Edwards was convicted of
six murders in 1989 and sentenced to seven consecutive life
terms in prison.

Other posses found a niche in cities as far-flung as Houston,
Dallas, Rochester, Boston, Buffalo, Denver, Hartford, Fort Laud-
erdale and even small towns in places like West Virginia, Mis-
souri, and Long Island. In each of those cities, their entrance into
the drug trade was accompanied by a rash of murders. The violence became so blatant that federal authorities and municipal
police departments around the country joined in cracking down
on the posses. It was the federal government's first use of broad
racketeering statutes against violent drug gangs. "The Jamaican
posses came in like Patton," said Chris Marzuk, a Manhattan assistant district attorney. "I've never seen a response from law enforcement like the one caused by these people."[35] In 1988, the
federal government indicted 34 members of the Miami-based
Shower posse—a J.L.P. ally that was described as the nation's
largest drug gang—for shipping suitcases full of cocaine to New
York, Los Angeles, Detroit and other cities. Two years later, the
FBI seized 17 members of the Gulleymen, a posse named after a
Kingston neighborhood called McGregor's Gulley, in a crackdown on narcotics peddling in Brooklyn and Dallas.

Many of the posse leaders who were not rounded up by authorities returned to Kingston and settled into lives as neighborhood "dons." Perhaps the most notorious don, Lester Lloyd
Coke—leader of the Shower posse and a key J.L.P. operative—
was burned to death in his Kingston jail cell in 1992 during a
bloody gang war sparked by the murder of his 24-year-old son,
Mark Anthony Coke.[36] Few large-scale posses are left in the
United States, and those that remain keep a lower profile than

their predecessors. Many criminals of Jamaican descent are still hawking drugs on the nation's urban street corners, but they have largely melded into the drug underworld of American blacks.

This migratory pattern is being copied by other big-city drug gangsters. Detroit's gangs have migrated to points throughout Ohio and Indiana, taking over the drug trade in big cities like Toledo, Columbus and Cleveland, and even smaller towns like Lima, Ohio. New York's black drug gangs, particularly from Brooklyn and the Bronx, have taken over drug trafficking in virtually every city in New York State that has anything resembling a black ghetto. They are in Rochester, Buffalo, Syracuse, Utica, Elmira, Newburgh, Middletown, Albany and many other cities. "I've talked to police all up and down the Hudson River, and they're all seeing the same thing," says Sergeant Alex Minor of the Binghamton, New York, police.[37] Drug dealing had gotten so bad in Schenectady, New York, by November 1993 that 500 state and local police swarmed through the city one morning and made 50 arrests. Almost all of the people arrested were from New York City.[38]

Still more disturbing, Chicago's long-established gangs are migrating out of the Windy City and forming alliances with Los Angeles gangs in Middle America. Unlike the Bloods and the Crips, Chicago's gangs are well organized and have solid leadership. Anyone who doubts that need only consider the case of Willie Lloyd.

The leader of the powerful Vice Lords street gang was not forgotten by his gang when he went to prison for three years. On the day he was due to be released from Logan Correctional Center in December 1992, gang members left a black-and-white leather outfit and a mink coat at the prison office so he would not look shabby upon his release. More than a dozen men and women, bedecked in leather, gold, fur and diamonds, showed up in a procession of five limousines to pick him up. When the short, 42-year-old gang leader walked through the steel doors of the prison, the supplicants rushed forward and placed a skullcap of black and gold on his head. Lloyd was pleased with the gifts and the loyalty of his troops. He raised his right hand in greeting and made a show of admiring his new clothes. "Mighty! Mighty!" he shouted.[39]

The damage that Chicago gangs could do if unleashed on the nation is even more frightening when one considers the case of Jeff Fort, the gang leader who led Chicago's Blackstone Rangers for a quarter-century. The Rangers were founded in the early 1960s by young men who wanted to protect themselves from other street gangs around 66th Place and Blackstone Avenue in the Woodlawn area of Chicago's South Side. Gathering other gangs under its umbrella, the Blackstone Rangers became the most powerful gang on the South Side. The gang's president was Eugene (Bull) Hairston. Jeff Fort was the vice president. The gang's bitter enemy was the Devil's Disciples, another large gang that formed in the neighboring Kenwood area.[40]

In the late 1960s, The Woodlawn Organization, a community group, came up with the bright idea of using the two gangs as tools to reach the South Side's troubled youth. Both gangs had displayed some political awareness and were credited with helping keep the South Side cool during the riotous summers of the era. So in June 1967, T.W.O. received a $957,000 grant from the federal Office of Economic Opportunity to set up four job-training centers in the territories of the two gangs. Amazingly, Hairston was hired as an assistant project director at a salary of $6,500. Fort was hired to a $6,000-a-year post as center director, responsible for hundreds of unemployed youths undergoing job training for $45 a week.[41] It turned out to be the first of a long line of scams for the rising young gang leader—as the citizens of Chicago soon found out.

The true character of Jeff Fort was revealed in the fall of 1967. He was first arrested for ordering three juveniles to kill a South Side drug dealer and then charged with pulling the trigger himself in the murder of a Devil's Disciple. The federal government had a thick glob of egg on its face. Senator McClellan's Permanent Subcommittee on Investigations launched a probe that revealed the sordid operation of the job-training program. A former Ranger named George Rose testified before the committee that

Jeff Fort, the longtime leader of Chicago's Blackstone Rangers street gang and its successor, the El-Rukns, testifying before a Senate sub-committee in 1968. (AP/Wide World)

Hairston and Fort were strong-arming teenagers to drop out of high school to join the unemployment program and then forcing them to kick back $5 to $25 of their weekly pay. Those who re-fused, he said, were beaten, shot in the arms, or even killed. Rose's revelations were a national sensation that not only helped ruin the name of the Office of Economic Opportunity but also started the legend of Jeff Fort, who took over the gang's presi-dency in 1968.[42]

After serving several years in prison, Fort was released in 1976 and resumed control over the gang, renaming it the El Rukns and wrapping it in the religious mantle of the Black Muslim movement. But nobody was fooled. The El Rukns operated more like a crime family than a religious cult—and the muscular, bearded Fort was the Godfather. The gang violently seized control of dope peddling over much of the South Side and shook down taverns, shoe stores, and other businesses for extortion payments. By the 1970s, the El Rukns' old nemesis also had a new name—the Black Gangster Disciples—and the two waged bloody wars for control of the drug trade in the city's housing projects.[43]

Fort and the El Rukns were taken down by a massive federal indictment in 1991, but their legacy continues to haunt Chicago. They were the inspiration for the formation of dozens of other gangs—gathered under the umbrellas of the Folk and People nations—that have made the streets of Chicago's black neighborhoods every bit as violent as those in Los Angeles. The sports world was shocked when Ben Wilson, the nation's top high-school basketball player, was shot dead after brushing against a hot-headed gang member in December 1984. But his was only one among many young lives taken. In the previous 11 months, 127 other Chicagoans under the age of 21 had been murdered, most of them in gang-related incidents.

The terror is now loose across the land. Even where the big-city gangs of Chicago, Detroit, New York and Los Angeles have not ventured, gangs have become a fixture in urban, suburban and even rural America. But the new alliances between the Chicago and Los Angeles gangs are especially frightening. The specter of the loyalty and organization that has been the hallmark of the Chicago gangs blending with the prolific mobility and brazen violence of the Crips and the Bloods gives a chill to gang experts. "I think what we are seeing is an embryonic Black Mafia," said McBride, the Los Angeles gang expert. "Right now, there is no charismatic leader. The gangs don't trust enough to organize. But if they ever get it together, we're in deep shit."[44]

10: The Corporation

The *South Florida Business Journal*'s list of the 50 wealthiest Dade County residents, published in 1987, was a compendium of wealth and influence. It was studded with people who had shaped Miami's economic and physical landscape, people like newspaper magnate James Knight, Miami Dolphins owner Joe Robbie, and Carnival Cruise Lines chairman Ted Arison, whose net worth of $400 million put him at the top of the list. The local media picked up on the list, but they barely noticed the shadowy occupant of the Number 10 spot, a man who ranked higher than Robbie, higher than an auto magnate, higher than the city's leading banker, higher than several media barons and corporate chairmen. This mercurial tycoon was José Miguel Battle, described tersely as a Cuban gambling kingpin whose net worth was $175 million. Neither the *South Florida Business Journal* nor any other media speculated on how a gangster virtually unknown to the public could have amassed such a fortune.

Battle is the most powerful gangster in South Florida and one of the wealthiest criminals in the country. He also has the most diverse resumé of perhaps any gangster who ever lived. Over three decades, Battle has been a Havana vice cop, a CIA operative, a counterrevolutionary, a Mafia confidant, a political power broker, and a reclusive millionaire businessman. But his most significant incarnation is that of crime boss. Battle's organization, known as "the Corporation," is a vast criminal empire that stretches across New York City, northern New Jersey, and Florida. He controls hundreds—some say thousands—of illegal numbers outlets in Manhattan, the Bronx, Brooklyn, Queens and Hudson County, New Jersey.[1] As the Mafia's traditional control over numbers has weakened over the last two decades, the Corporation and other Cuban crime groups have eagerly filled the void, moving into neighborhoods where policy games were until recently controlled by Mafia families. In Florida, Battle controls another lottery network as well the distribution of video poker machines and what the Broward County Sheriff's Office described in 1988 as perhaps the wealthiest bookmaking operation in the country, if not the world.[2]

Battle, known as *El Gordo* (the Fat Man) or *El Padrino* (the Godfather) has been a powerful rackets figure since the 1970s. He is said to have ruthlessly taken over policy turf by terrorizing independent operators with murder and arson. But he was virtually unknown to the media and many law enforcement agencies until 1985, when the President's Commission on Organized Crime held a hearing that outlined his operation. According to testimony by law enforcement officers and former members of Battle's group, the Corporation had 2,500 members and controlled more than 4,000 numbers outlets in New York City alone. Some investigators have since concluded that the number of outlets was an exaggeration—the real figure is probably in the hundreds—but the commission's estimate that the Corporation was grossing $45 million annually from New York's numbers racket was almost certainly accurate. It was based on a tally sheet seized from the Corporation itself. Battle's son and heir apparent, José Miguel Battle Jr., was arrested at Kennedy Airport in 1983 with $439,000 in cash wrapped up in Christmas presents that he was taking with him on a return trip to Miami. Though the men denied they owned the money, documents that Battle tried to tear up and throw in an ashcan before he was seized showed that the take from the Corporation's New York City gambling operations that week was $2.1 million.[3]

Strangely, Battle has gotten almost no media attention since

Jose Miguel Battle, reputed leader of a Cuban crime syndicate known as the Corporation, at a 1985 hearing of the President's Commission on Organized Crime in New York. (AP/Wide World)

the commission hearings, and his empire has remained intact. His operation has not been a priority for the FBI and other law enforcement agencies, partly because the public views street numbers as a benign form of racketeering. "The Battle organization is stronger than it ever was," Colonel Justin Dintino, superintendent of the New Jersey State Police and an expert on organized crime, said in 1993. "But the concentration against them by law enforcement has not been as strong as with the Mafia."[4]

Battle's organization is only one of the Hispanic crime groups that have gained enormous influence in American cities in the past 25 years. While the Corporation's empire rests on gambling, the reason for the success of most Hispanic crime groups can be summed up in one word: cocaine. Distribution of cocaine was one of the biggest moneymakers for the underworld in the 1980s, and Hispanics had a leg up on other crime groups because of their language and cultural ties to the Colombian cartels. The Colombians will generally deal with Cuban, Dominican or Mexican distributors before they will deal with American blacks. So Hispanics have largely played the role of middlemen between the Colombian importers and the black street gangs that distribute drugs on street corners.

That is not to say that all Hispanic crime groups have evolved at the same pace. Cubans and Dominicans have made the biggest impact on the American underworld. Cubans have huge gambling empires and control the distribution of cocaine in the southeastern United States. Dominicans dominate drug distribution in the Northeast and have made forays into gambling, numbers, loan-sharking, and other rackets. On the other hand, Puerto Ricans have made fewer strides in organized crime. Though they have a role in illegal numbers sales in many predominantly Hispanic neighborhoods in New York City (a Puerto Rican named Spanish Raymond Marquez has been one of the city's numbers kings for years) and have been active in heroin distribution, they have formed almost no large and enduring crime groups over the years.

It would be tempting to dismiss the Puerto Ricans entirely as an organized crime threat were it not for the Latin Kings and the Netas, two gangs that have established a frightening presence in cities and prisons around the Northeast. Their wars with other gangs cost dozens of people their lives in the early 1990s in New York and several Connecticut cities, especially Hartford. The Latin Kings have been able to attract thousands of young Puerto Ricans to their ranks by appealing to their ethnic pride and giving them a sense of identity in prison. Claiming to represent the aspirations of the Puerto Rican people, the gang holds huge outdoor meetings at parks in the Bronx, Queens, Brooklyn and neighborhoods in various other cities. With the number of young people attracted to this criminal movement on the rise, Puerto Ricans may be on the verge of greater criminal sophistication.

Mexican-Americans have made forays into organized crime in Houston, Los Angeles and other southwestern cities, in part because of their access to Colombian cocaine being smuggled through Mexico. One of the most notorious of these gangs is the Mexican Mafia, a criminal syndicate that has operated in Los Angeles for more than two decades. Having begun as a prison gang, the Mexican Mafia became a well-disciplined crime group in the *barrios* of Los Angeles, where the gang is known on the streets simply as *La EME*—Spanish for the letter M. Federal authorities who indicted 22 members of the Mexican Mafia in May 1995 said the gang had demanded a street tax from other drug dealers in Latino districts of Los Angeles. "People who don't obey their commands are hit, are silenced," said Charlie Parsons, an FBI agent in Los Angeles. The gang took offense at the 1992 release of *American Me*, a film that depicted one of the gang's most respected leaders as having been sodomized in prison and then stabbed to death by his own followers. The film's star and director, Edward James Olmos of *Miami Vice* fame, received death threats and two of his consultants were murdered.

Whatever the exploits of the Mexican Mafia and Latin Kings, it is clear that Hispanic crime groups of all kinds are a growing force. The sheer weight of the Hispanic population is likely to give them greater influence in a number of cities around the country. Mexicans are or will soon be the majority ethnic group in several major cities in the Southwest. And Hispanics are expected to surpass blacks as New York City's largest minority group within the next five years, according to a recent study by the city's Department of City Planning. The study projected that New York's Hispanics will add 400,000 to their number in this decade and by the turn of the century will comprise 29 percent of the city's population, compared to 26 percent for African-Americans. In the Bronx, Hispanics are expected to make up 52 percent of the population.

So far, the Hispanic crime groups in this country that have reached the highest level of sophistication are the Cuban gangs. The Cuban Mafia, as it has sometimes been called, was the first organized-crime group created in part by the "blowback" from a CIA operation. Many of the earliest Cuban-American racketeers were veterans of the failed Bay of Pigs invasion of 1961, in which exiles trained by the CIA had attempted to overthrow the Communist government of Fidel Castro. Among the soldiers in Brigade 2506 were thugs who hit the beaches not out of patriotic fervor but as a means to regain the privileged positions they had held in the regime of Fulgencio Batista, the dictator whom Castro had overthrown in 1959. Under Batista's corrupt rule, Cuba had been wide-open territory for American mobsters, who ran gambling casinos, brothels and loan-sharking just 90 miles from Miami—but out of the reach of U.S. authorities.[5]

Batista, of course, was not the only Cuban cozying up to the American mob. A significant portion of Havana society played ancillary roles in the operation of the casinos and in the prostitution, loan-sharking, and other criminal activities that went along with the gambling. Cuba's armed forces and national police were flush with men ready to lend favors to Batista's friends in the Mafia. So when Castro overthrew Batista's regime in 1959, the mafiosi weren't the only crooks who packed their bags and headed for the United States. So did plenty of crooked cops, venal government officials, and shady businessmen who had been facilitators in the Havana underworld.

These criminal elements wanted badly to regain a foothold in Cuba and were more than willing to lend the CIA a hand in undermining Castro through the Bay of Pigs invasion and an assassination plot. As it turned out, both plans failed. Miami was suddenly inundated with returning Bay of Pigs veterans who had been trained in the use of automatic weapons and explosives. Some of them turned to their old Mafia connections to resume the profitable relationships they had enjoyed in Havana. These unsavory few, who made a mockery of the honest soldiers who gave their lives at the Bay of Pigs, became part of the so-called Cuban Mafia. They sold numbers and dope in Little Havana, the

Cuban ghetto of Miami, and slowly made inroads into the Hispanic neighborhoods of New York City and nearby Hudson County, New Jersey.[6]

To sell numbers in New York City and Miami, the Cubans had to give a percentage of the take to the Mafia. But one racket they had all to themselves was the wholesale distribution of marijuana and cocaine. In the mid-1960s, police pressure made it more difficult for the marijuana smugglers to move their loads across the Mexican border. So they began boating the stuff across the Gulf of Mexico and landing it along the vast shoreline of southern Florida. Miami's Little Havana, a quiet middle-class neighborhood at Flagler and 8th streets flush with Cuban exiles, became a marijuana distribution center for much of the country. Big black Cadillacs with New York plates became a fixture in the neighborhood—and so did young Cuban drug dealers with ostentatious wealth. One of them, Herman Lamazares, made his headquarters in the Yumuri Restaurant, from which he would send marijuana to New York in shipments of two to three thousand pounds. "The first Cubans attracted into the drug business . . . were making fortunes for themselves," Donald Goddard wrote in *Easy Money*. "In a matter of weeks sometimes, they would graduate from roach-trap apartments to $75,000 houses with swimming pools, and break out in a rash of silk shirts and diamond pinky rings."[7]

Even bigger money would eventually grow out of cocaine. The flaky white powder that would take the nation's cities by storm in the 1980s was, a decade earlier, primarily a drug for the well-to-do. It was popular with the jet-setters, the show-biz and night-club set, not something that ghetto kids sold on street corners. But cocaine was gaining popularity, and Cubans were well positioned to dominate its distribution. After the Bay of Pigs fiasco and the loss of CIA financing, some Cuban exiles had set up bases in South America to strike at Castro. Once there, they took to exporting cocaine to the United States as a means to finance their counterrevolution. Drug smuggling thus became intertwined with anti-Castro politics, a nexus that gave the business legitimacy in the eyes of some otherwise law-abiding Cubans and initially caused the federal government to turn a blind eye. Bay of

Pigs veterans armed with grenades, automatic weapons, and si-
lencers became troops in the Cuban Mafia, and suddenly narcotics intelligence files in Dade County were replete with the
names of Cubans whose dossiers bore the notation "Bay of Pigs
veteran," "experienced in explosives" or "former CIA operative."[8]

Cubans had connections in Colombia, Bolivia and other South
American countries, and they—not the Italians—became the
dominant importers and wholesalers of cocaine in the 1960s and
early 1970s. By allowing Hispanics to control what would become the most profitable illegal enterprise since Prohibition, the
Mafia had helped seal the doom of its monopoly on big-time organized crime. Cubans would later be eclipsed by the Colombians as the dominant importers of cocaine, but they have remained important wholesalers and distributors in cities around
the country.

Cuban organized crime in the United States took on a new dynamic with the exodus of tens of thousands of refugees from the
Cuban port of Mariel. Among the people fleeing the Caribbean
island were thousands of hardened criminals whom Castro had
freed from prisons as sort of a cruel joke on the Americans. Immigration officials screening the refugees routinely came across
people with tattoos on their bodies that denoted their criminal
specialty, such as murder, hijacking or kidnaping. Since Castro
was not about to provide records on their criminal pasts, the
convicts were admitted into the United States right along with
thousands of law-abiding "Marielitos."

These newly arrived Cuban hoods had a reputation for ruthlessness and were recruited into the lower ranks of the drug underworld. Many of them became mules who shuttled drugs from
Miami to other parts of the country, some staying behind to set
up wholesale distribution operations. One example of the new
breed of Cuban drug dealer was Rodolfo Moreno-Ponce, who allegedly set up a distribution operation in the Hispanic community of southwest Detroit in 1985. Known as "Bolo" on the
streets, Moreno-Ponce was said to have brought thousands of
kilos of cocaine to Detroit from Miami and California. The drugs
would be transported in hidden compartments of cars driven by

couriers whom he paid $2,000 per trip. By the time Moreno-Ponce and 16 of his men were indicted in October 1992, the organization was the biggest cocaine wholesaler in Detroit, bringing in an estimated $20 million a year.[9] But the kingpin never came to trial. The federal government housed Moreno-Ponce in rented space at the Macomb County Jail, where officials confused him with another inmate by the same name and accidentally released him in January 1993. Despite a substantial amount of money being offered for his capture, Bolo hasn't been seen since.

Union City, New Jersey, is a dense, mile-square city that sits on the palisades overlooking Manhattan's West Side. It has almost no parks, no lawns, no open spaces, just row after row of attached homes and apartment buildings that crowd the narrow streets, as claustrophobic a city as can be found in the United States. Since the early 1960s, Union City and neighboring West New York, New Jersey, have been home to the largest community of Cuban-Americans outside of South Florida. Cubans breathed new life into the sagging downtown strip of Bergenline Avenue in the 1970s, turning it into one of the most vital commercial corridors in New Jersey. They opened restaurants, nightclubs, groceries, pharmacies, liquor stores. Bergenline Avenue became Little Havana North, a place where English is a second language and most of the stores' signs are in Spanish.

The area has long seethed with the same political passions as Miami's exile community. Anti-Castro terrorist groups like Omega Seven operated in Union City, occasionally bumping off people suspected of being disloyal to the cause. And the intertwining of criminal and political activities that blurred the line between good guys and bad guys in Miami was also present in northern Hudson County. No one walked this line between crime and patriotism more skillfully than José Miguel Battle, who arrived in Union City in the mid-1960s and soon became known as *El Padrino*, the Godfather, the man you went to for favors when you had nowhere else to turn.

Battle's introduction to organized crime took place in the late

1950s. As a vice sergeant in Cuba's national police, he became acquainted in Havana's gambling casinos with Meyer Lansky and Santo Trafficante Jr., the Mafia boss of Tampa, Florida. Landing in Miami after the Cuban revolution, Battle was one of those trained by the CIA to take part in the Bay of Pigs invasion. His role in the failed mission earned him a commission as a lieutenant in the U.S. Army. But the real benefits he gleaned from his Cuba days were his Mafia connections, which he parlayed into permission to open the first Cuban-controlled gambling operation in Miami.[10]

Battle was not a known organized-crime figure when he moved to Union City. Hudson County rackets investigators only became aware of him in 1967, when the 38-year-old Cuban opened a go-go bar in Union City. By then, he was already making his mark on the New Jersey underworld. He had allied himself with Joseph (Bayonne Joe) Zicarelli, a captain in the Bonanno crime family and a legend in the Hudson County rackets. Zicarelli authorized Battle to handle the numbers in Union City and West New York so long as he turned over a percentage to the mob. He also make alliances with other mobsters, including James Napoli, a *capo* in the Genovese crime family.

Battle became the Cuban Godfather, the leading vice merchant in northern Hudson County. A tall, barrel-chested man of some 240 pounds, he became a fixture on Bergenline Avenue with his somber dark suits and Havana cigars. He used a Union City store that sold jewelry and religious items as a headquarters for a numbers operation that included nine major banks in Hudson County and upper Manhattan. Zicarelli went to prison in 1971, but Battle stayed in touch with other mobsters, including Carmine and Sonny Lombardozzi of the Gambino crime family.

Using Bay of Pigs veterans as enforcers, Battle further enlarged his empire by taking over the territories of independent numbers operators. The CIA-trained hit men did not hesitate to use the automatic weapons and bombs that were the tools of their trade as counterrevolutionaries. One way they had of dealing with an adversary was by attaching a grenade to the underside of his car and running a fishing line from its pin to the wheel. When the car moved, the pin was yanked out and the grenade exploded.[11]

They had a different treatment for store owners who refused to stop selling unauthorized numbers or become affiliated with "the Corporation." Two or three men would walk into the store, douse the floor with gasoline, back up, and light a match, sometimes while the employees were still inside. Murder by arson became one of the Corporation's most effective weapons.[12]

The group also occasionally had skirmishes with Puerto Ricans and other Cuban exile groups for control of the numbers trade in Washington Heights and the Bronx (though Battle managed to avoid running afoul of black operators and their partners in the Genovese and Lucchese crime families, who ran the numbers in Harlem). In one such skirmish, Battle's 38-year-old brother, Pedro, was shot down in an upper Manhattan bar, setting off a shooting war between the Corporation and another Cuban group that left eight people dead. Pedro's killer, José (Polulu) Enrique, was eventually shot and wounded by Corporation henchmen as Battle stood by and laughed. Enrique was in intensive care in St. Barnabas Hospital in the Bronx when someone walked into his hospital room at three o'clock in the morning and finished the job with two shots to the head.[13]

Battle was particularly ruthless with disloyal members of his own organization. Ernestico Torres was once one of The Corporation's prized killers, famous for the wigs he wore as disguises and the trench coat that he had tailor made to hide a sawed-off M-1 rifle. Though he was only in his early 20s, Torres had already been linked to 13 murders in New York and New Jersey in the first half of the 1970s. But Battle and Torres collided over the hit man's gambling debts and his habit of arranging drug deals and then robbing the supplier. The last straw came when Torres began kidnapping numbers bankers for ransom and ended up wounding one of Battle's top policy men.

One morning just before Christmas in 1975, Torres started up his turquoise Lincoln Continental Mark IV outside his home in Cliffside Park, New Jersey, without knowing that a grenade was wired underneath. He had just started to roll when he heard the metallic sound of the pin being yanked out by the fishing line. He dove out of the car just as it exploded.

Five days later, Torres was shot and wounded as he walked out of an upper Manhattan bookie joint. He told his girlfriend they had to get out of town, and the two fled to Miami. But Battle wasn't going to give up. Carlos (Charlie) Hernandez, another Corporation hit man, later testified in court that Battle summoned him, put six .38-caliber bullets into his hand, and told him to make sure one of them went between Torres' eyes. "I know you love your son very dearly," Battle told Hernandez. "If anything goes wrong, he is the first one we are going to kill."[14]

Instead of carrying out the killing, Hernandez went to Florida and warned Torres. Battle learned of Hernandez' double cross and sent three other men to take care of the hit. They burst into Torres' apartment in suburban Opa-Locka, Florida on June 16, 1976, while the hit man was sleeping and his girlfriend, Idelia Fernandez, was watching *General Hospital* on television. She was shot and gravely wounded and Torres was killed. One of the bullets was put squarely between his eyes.[15]

The Corporation's repeated attempts to kill Torres were almost Battle's undoing. Hernandez was picked up on a weapons charge in Union City in 1976 and, still fearing Battle's vengeance, started talking. Battle was arrested and convicted for Torres' murder in 1977, but he appealed the verdict and had the conviction overturned. It would be the last time law enforcement even came close to laying a glove on José Miguel Battle.

In the early 1980s, the Corporation began a violent campaign to take over an even larger share of the city's numbers racket. Battle's henchmen firebombed and torched the storefronts of rival numbers outlets—some controlled by Spanish Raymond Marquez, the legendary Puerto Rican numbers kingpin. Dozens of gambling joints in Brooklyn, the Bronx, and Manhattan were torched during the war, and more than a few people died in the flames. In October 1985, city police arrested Conrado (Lalo) Pons, Battle's 42-year-old enforcer, and 10 other Corporation members on charges that they had killed 11 people in the arson war. Listed in the charges were eight fires in Brooklyn, two in the Bronx, and four in Manhattan. In one of the fires, a three-year-old girl and her baby-sitter were trapped by flames in the rear of a shoe-repair shop at 411 West 56th Street in Manhattan.[16]

Pons faced life in prison on the murder charges, but he refused to make a deal and rat on his boss. Battle was never charged in the arson spree. In fact, he moved from New Jersey to Florida in the middle of the investigation; his last known sighting in New Jersey was at the December 1985 funeral of his father in North Bergen.

The crime boss had learned his lesson in the Torres affair, and from then on deeply insulated himself from the crimes of the Corporation. There would always be at least one buffer between *El Padrino* and his numbers bankers and henchmen. He even had a man designated to take care of the politicians in Hudson County, New Jersey. Eusebio (Chi Chi) Rodriguez was more than just a bagman who paid off politicians. He was an important figure in Union City's political establishment—and he stayed in regular phone contact with Battle in Florida.

A Hudson County grand jury probed the relationship between Rodriguez and city officials in 1985. Although the investigation produced no indictments, its final presentment painted a devastating portrait of the Corporation's control over Union City government.[17] Rodriguez was a well-known gangster and numbers runner whose gambling arrests dated to the 1970s. He had been named as an unindicted coconspirator in the 1977 indictment of Union City Mayor William Musto and several police officials, who had been accused of protecting gambling operations. Yet even with this background, Rodriguez in the 1980s had regular access to police officials and members of the city commission. When someone in town needed a city job or wanted something quashed in municipal court, they didn't go to a commissioner or the mayor. They went to Rodriguez, and he got the job done. The portly, balding gangster even transported his lottery receipts in a minivan owned by the Department of Public Works.

The grand jury presentment also implicated Rodriguez' girlfriend, Mayra DeLaRosa, who was putatively a secretary in City

Hall, but had influence over all sectors of city government. She allegedly could get advance information on the planning of gambling raids and even had free access to the Police Department's computers, which Rodriguez would use to run license plate checks on cars he suspected were being driven by federal investigators or state police. In April 1985, DeLaRosa went to police headquarters and asked a computer operator to go into the National Criminal Information Center database and learn the criminal record of José Miguel Battle's brother, Sergio Battle. When the operator refused, DeLaRosa took the matter to Deputy Chief Walter Gerrity, who headed the detective bureau and was responsible for drug and gambling investigations in Union City. Gerrity upbraided the computer operator and ordered him to give DeLaRosa the information. A wiretap later recorded DeLaRosa telling Rodriguez what she had found about Sergio: "He has a number assigned with the federals. And from what the [computer operator] made out of it . . . the guy seems to be an informer. Please, don't let it come out from you."

The incident that sparked the grand jury probe, however, was Battle's attempt to get rid of the city's police chief, Herman Bolte. With the detective bureau doing nothing about gambling, Bolte had set up a special vice squad that began raiding numbers joints and card games. According to the grand jury presentment, Anthony Dragona, the city's public-safety director, pressured Bolte to halt the operations and then tried to assign Chi Chi Rodriguez' son, Police Officer Julio Rodriguez, to the new unit. But the city's charter gave the chief independence and he resisted the pressure, keeping the heat on Battle's operations. In early 1985, Hugo DeLaRosa, Mayra's ex-husband and a former Union City police officer who had moved to Miami, called Bolte and warned him that Battle was plotting against him. He told the chief "to be very careful because you are going to be in trouble." Wiretaps also picked up Rodriguez talking to people about getting rid of the chief. Sure enough, the city's Board of Commissioners on February 7, 1985, voted 5–0 to introduce an ordinance to abolish the position of police chief and turn over his powers to the public-safety director. The proposal inexplicably was withdrawn at a subsequent meeting, but the incident left no question about who was in control of Union City.

The grand jury's 1987 presentment summed up the degree to which the commissioners did the bidding of the Corporation: ". . . all the commissioners acknowledged that they were aware that Rodriguez was reputed to be actively involved in organized criminal gambling. Nevertheless, they sought and accepted Rodriguez' political support and interacted with him in such a way as to allow a known criminal actor to be perceived publicly as having intimate and influential connections with governmental officials."

One commissioner, said the presentment, "explained that he was able to conceptually separate Rodriguez 'the gambler' from Rodriguez 'the political supporter' and therefore was only dealing with the latter without compromising himself or his official position." Another said he wanted to disassociate himself from Rodriguez but "in a way that I wasn't going to make an enemy of him, because he happened to be a popular guy in town as far as knowing a lot of people."

Unfortunately, a 40-page presentment outlining the extent of corruption in Union City was the only result of the grand jury probe. The wiretaps had led to gambling and narcotics charges against Rodriguez and a slew of other Corporation members, but the grand jury's inquiry into corruption produced no indictments. As usual, Battle walked away with no charges.

For the next decade, Battle seemed to have all but disappeared from the radar screen of law enforcement and the media. The Florida Department of Law Enforcement was alone in consistently tracking the elusive crime boss, who reportedly spends some of his time at an estate in Lima, Peru. But the agency has brought no charges and his operation has grown even larger. In South Florida, Battle's operation is as diverse as that of a traditional Mafia family. Besides the *Bolita*—the Spanish name for the numbers game—the Corporation has stationed hundreds of video poker machines in bars, grocery stores, and other businesses in Latino neighborhoods. It has an estimated 500 such machines just in Hialeah, a predominantly Cuban suburb of Miami.[18] Battle has also allegedly operated one of the best-financed sports betting rings in the country. Lieutenant David Green, formerly a seasoned organized-crime investigator for the Broward County Sheriff's office, posed as an Irish-American tavern owner in 1984 and found himself placing bets with Alfonso Ramos, reportedly a Corporation-linked bookmaker in Miami. To his amazement, Ramos placed no limits on the amount one could wager. Green said he learned that a drug dealer from Ocala, Florida, put down $250,000 in a single bet. Green was perhaps the nation's leading expert on bookmaking, having instructed investigators from 35 states on how to infiltrate the local betting. From each of these investigators he learned a little about how bookmaking operated in their city. But the Corporation was the only crime group he had ever come across that would accept bets of unlimited size. "I consider Battle the king of illegal gambling in the country," Green said in 1993. "You could take all the mob families in the country and you won't find one as strong as this."[19]

When he was in this country in the early 1990s, Battle was not the man about town he was in his Union City days. He stayed behind the walls of El Ranchero, his 19-acre estate in southern Dade County, Florida, which included a home and a ranch. For years he has been hiding income in several legitimate businesses in Florida and New Jersey. Other money is shipped abroad to Swiss banks or funneled into money-laundering schemes. One method of laundering money is the Corporation's purchase of tens of thousands of lottery tickets in Puerto Rico, which are then distributed in the United States. When someone wins, the Corporation offers them the cash up front for the ticket, giving the gangsters a convenient way to launder millions of dollars.[20] (The Cubans are apparently are not the only ones who have tried this scheme. In 1991, the Massachusetts Lottery Commission reported that one of the winners of a $14.3 million jackpot was none other than James (Whitey) Bulger, boss of the Irish rackets in South Boston).

Battle may be keeping a low profile in Miami and Peru, but his presence looms large in the *barrios* of New York. The Corporation is continually conquering new territory in the city, most recently opening gambling parlors in sections of Harlem that were once the stronghold of the Genovese and Lucchese families. Most of the law·enforcement personnel who keep tabs on Battle's organization in New York believe he has gotten big enough so that he no longer has to pay tribute to the Mafia.[21] He just gives the Italians the same courtesy they give each other—and that means never opening a numbers joint within two blocks of a competitor. One measure of the Cuban mob's power in the underworld came in June 1985, when FBI agents bugging the Staten Island home of Gambino family underboss Aniello Dellacroce heard him discussing the need to give Cubans a 35 percent cut from some of the family's Staten Island gambling operations to avoid a war. This may have been the first time the Mafia has been caught paying tribute to *somebody else*.[22]

José Miguel Battle last flexed his muscles publicly in May 1993, when competing numbers runners began paying higher odds than the payoff then prevailing on the streets. The Corporation responded by posting signs in Spanish and English in *bodegas* across the city that laid out the payoffs for the three common numbers games and warned that odds would be "strictly supervised."

About the same time, men who said they were from the Corporation visited a candy store at Amsterdam Avenue and 163rd Street and warned owner José Salazar to stop selling numbers. Salazar, who was having trouble making his rent, ignored the warning. A few days later, two men carrying guns and gasoline cans walked into his store in broad daylight, doused the store with gasoline and set it on fire. Salazar's wife, Leny, suffered burns from her face to her feet. "All the stores take numbers," Salazar said after the incident. "I am confused. Why can other stores take numbers and I can't?"[23]

A major profile of Battle that ran in the New York *Daily News* after the arson incident prompted the crime boss to leave Florida for South America, fearing that the heat was coming down on him.[24] And he may have been right. The arson also helped kick off a year-long investigation by the New York Police Department's Public Morals Division that culminated in the arrests of dozens of Battle's numbers operators in a series of police sweeps in October 1994. The crackdown hit hard at the Corporation's operation in New York. But it swept up none of the crime group's top leaders, such as Battle's son or his brothers. And, as usual, El Padrino himself was safely out of the line of fire.

Washington Heights is a neighborhood of cliffs and canyons that rises between the Hudson and Harlem rivers in northern Manhattan. For much of this century, its sturdy brick apartment buildings were home to Italian, Jewish, and Irish workers who had scraped up enough money to flee crowded downtown ghettos and seek refuge in the cleaner, safer neighborhoods north of Harlem.

The neighborhood is still an immigrant refuge, but of a different sort. Beginning in the early 1980s, hundreds of thousands of immigrants from the Dominican Republic flooded into Washington Heights, fleeing the grinding poverty of their Caribbean island and hoping for a better life in *Los Estados Unidos*. In place of Irish bars and Jewish delis there are now Latin nightclubs and restaurants with names like La Malicon and Sambuca. The frantic rhythms of *merengue*—music that is practically a national religion in the Dominican Republic—blare from cars and tenements and storefronts, a constant background noise on such thoroughfares as upper Broadway and St. Nicholas Avenue.

Washington Heights has been transformed from a quiet working-class white neighborhood into a bustling center of Latino life with surprising affluence. Unlike Harlem and other depressed neighborhoods in northern Manhattan, there isn't an empty storefront to be found along the commercial corridors of Washington Heights. Grocery stores, pharmacies, clothing stores, jewelers, beauty salons and electronics stores do a brisk trade on Broadway and St. Nicholas Avenue. Crowds of people browse sidewalk tables and racks thick with clothing and household items. In the streets, young men in baseball caps and gold chains double park BMWs, Range Rovers, Pathfinders and Land Cruisers. In a neighborhood where many immigrants arrive illegally, with little more than the clothes on their back, the prosperity is astounding. It is also a testament to the enormous wealth generated by the cocaine trade.

For it does not take a practiced eye to notice that the principal commerce of Washington Heights is in cocaine. Young men with beepers stand conspicuously on street corners. Cars with New Jersey, Connecticut, and even Pennsylvania license plates cruise slowly through the streets, looking for signals from the drug steerers. The very nature of the storefronts betrays the neighborhood's dirty little secret. On almost every block there are beeper stores and telephone parlors and money-wiring houses.

No one can hide the fact that Washington Heights is the busiest drug bazaar in the country, the epicenter of Dominican control over cocaine distribution throughout the Northeast.[25] The mules for the Colombian cartels bring the cocaine to New York by the hundreds of kilos and sell it to Dominican wholesalers who then become the suppliers for both lower-level Dominican dealers and drug gangsters of every other ethnic stripe. From Washington Heights, Dominican dealers transport the drugs to Philadelphia, Boston, Hartford and dozens of other old industrial cities. The frantic pace of the drug trade has made Washington Heights one of the most violent and corrupt neighborhoods in the city. Homicides in the 34th Precinct, which covers the neighborhood, increased from 57 in 1987 to 122 in 1992, the year it was the deadliest precinct in the city. In the spring and summer of 1994, more than two dozen cops were arrested in the 30th Precinct—the tabloids called it the Dirty 30—for protecting Dominican drug dealers or violating suspects' civil rights. Those dealers who didn't pay off often found that the police would converge on their apartments and automobiles, steal drugs and money, and then disappear into the night without making an arrest.

The drug trade has left its indelible mark on every facet of life in the neighborhood. So much drug money has been pumped into the community that the local economy is hyperinflated.

Commercial rents in the district are much higher than they are in other northern Manhattan neighborhoods. Clothing and electronics stores that would have trouble surviving in other poor communities flourish on almost every major commercial block in Washington Heights. Perhaps the most conspicuous sign of the drug economy is the number of small grocery stores known as *bodegas*. There are dozens of them on such thoroughfares as Broadway and Amsterdam Avenue, sometimes three or four to a block, far more than could survive if their sole reason for existing was to sell groceries. A single block can only devour so many green bananas and bags of rice. Many of the *bodegas* are honest businesses, but clearly a significant percentage exist solely to launder drug money or to act as fronts for drug sales or illegal numbers joints.

But for every drug dollar that lingers in Washington Heights, many more are shipped back to the Dominican Republic, where the influx of cash has had an even bigger impact than it has in New York. Washington Heights streets are lined with money-wiring businesses that act as laundries for drug money. Most of the wiring houses, known as *envios de valores* in Spanish, are unlicensed and ship money illegally. Federal and state law-enforcement agencies have repeatedly cracked down on them. New York State authorities in November 1988 seized $160,000 from one unlicensed wiring operation, Dominican Dollar Express on West 181st Street, and calculated that it had been transferring $70 million a year. But the crackdowns have not stopped the businesses from blatantly advertising their services. They are among the most ostentatious of the neighborhood's storefronts, with huge colorful awnings, flashing lights and *merengue* blaring from public-address speakers outside.

Federal agents and city drug investigators estimate that as much as $100 million is shipped from Washington Heights to the Dominican Republic every year. Even if the figure is only half that, it is an astounding amount for a country whose total foreign aid from the United States in some years has only been about $200 million. And the money's impact is enormous. Perhaps the most conspicuous drug-related wealth in the Dominican Republic is found in San Francisco de Macorís. Most of the center of San Francisco is still dusty streets and run-down buildings, but the city's outskirts look like Bel Air. One pastel-colored cinder-block mansion after another is rising in environs dubbed Man-hattan and El Bronx. The "Dominican Yorks," as the returning drug dealers are called, live in homes with swimming pools, satellite antennas and luxury automobiles.

San Francisco is where the wealth is the most ostentatious, but its effect is felt elsewhere in the country. The streets of the capital, Santo Domingo, are filled with Monteros, Pathfinders, BMWs and other cars that are so expensive to purchase and ship into the Dominican Republic that they are out of reach even for much of the country's elite. But they are standard issue for suc-cessful drug dealers. The capital's real estate values have soared in the past few years—an inflation caused in part by the flood of American dollars into the country.

The Dominican drug underworld is not organized crime as we have understood it in the past. The Dominicans' role in the co-caine trade has been almost impossible for law enforcement to control. The Drug Enforcement Administration, the Bureau of Al-cohol, Tobacco and Firearms, and city narcotics units are con-stantly making cases against the uptown drug trade. The criminal docket in U.S. District Court in Manhattan is crowded with Do-minican drug cases. On any given day, one can walk into the fed-eral magistrate's office and see benches filled with young Do-minican men in handcuffs. But all the arrests have been useless. The drug trade in Washington Heights is big business, but it can-not be dislodged by the tools the federal government usually uses against organized crime. Many of the drug organizations have no large hierarchies for the Feds to rope into a RICO indict-ment. "There is no Mr. Big," a Washington Heights drug dealer told the author. "Every corner has a Mr. Big. Some corners will supply other corners, but a lot of people have the Colombian connections. They don't need a boss."

The drug trade has led many in law enforcement and society at large to saddle Dominicans with the same kind of criminal stereotype that has been foisted upon immigrants for more than a century. They are often dismissed as bands of criminals. A county judge in Syracuse, New York, was even censured by the state's Commission on Judicial Conduct after he praised a jury that had convicted a Dominican drug offender. "Dominican people are just killing us in the courts," the judge said. But Dominicans are not inherently immoral, lazy or criminal. They just come from a country that is frighteningly impoverished and whose emigrants, through accidents of timing and geography, have found themselves being tempted more than other ethnic groups by the siren call of the drug trade.

Much of the Dominican Republic is still the unspoiled tropical oasis that Christopher Columbus found when he stumbled across the island he named Hispaniola (Little Spain) in 1492. The island's northern coast is a nearly undisturbed paradise of pristine white beaches, palm-covered hills and peasants with sun-dried skin hawking coconuts and live crabs by the side of the road. The great green mountains of the *Cordillera Central*, the highest range in the Caribbean, sprawl through the country's interior, looming over vast flat acres of rice, coffee and sugarcane.

But if the Dominican Republic has a wealth of natural beauty, it has little else. After Haiti, which lies on the other half of the island of Hispaniola, it is the poorest country in the Western Hemisphere. The average annual per-capita income is only a little more than $1,000. Even high-ranking government employees like army officers are paid the minimum wage, about $100 a month. The capital, Santo Domingo, has swelled into a city of more than a million people in the last two decades as thousands of impoverished peasants from the countryside have migrated to the city in search of work. Throughout the capital are hastily-built shantytowns where children run naked through alleys clotted with running sewage and rotting food. This is not a situation of much consequence to the Dominican elite, the whites of pure Spanish descent whose children can be found in the classy nightclubs and hotels that line the ocean-front drive known as the *Malecón*. But the vast majority of the country's population is people of mixed race for whom life is a daily struggle.

No one looks to the government to solve the nation's mounting social problems. The Dominican government for decades has been rent by coups, civil wars, rigged elections and dictatorships; the one constant throughout this century has been a mind-numbing system of graft. Rafael Trujillo, the murderous dictator who ruled the country for 30 years, was assassinated with the blessing of the CIA in 1961. But his legacy lives on. One of his former ministers, a now nearly blind intellectual named Joaquín Balaguer, has been president for the last decade. He was re-elected in 1994 only after international observers concluded that he had stolen the election. Balaguer's government is primarily about maintaining the perquisites of his followers. Government housing units built for the poor are routinely turned over to government bureaucrats. Army officers who earn only the minimum wage somehow manage to live in big houses and drive fancy cars. Police who pull over speeders on the highways approach cars with hands out, always eager for bribes to augment their paltry wages. Balaguer is a godlike figure to his followers, but his name is spoken with bitterness in the country's slums, where the Dominican government is regarded as little more than a band of thieves.

The one hope that the average Dominican has for a better life is passage to the United States. Assisted by corrupt government officials, they escape by the boatload across the Mona Passage, a 100-mile body of water that separates the Dominican republic from Puerto Rico. It is a perilous journey, one that all too commonly ends with boats capsizing and their inhabitants being devoured by sharks. But once in Puerto Rico, a self-governing commonwealth in association with the United States, Dominican illegals can easily purchase fake Puerto Rican birth certificates and fly to New York with a phony claim on legal immigrant status. Since so many claim to be Puerto Ricans, nobody really knows how many Dominicans there are in New York City. The 1990 census found that they had emigrated to New York in greater numbers than any other ethnic group, totaling 332,713 by the end of the decade. But most estimates put the total much higher, probably closer to 500,000. Dominican immigrants have settled in Queens, Brooklyn, Paterson, New Jersey, and Lawrence, Massachusetts. But by far the greatest number of them have swarmed into Washington Heights, neighboring Manhattan districts like northern Harlem and Inwood, and the nearby University Heights and Highbridge sections of the Bronx.

Their gravitation to the drug trade was inevitable. Dominicans are natural entrepreneurs, opening small businesses and restaurants no matter where they settle. Turning these skills toward cocaine has been hard to resist for a certain percentage of the Dominican population. After all, the neighborhood they have chosen as the promised land has always been a major source of drugs. Its proximity to the George Washington Bridge and Interstate 95 has made it a convenient shopping area for hordes of suburban New Jersey drug users at least as far back as the late 1960s.

What is more, Dominicans arrived in large numbers in the 1980s just as the popularity of cocaine was soaring, and the Colombian cartels needed reliable partners to get the drug onto New York's streets. The reputation of the Colombian cartels has always been that of hyperviolent "cocaine cowboys" who murderously pushed aside any competition for the drug trade. This reputation first developed in Miami in the 1970s, when the Medellín cartel wiped out Cuban competitors and took over South Florida's coke trade, not only importing the stuff but handling most of the wholesale distribution around the country. But by the mid-1980s, the Colombians' methods had changed. New York's cocaine market now came under the control of the Cali cartel, a more businesslike operation that preferred not to dirty its hands with midlevel wholesaling. It concentrated on importing tons of cocaine and began relying on Dominicans to handle the distribution.[26] Dominicans and Colombians had had a business relationship since the early 1980s. When the Cali cartel began using Caribbean islands as transshipment points between South America and the United States, the Dominican Republic turned out to be perfectly suited. It had remote areas and plenty of corrupt army officers willing to turn a blind eye to shipments of cocaine being dropped off the coast or flown into remote landing strips. In the mid-1980s, as political instability gripped Haiti and Panama—two other favorite transshipment points for Colombians—the Dominican Republic became an even more important way station for the cartels. The transshipment arrangements provided the Colombian connections for many of the Dominican kingpins who emerged in Washington Heights in the second half of the 1980s.[27]

Initially, dope dealing in Washington Heights was dominated by drug dealers from Santiago, the island's second largest city, and San Francisco de Macorís, a city of some 65,000 people that has become almost as notorious in the drug trade as the Colombian city of Medellín. So many Washington Heights drug dealers have hailed from San Francisco that law-enforcement officials began talking in the mid-1980s of the "San Francisco cartel." Between 1985 and 1993, an estimated 400 young men from San Francisco were slain in the New York drug trade.[28]

By the early 1980s, Washington Heights was swarming with drugs. Some entire blocks were lost to the drug trade. In some buildings, as many as two dozen apartments would be controlled by a single drug organization. One apartment would be used to store the drugs. Another would be used to store cash. Yet another would be the place where drug dealers would meet their customers. If the dealers were selling to an undercover cop, all the police would seize would be the few grams of cocaine on the table. Dominicans' success in foiling narcotics investigators in Washington Heights has become legendary. Drug gangs employ electronic devices that street spotters use to sound an inside alarm when cops are approaching. Investigators often find that the doors they are trying to ram are fortified with heavy chains that cops in other northeastern cities have begun to call "New York locks." Cocaine is often concealed ingeniously in hidden traps in the floors and walls, some secured with magnetic locks that need to be deactivated with a special device.

One of the Dominicans who pioneered the drug trade in Washington Heights was a Santiago native named Santiago Luis Polanco-Rodriguez. Known on the streets as "Yayo," Polanco-Rodriguez was only 21 years old when he and several relatives began distributing cocaine in Washington Heights around 1982. For the first three years, they were run-of-the-mill drug dealers. But then they discovered crack, the drug that would make them millionaires. Yayo is considered the marketing genius behind the spread of crack in upper Manhattan. His gang was among the first to move the drug in any quantity, and his retail distribution network became for a time the largest in the city. The Drug Enforcement Administration estimated in 1987 that Yayo's group was selling about 10,000 vials of crack a day, marketing them under the brand name "Based Balls." His men would stand on dozens of street corners throughout Washington Heights and the South Bronx.[29]

In the middle of his reign as crack king of New York, Yayo got into a gun battle with police and was forced to flee to his native Santiago. There he opened a discotheque and drove around the city in a gold-winged Cadillac. From his remote Caribbean base, Yayo no longer inspired fear in his followers more than a thousand miles away. They began taking over their street corners and keeping the profits for themselves. Yayo dealt with the problem by sending two hit men to New York to take care of some of the renegades. Tipped off to their presence, police put a tail on them. Detectives followed them to a Bronx apartment, where they arrested them just as they pulled an Uzi on four Puerto Ricans. The only thing that saved the Puerto Ricans' lives was that the Uzi jammed. "They were going to shoot them, there's no doubt about it," said William Mockler, an assistant special agent in charge at the DEA office in New York. Not only did Yayo's plan to regain control of his drug empire fail, but even his hit men ended up at each other's throats. While the two were out on bail, one shot the other to death in an argument. In July 1987, authorities rounded up nearly the entire organization in a 58-count RICO indictment. Yayo, however, was never caught and remains a fugitive from American justice.

Yayo's group was only the beginning of the Dominican invasion of the northeastern drug trade. While Yayo and other early Dominican gangs were known for keen marketing techniques— including such gimmicks as two-for-one sales and ladies' day specials—their successors in the 1990s would rely on violence to mark out their territories. The Jheri-Curl gang was especially notorious. Led by the five Martinez brothers—Rafael, Papin, Augusto, Loren, and Daniel—the Jheri-Curls for some three years maintained a $5 million-a-year crack business on West 157th Street between Broadway and Riverside Drive. Rafael Martinez, the founder, purposely made the Jheri-Curls a violent and high-profile gang to cow neighborhood residents and competing drug dealers. He required gang members to get the same haircuts—shaved close on the sides and a pile of jheri-curls on top—and made them paint their luxury automobiles a flamboyant gold.[30]

Between 1989 and late 1991, the Jheri-Curls made life hell for residents of 157th Street. They virtually took over the building at 614 West 157th Street and clotted the sidewalks with drug dealers, who hassled women and fired their guns in the air to let residents know they meant business. "This was a really vicious gang—even other drug dealers were intimidated by them," said James Gilmore, a young beat-walking police officer who was relentless in his campaign to get the Jheri-Curls off the street. "The people on the block kept their children inside. People were just afraid to go out."[31] One person who refused to be intimidated was José Reyes, a 66-year-old retired city worker who had lived on the block for 20 years. Reyes confronted the gang members blocking the sidewalks, but they just laughed at him. Then he organized his fellow tenants at 614 West 157th Street to press the police for action. The Jheri-Curls stopped laughing and began plotting his death. In May 1991, while Rafael Martinez was conveniently in the Dominican Republic, a hired hit man named Roberto Gonzalez walked up behind Reyes as he walked on Broadway in the middle of the day and put a .45-caliber slug in the back of his head. Outraged, Gilmore stepped up his pressure on the gang, braving regular death threats against him called into the 34th Precinct station house. But after Reyes' murder, he wasn't alone anymore. A state-federal task force joined in targeting the Jheri-Curls and put 23 of them behind bars by October 1991.[32]

But things would get even bloodier in Washington Heights.

The five Martinez brothers, leaders of the Jheri-Curl gang in upper Manhattan; from top left, Rafael, Papin, Augusto, Loren, and Daniel.

Even the Jheri-Curls' violence was surpassed by a group called the Wild Cowboys, the first major drug gang headed by American-born Dominicans. The gang's leaders met each other at George Washington High School in the mid-1980s and went on to form one of the most vicious gangs the city had ever seen. They are believed responsible for as many as 30 murders in Manhattan, the Bronx and Brooklyn. And the violence was not random: It was carefully targeted to maintain the gang's control over a crack-distribution business that grossed $20 million a year.[33]

Led by brothers Lenin and Nelson Sepulveda, the Wild Cowboys had a corporate-like structure in which street dealers, known as "pitchers," and a squad of enforcers answered to higher-ups known as "managers" and "supervisors." The gang was headquartered at 171st Street and Audubon Avenue in Washington Heights, but its main selling point was 348 Beekman Avenue in the Bronx. From that location, the gang every week distributed thousands of crack vials under the brand names

LENNY SEPULVEDA   NELSON SEPULVEDA

Leaders of the Wild Cowboys, a murderous Dominican gang in New York City.

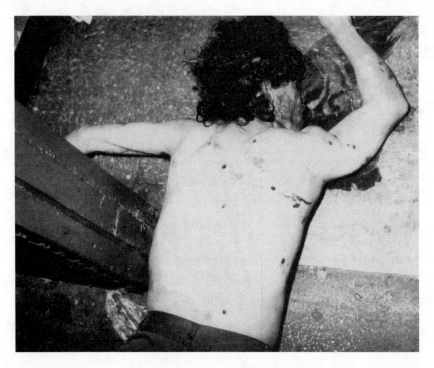

*Manuel Vera, one of four people gunned by the Wild Cowboys in a
1991 massacre on Beekman Avenue in the South Bronx.*

"Red Top" and "Orange Top," which referred to the color of the
caps on the vials.

The Wild Cowboys were as ruthless with their employees as
they were with rival drug dealers. One gang member accused of
stealing money, Oscar Alvarez, was executed in May 1991 on a
rooftop at 592 East 141st Street. Another, Eddie Moldonado, was
repeatedly stabbed and ultimately disemboweled in November
1991 in an attack in broad daylight at St. Mary's Park in the
Bronx. But the incident that led to the Wild Cowboys' downfall
was the most brutal of all. It stemmed from a dispute the Cowboys were having with a gang that had begun selling a competing
brand of crack, "Yellow Top," from the building next door to the
Beekman Avenue headquarters. On December 16, 1991, five
members of the Cowboys—including two of the gang's designated enforcers—pulled up to the Beekman alley in a white compact car and opened fire on Anthony Green, a 17-year-old mem-

Another victim of the Beekman Avenue shootings; this one was never identified by police.

ber of the rival gang. The sixty shots fired from the Cowboys' 9-millimeter handguns killed not only Green but also three innocent victims walking with him—a man and a woman in their twenties and a teenaged boy. The massacre so outraged authorities that a three-county task force was put together to target the gang. After a two-year investigation, the Sepulvedas and 33 of their followers were indicted in September 1993 on a wide range of charges. Nelson Sepulveda fled the country but was arrested in the Dominican city of Santiago in April 1994 and returned to the United States.[34]

As their connections with the Colombian drug cartels have solidified, many Dominican criminals in the 1990s have graduated from retail drug sales to wholesale distribution, acting as middlemen between the Colombians and smaller drug gangs. Typical of these new wholesalers was Euclides Rosario Lantigua. A native of San Francisco de Macorís, Lantigua ran an operation that controlled 20 apartments in a building on West 165th Street, with dozens of foot soldiers either posted out front as steerers or working inside as cutters and salesmen. The eighth floor of the building was reserved for major deals, such as purchases from Colombian importers. In Lantigua's office on the eighth floor, police tapped a telephone and recorded more than 4,000 incoming and outgoing calls over a six-week period in the summer of 1992. "This was like a pizza delivery service," said Assistant District Attorney Chris Marzuk. "They were doing big volume on short orders." The volume amounted to about 15 kilos a day at $20,000 apiece.[35]

Even higher up in the chain of international drug smuggling was a Dominican named Ramon Velazquez. Before his arrest in the spring of 1992, Velazquez was an important partner of the Cali cartel. He not only bought cocaine from the cartel by the hundreds of kilos, but smuggled the stuff in himself through Mexico, Panama and other Latin American countries. Velazquez was a far different breed from the men who stand on Washington Heights street corners with baseball caps and baggy-legged blue jeans. His tastes ran more in the line of grey or black business suits, and he conducted much of his business from an apartment on Central Park West. "The guy would be on the mobile phone while he was doing the dishes in his apartment, telling people to bring 50 kilos here and 30 kilos there," said DEA Special Agent Harry Brady.[36] Federal agents first detected the enormous scope of his operation when they searched a warehouse on 44th Avenue in Long Island City, Queens, and found 5.5 tons of cocaine concealed in drums of sodium hydroxide. At the time, it was the largest amount of cocaine ever known to have been brought into this country by a Dominican smuggler. Instead of sending all his money back to the Dominican Republic, Velazquez invested in luxury homes in suburban Westchester County as well as in businesses in Manhattan and the Bronx.

With all this new clout in the international drug trade, Dominicans have branched out of Washington Heights and set up distribution networks in cities around the Northeast. Dominican drug dealers with roots in Washington Heights are in the Pennsylvania factory towns of Allentown and Reading, and as far north as Lewiston, Maine. They have swarmed into Northeast Philadelphia; Paterson, New Jersey; Providence, Rhode Island; Hartford and New Haven, Connecticut; Brockton and Worcester, Massachusetts; and a score of other cities. "They're coming here in droves," Sergeant Norberto Huertas of the Hartford police narcotics unit told the author in the summer of 1993. "We make arrests at a location, and they have replacements there in an hour."[37]

The shoe and textile mills that sprawl along the Merrimack River were once the lifeblood of Lawrence, Massachusetts, the reason thousands of European immigrants crowded into its wooden three-family houses. But many of the mills have closed, and the Italian, Irish and Polish workers have moved to the suburbs or left the region altogether. The city's big industry these days is cocaine—and Dominicans are in control. Dominican drug gangs that began migrating to Lawrence in the early 1980s have reached into every corner of the city, from the downtown shopping district to the remotest slum neighborhood. Narcotics detectives can look out the window of their downtown headquarters and see drug customers lined up outside apartment buildings. "We're buried," said Lieutenant Michael Molchan, commander of Lawrence's detective squad. "Even if I had ten more detectives I couldn't keep up with it."[38]

Lawrence, rather than Boston, has become the headquarters for Dominican drug distribution in New England. New York's cocaine flows freely into the city aboard the "cocaine express," the name locals have given to the express vans that shuttle Dominicans between Lawrence and Washington Heights. In the first half of 1993, Lawrence police and federal immigration agents seized drugs from six vans driving along Interstate 495 on the city's outskirts. The seizures netted four kilos of cocaine, 1,400 small bags of heroin and a pound of marijuana. As is the case with detectives in many other northeastern cities, Lawrence police have met nothing but frustration in trying to stop the migration of drug dealers. They executed some 300 drug raids in 1993, but rarely came across the big stashes, since only small amounts of drugs are kept at selling locations. They arrest small-time drug dealers only to watch them disappear from the city after making bail. Most of the Dominicans arrested have three or four aliases and phony documents to back them up. Often police never learn their true identities. "We had one guy who gave us the name Joaquín Balaguer," said Lawrence Detective Brian Burokas. "We only found out later that Joaquín Balaguer is the president of the Dominican Republic."

In Washington Heights, law-abiding Dominicans are powerless to stand in the way of this drug underworld. With so many guns floating around the neighborhood, few would dare to raise their voices. Police who look for help from tenants of drug-infested buildings usually find a lot of closed mouths. And who can blame them? No one is going to rally around a person who combats the Dominican drug trade. Even many of the so-called business leaders in the community are too busy making money off drugs and other illegal activities to do anything about them.

A federal immigration agent named Joseph Occhipinti found out the hard way how deeply wired the drug trade is to the Dominican business community. Occhipinti interpreted his mandate as an immigration agent far more broadly than some of his other colleagues. He saw it as his duty not only to combat smuggling of aliens into this country but also to crack down on crimes committed by illegal immigrants. Occhipinti is a short, stocky, and tenacious lawman who goes after his targets like a pit bull.

In the late 1980s, Occhipinti began raiding *bodegas* owned by people suspected of being involved with the drug trade. The raids turned up drugs, illegal numbers slips, untaxed rum, firearms, and other illicit items. Some of the operations resulted in the seizure of tens of thousands of dollars in cash. Project Bodega, as the operation was known, confirmed Occhipinti's suspicions that grocery stores were the centers of criminal life in Washington Heights.[39]

But Occhipinti didn't realize whose toes he was stepping on. Many of the *bodega* owners feeling the sting of his raids were members of the Federation of Dominican Merchants and Industrialists, a politically savvy business group. Through their attorneys, the Federation members began making plans to "get Occhipinti," and they had ample room to do so. The aggressive immigration agent had left himself wide open for attack by conducting all but four of his 56 searches without warrants. Prior to each of these searches, Occhipinti claims, someone in the *bodega* had signed a form giving consent for the warrantless search. But Federation members began complaining to the administration of then-Mayor David Dinkins. They said that Dominican immigrants with no knowledge of the American system were being pressured to sign the forms after the searches. Project Bodega, they charged, was an effort by the federal government to make Dominicans wary of federal officials and thus subvert an accurate census count in Washington Heights. Too low a count would mean less federal money for the area.

Dinkins expressed some support for the Federation's position, especially after its members held a demonstration in 1990 on the steps of City Hall. Ultimately, federal prosecutors indicted and convicted Occhipinti of civil-rights violations, despite the perjured testimony of some *bodega* owners in court that they had no criminal records or connections to the underworld. Occhipinti spent seven months in jail before President Bush commuted his sentence in January 1993. With the backing of Staten Island Borough President Guy Molinari and other Republicans, Occhipinti has since been fighting a losing battle to have his conviction overturned entirely.

Occhipinti may have left himself open by being reckless in his investigative techniques and perhaps by breaking the law. But it is hard not to be awed by the ability of the *bodega* owners, who no one seriously doubted were involved in illegal activity, to so effectively derail a federal investigation of drug trafficking. Even if he has himself to blame, there can be no doubt that Occhipinti was set up and knocked down by the Dominican underworld.

11: The Organizatsiya

On Saturday morning, May 4, 1985, Evsei Agron, a middle-aged Soviet emigré, was preparing to leave his apartment at 100 Ocean Parkway in Brooklyn for his weekly trip to the Russian and Turkish Baths on Manhattan's Lower East Side. He said goodbye to his common-law wife, a platinum-blonde cabaret singer, and stepped out into the hallway outside his sixth-floor apartment at 8:35 A.M. With his ill-fitting blue striped suit and balding pate, Agron could have been mistaken for a retired merchant going on a Saturday-morning errand. But any illusions that the tenants of 100 Ocean Parkway may have had about their neighbor were dispelled on this Saturday morning. As Agron stood in the hallway waiting for the elevator, two gunmen stepped from behind a corner and cut him down with small-caliber bullets.

Few tears were shed for the slain Russian among the tens of thousands of law-abiding Jewish emigrés in Brooklyn's Brighton Beach section. Agron was a diminutive man weighing less than 140 pounds, but despite his mild appearance he was a ruthless gang leader who had survived 10 years in harsh Soviet prisons and had come to these shores a dangerous criminal. He had been extorting money from Brighton Beach businessmen since the early 1970s, making his rounds with a cattle prod that he used on recalcitrant victims. Agron was said to have extorted $15,000 from one emigré by threatening to kill his daughter on her wedding day. Not surprisingly, his slaying was only the last of several attempts on his life. After one gunman's attempt, outside Agron's apartment in 1984, the surgeons operating on him found several bullets in his body left over from previous shootings.[1]

Agron was a pioneer of a new organized-crime threat that has sprung up in the last 15 years in several major American cities—a loose-knit assortment of thieves, extortionists, confidence men and white-collar swindlers that has been dubbed the "Russian Mafia." These cunning and extremely sophisticated criminals—they call themselves the *Organizatsiya*, or organization—are the newest cast of gangsters to gain a foothold in the United States, and they are proving to be among the most insidious. Most were veteran gangsters in the former Soviet Union, where survival in the criminal underworld meant evading the dreaded KGB and carrying out their activities within the tight confines of a totalitarian system. The Soviet police did not need search warrants to sweep through a gang's headquarters, and beatings and torture were the favored interrogation techniques. By comparison, Russian gangsters have found police in this country to be pushovers. "I had one guy in here for questioning whose leg looked like a pretzel," a Brooklyn detective said a few years ago. "It was broken in a dozen places in a Soviet prison. He showed it off and said, 'You're going to do worse to me?'"[2]

Criminal life in the Soviet Union equipped many Russian gangsters with skills perfectly suited to white-collar crime in the United States. Soviet citizens were forced to negotiate their way through the vast communist bureaucracy with a never-ending flow of documents: papers were needed to work, to travel, to buy certain consumer goods, to get medical care, to buy a car. In order to survive, criminals had to master the bureaucracy and learn the fine arts of forgery and counterfeiting. In America, those skills have brought Russian gangsters fortunes from white-collar crimes so sophisticated that they confound all but the most highly trained federal agents.

The most ingenious of these crimes are the so-called "daisy chains" of bogus-fuel wholesalers that beat the federal government out of hundreds of millions of dollars in gasoline and diesel fuel excise taxes. The scam is not all that complex. Since 1982, federal law had required that fuel wholesalers collect the taxes on all their sales and then turn the tax money over to the Internal Revenue Service. Russian crime groups made enormous amounts of money by passing the wholesale fuel through a string of companies and then dissolving the company that sold to the retailers and collected the tax. When the IRS came looking for the hundreds of thousands or even millions of dollars it was owed, the company no longer existed and its officers turned out to have been fictitious. The scam has been used with the sale of both gasoline and No. 2 oil, which can be used as either diesel fuel or home-heating oil. Since no tax is levied on home-heating oil, mobsters would pose as home-heating companies when purchasing No. 2 oil and then turn around and sell the product as diesel fuel, pocketing the taxes they collected from retailers. Among the first Mafia figures to see the potential in the fuel-tax scams was Sonny Franzese, the Colombo family underboss. In the early 1980s, he formed a partnership with several Russian mobsters in a gas scam that was broken up by a federal task force on Long Island.[3] After that, the Russians became the masterminds of most large-scale fuel scams, but they have been required to give the Italian Mafia a cut of every gallon they sell. And still there is enough money to keep everyone happy. John Gotti almost burst with excitement when an underling told him about the scam in 1986. "I gotta do it right now!" Gotti was heard saying over a wiretap. "Right now I gotta do it:"[4]

And Gotti wasn't just shooting off his mouth. In 1993, federal authorities in New Jersey uncovered a $100-million fuel-tax-evasion scam engineered by Anthony Morelli, one of Gotti's captains in the Gambino family, and several Russian mobsters. The mobsters formed a fuel-oil industry association that attempted to control the wholesale market for fuel oil in New Jersey and parts of Pennsylvania while evading much of the federal and state taxes. Under the code name Operation Red Daisy, the FBI and IRS set up a phony fuel wholesaler in Ewing Township, New Jersey, in May 1991 and began competing with the mobsters in selling bootleg fuel. Within a few months, a Gambino family associate named Edward Dougherty approached the company and told them they would have to pay a mob tax to stay in the bootleg business. The investigation led to the indictment of 12 people—including six Russian mobsters. All of them were convicted or pleaded guilty.

The amount that the fuel-tax-evasion schemes were costing the public only became known for certain after federal authorities clamped down on the daisy chains. On January 1, 1994, a law went into effect requiring taxes to be paid when the wholesaler draws the fuel from the terminal. The new law also requires that No. 2 oil be dyed red if it is to be used as home-heating oil. That means that any clear oil that police now find in a home-heating truck can be assumed to be part of a fuel-tax-evasion scam. The savings to the taxpayers produced by these reforms have been stupendous. The Federal Highway Trust Fund, which is the recipient of fuel excise taxes, projected that its revenue would increase by $1.3 billion in 1995 because of the clampdown. The largest share of that savings is believed to have come out of the pockets of Russian crime groups.

But that does not mean that fuel-tax evasion is over. Russian mobsters in the New York area are pushing another scam: they buy gasoline and diesel fuel at New Jersey terminals and sell it in New York without paying the Empire State's steeper sales tax. Robert Shepherd, the top enforcement official in the New York State Department of Taxation and Finance, estimated in June 1995 that Russian crooks were netting up to $1 million a week in the scam.[5] The Russian mob is also believed to be evading fuel taxes by mixing gasoline or diesel fuel with cheap waste oil and selling the concoctions to retailers. That scam is known as "cocktailing." "They have some involvement in almost every aspect of gasoline and diesel fuel distribution," said Robert Buccino, an organized crime investigator with the New Jersey Attorney General's Office.[6]

Russian gangsters are fanning out across the United States. The headquarters of the Russian Mafia is southern Brooklyn, which is home to about a quarter of the 200,000 emigrés who have come to the United States in the last two decades. But the FBI says Russian gangsters also operate in Los Angeles, Boston, Philadelphia, Miami, Detroit, Seattle and other cities. FBI Director Louis Freeh told a congressional committee in May 1994 that the bureau had elevated the Russian Mafia to its highest investigative priority after an internal survey of field offices in April 1992 counted 81 investigations involving Eastern European criminals. Thirteen of those investigations involved organized crime, a number that had nearly tripled by early 1994.[7]

The Russian Mafia is particularly brazen in New York and Los Angeles. Brighton Beach and nearby neighborhoods have been the scene of nearly two dozen gangland slayings involving Russians since 1982. Everyone in the tight-knit Russian neighborhood, often called "Little Odessa," knows who the gangsters are—and indeed they are not hard to spot. Their Cadillacs and BMWs can be seen double-parked at night spots like Rasputin on Coney Island Avenue, where portly mobsters and their fur-clad women reserve the best tables for views of the ostentatious floor shows.

The emergence of Russian organized crime in this country is rooted in the Cold War. In the early 1970s, as the Nixon administration's policy of détente began thawing the deep freeze in East–West relations, the United States pressured the Soviets to prove their good intentions on the world stage by allowing the emigration of Soviet Jews. While anti-Semitism was officially proscribed in the Soviet Union, the centuries-old patterns of repression still ran deep. Jews were effectively barred from the highest echelons of the Communist Party, the military, and other important circles. And anti-Semitic tracts were common in the press. So when President Gerald Ford signed into the law the Jackson-Vanik Amendment, which required the Soviet Union to grant exit visas to increasing numbers of Jews in order to receive the benefits of trade with the United States, there was no shortage of people waiting to emigrate. Between 1975 and 1980, some 90,000 Soviet Jews immigrated to the United States. The number leaving the Soviet Union climbed every year after the amendment, peak-ing at 51,000 in 1979. And though emigration dropped off after a new freeze in U.S.–Soviet relations in the 1980s, it has resumed its growth since the fall of the old Soviet Union in 1989. In 1990 alone, 185,000 Jews left the Soviet Union.

Estimates put the number of Russian emigrés in the United States at 200,000, the majority of whom have settled in southern Brooklyn. Brighton Beach, a dingy working-class Brooklyn neighborhood just east of Coney Island, has become the city's center of Russian emigré life. Russians restaurants, bakeries and meat shops line Brighton Beach Avenue, and the rough cadences of Russian can be heard among the groups of people strolling the wooden boardwalk on summer nights. In more recent years, thousands of Russian Jews have moved into Bensonhurst, Brooklyn, a traditionally Italian neighborhood. Additional neighborhoods of Soviet Jews have also sprung up in Los Angeles, Chicago, Philadelphia and other cities. For the most part, Russian Jews are honest and hard-working people who open small businesses and strive to send their children to good colleges. Rita Simon, a University of Illinois researcher, surveyed 100 families of Russian Jews in 1983 and found that virtually all of the fathers and most of the mothers had the educational equivalent of four years of college. Among the respondents she found doctors, engineers and others with advanced and highly technical skills.[8]

But among those law-abiding and industrious emigrés, an organized criminal element was present from the very beginning. The Russian *Organizatsiya* is distinct from some other ethnic-crime groups in not having grown out of its members' immigrant experiences. Russian mobsters were not groomed in adolescence in overcrowded immigrant neighborhoods where the only place to find a sense of belonging was in a street gang. Russian emigrés face many of the same pressures as other immigrants—the same feelings of cultural alienation, the sense that they are not welcome in this country and have to work harder than others to get a fair shake in the job market. But for the most part, Russian Jews came to this country with far more education and technical skills than most other immigrant groups. And their integration into the American economy has been fairly swift. The Russian criminal class is not a product of economic disadvantage. And that's what makes the Russian Mafia unique: most of its mobsters were already hardened criminals when they arrived here. They came here looking for economic opportunity, just like every other emigré. To them, says Lieutenant John Gallo, a Philadelphia police investigator, "the U.S. is like a big candy store with no one minding the store."[9]

The white-collar background of Russian criminals meant that they did not have to follow the pattern of other ethnic-crime groups and huddle within their own neighborhoods for a generation, forming crude street gangs and sucking the blood out of immigrants like themselves. Though they had no qualms about preying on other emigrés, they arrived here almost immediately ready to prey on the community at large. The victims of their earliest swindles were major credit-card companies, banks, the Internal Revenue Service, and even major department stores, which they looted of millions of dollars with their sophisticated shoplifting and burglary rings.

Federal law enforcement is more accustomed to letting new ethnic crime groups go through their crude street-gang phase before cracking down on them. In the case of the Russians, there was no such phase. They were playing in the big leagues from the day they arrived. But because they did not fit the usual model of an organized-crime group, many federal agencies ignored them. The U.S. Secret Service investigated specific counterfeiting and credit-card schemes. The IRS set up task forces to crack down on gasoline-tax scams. But no one looked at Russian organized crime in its totality. The FBI did not set up a Russian squad until 1994, and as late as 1995 its top officials were admitting that they still knew little about the Russian crime groups in the United States.

The first Russian gangsters in Brighton Beach formed organized bands of swindlers who preyed on other emigrés in the 1970s with an array of confidence schemes. One early Russian crime group was known as the Potato Bag Gang because of a ruse it repeatedly used to steal from emigrés. A member of the gang would tell an emigré that he had just arrived from the Soviet

Union with all his money in antique gold rubles. The victim would be shown one of the gold rubles and told he could have a whole bag for a sum of cash. After paying the money and bidding farewell to the new immigrant, the victim would open the bag and find that it was filled with potatoes.[10]

Russian hoods became involved in a mind-numbing array of scams. They pulled off jewelry-store robberies and fur robberies. They pawned off fake diamonds and other jewelry. One group of Russians posed as representatives of Volvo International interested in doing a luggage promotion. They managed to walk away with tens of thousands of dollars in luggage from a Suffolk County distributor without putting down a cent.

One particularly harrowing crime occurred in October 1981. A Russian woman named Larisa Schulman arrived in Philadelphia to invest in a condominium for a friend. After she had chosen the apartment in Northeast Philadelphia, her friend, an Austrian businessman named Richard Egit, was to wire $50,000 in cash to New York. Gary Esterman, a Russian business associate of Egit's who was living in Philadelphia, offered to drive Schulman to New York to pick up the money. Esterman's little nephew accompanied them on the trip.

Inexplicably, Esterman drove around New York for several hours after they picked up the money in the bank. At one point, he left the woman and the small boy in the car for three hours while he was supposedly attending an antique auction. The real reason for the delay became apparent when the three pulled up in front of a home in Northeast Philadelphia later that evening. Three men descended on the car. One of the men Maced the woman and the boy and another grabbed the purse with the $50,000. Police believe the heist was set up by a Russian gang in New York. Schulman originally identified two of the robbers but, scared to death, she later fled the country and the charges were dropped. Police later discovered that she had hidden out by signing herself into a mental institution in Switzerland.[11]

Out of this rabble of con men and swindlers, Evsei Agron emerged as something of a kingpin in the early 1980s. The Leningrad-born gangster had been a killer and black marketeer in the Soviet Union and had spent years in prison. He was obviously feared on the streets of Brighton Beach, but police learned only so much about him. "He was a grandfatherly type guy," said Joel Campanella, a U.S. Customs investigator who was then a detective in the New York City Police Department's intelligence unit. "He wasn't a big person. But he was tough. We talked to him in the hospital the first time he was shot, and he said, 'Don't worry. I'll take care of it.'"[12]

Agron was a rogue who even at his advanced age liked to pick fights in the nightclubs of Little Odessa. He left the deep thinking to his chief financial adviser, Marat Balagula, a Russian-born criminal who came to the United States in 1977. Balagula had picked up degrees in business and economics back in the old Soviet Union and had spent years making money in that country's black market. He had a much greater knack than his boss for the kind of white-collar swindles that would propel the Russian Mafia into big-time crime. And the biggest swindle of them all, the one that would give the Russians their alliance with La Cosa Nostra, was the gasoline-tax scam.

Balagula was reportedly making millions on the gas scam by the mid-1980s. He lived lavishly, driving expensive automobiles and spreading money around Brighton Beach nightclubs. Freelance writer Robert Friedman quoted an underworld source as saying that Balagula would cruise around New York Harbor in luxury yachts and drive around in a white stretch limo. "Marat throws around diamonds the way we throw around dollar bills," a Genovese family soldier was overheard saying on a wiretap.[13]

The FBI was not investigating Russian organized crime in the early 1980s, and the police department had only a skeleton crew with no wiretaps or informants.[14] So it is not known how Agron reacted to his underling's success in the gas scam. But Balagula is not likely to have wanted to take orders from a ruffian like Agron when he was making millions of dollars in white-collar crime on his own. What is known is this: Agron was murdered with his own bodyguard, Boris Nayfeld, standing in the street below. Nayfeld then became Balagula's bodyguard. What is more, Balagula took over ownership of El Caribe, Agron's Brooklyn health club. "Balagula moved into Agron's shoes in all respects," said Campanella, the IRS investigator. "This is the classic type of thing you see when a traditional organized-crime boss dies."[15]

It would not be the last time investigators would suspect Balagula of playing a role in a murder. In 1986, Boris Nayfeld and his brother Benjamin—both loyal employees of Balagula—became embroiled in a dispute with a Russian mobster to whom they had just sold a gasoline dealership, the MVB Energy Company in Linden, New Jersey. The purchaser of the company, Michael Vax, accused the Nayfelds of trying to swindle him by selling a dealership that owed gasoline taxes to the federal government. On February 3, 1986, Vax went to the Platenum Energy Company in Sheepshead Bay, Brooklyn, a gasoline dealership owned by the Nayfelds. Vax confronted them about the back taxes. While they were arguing, two men opened up with automatic weapons through Platenum's side door. Alex Zeltser, the Nayfelds' partner, was killed and Boris Nayfeld was wounded in the thumb. Vax disappeared during the gun battle but later that day showed up at Coney Island Hospital with bullet wounds in his chest.

No one would talk to police about the shootings and the authorities never made a case against Vax. But it was well known in the Russian underworld that Vladimir Reznikov was one of the gunmen. Reznikov had a reputation as a renegade gun for hire in the *Organizatsiya*, a man whose name had surfaced in more than a few Brooklyn murder investigations. "Everybody was afraid of him," said Campanella. "He didn't align himself with anyone. He was a complete cowboy." In this case, a few friends might have helped. On June 13, 1986, he walked out of the Odessa Restaurant on Brighton Beach Avenue and got into a brown Nissan parked at the curb. As he pulled the car out of the parking space, a man approached the driver's-side windows with a .380-caliber handgun and shot him dead. Campanella later found out that Balagula had warned a friend to stay away from the Odessa that night, showing that he had advance knowledge of the rub-out.[16]

Balagula was not on the streets of Brighton Beach for long after Reznikov's murder. Along with the Nayfelds and several others,

The body of Vladimir Reznikov, a maverick Russian mobster shot to death on Brooklyn's Brighton Beach Avenue in 1986. (Todd Maisel)

he was convicted in Philadelphia on charges of heading a scheme in which the credit-card numbers of Merrill Lynch customers were stolen and used to buy more than $300,000 in furs and furniture at Brooklyn stores. Rather than face prison, Balagula fled the country. There were sightings of him in Atlantic City, California, Paraguay, South Africa, and Hong Kong before he was arrested and extradited to the United States in 1989. He is now in federal prison.

Until the early 1990s, the *Organizatsiya* was composed of about 2,000 members nationwide who operated in small criminal cliques. The structure and memberships of these gangs constantly shifted, and police were unable to identify a single person who acted as the boss of a large criminal organization. The FBI did not even include the Russians on its list of ethnic-crime groups in need of close scrutiny.

But the picture changed drastically around 1992. The crumbling of the old Soviet Union in 1989 set off a tidal wave of organized crime that flooded Moscow, St. Petersburg, and other Russian cities. Gangsters placed a stranglehold on many of the private enterprises struggling to emerge in Russia's new market economy. Their power in Russia's new capitalistic society has been compared to that of criminal syndicates the United States during Prohibition, but that is far too modest a comparison. Russia's new criminal syndicates far exceed in reach and power even the old Capone-Torrio mob. As it makes the difficult transition from state-controlled industry to a private economy, Russia is wide open for plundering by the 5,600 organized-crime groups said to be operating in the country. Russian officials have erected none of the safeguards that the United States employs to prevent criminality. Russia's banks and securities, for instance, are completely unregulated. In this tumultuous period, as millions of new entrepreneurs fuel the growth of Russia's newly liberated economy, organized crime has turned commerce into a bloody free-for-all. Gangs openly extort money from many of the new industries that have sprung up in the country. Even some American companies operating in Russia have had to hire armed guards to fend off extortion attempts.[17] Russian President Boris Yeltsin has called organized crime the biggest threat to Russian society in the 1990s. Nearly 40 percent of the country's new businesses and two-thirds of its corporations, Yeltsin has said, have ties to organized crime. "Organized crime is trying to take the country by the throat," he said in one speech.[18]

Bombings and assassinations linked to organized crime have become commonplace, even in the middle of bustling neighborhoods. Five people were slain by gangsters in downtown Moscow in one week in February 1994. One was Sergei Dubov, publisher of the weekly magazine *New Times*. Dubov, who was shot in the head while walking to his car one morning, had been getting extortion demands from gangsters. Another victim, the manager of a luxury food store's foreign-currency department, was shot down outside his apartment. His briefcase was untouched, so authorities ruled out robbery. In some cases, the assassinations have been of major crime figures whose funerals were of the lavish variety once favored by Chicago gangsters.

Some of the gangs are commanded by *vory v zakone*, or "thieves-in-law," who made up an elite group of criminals in the old Soviet Union. In the harsh Soviet prison system, the thieves-in-law were the thugs most feared and respected by their fellow inmates. One could only be named a thief-in-law by the recommendation of another, and there was usually an elaborate coronation ceremony. Thieves-in-law are paid homage by other criminals when they are back on the street. They were naturals to take the helm of the new gangster state emerging in Russia, but they have not gone unchallenged. Some of the toughest new mobs in Russia are ethnic gangs that have their roots in other former Soviet republics, such as Chechnya and Azerbaijan.[19]

As Russian crime groups have grown in sophistication, they have begun dispatching emissaries to Western Europe and the United States to conquer new territory. Russian gangsters are now responsible for much of the organized crime in Poland, Germany and other European counties. And a new generation of gangsters has been appearing in New York, Los Angeles and other U.S. cities. Part of the reason is the new influx of Russians coming to the United States on tourist visas. In 1992, for instance, there were more than 129,000 nonimmigrant U.S. visas issued to residents of Russia, the Ukraine and Belarus, compared with some 3,000 in 1988. Between 10 and 20 percent of the visa holders do not return to Russia before the documents expire, and authorities say many of these overstaying their welcome are gangsters.[20] Indeed, police have seen dozens of cases where Russian hit men or swindlers are brought into the country to commit specific crimes and then shuttled out of the country.[21]

U.S. authorities have watched with alarm as gangsters well known to the Russian authorities as top crime bosses have started showing up in Brooklyn, Los Angeles and other cities. The authorities fear that these newcomers will forge crime groups that are far more dangerous and organized than their predecessors in the Russian-American community. "Before we had the second stringers," said James Moody, chief of the FBI's organized crime program in Washington. "Now we're getting the first team."[22]

The most closely watched of these new arrivals was Vyacheslav Ivankov, who goes by the nickname Yaponchik, or "Little Japanese." Ivankov, known to Russian police as one of the most respected *vory v zakone*, slipped into Brooklyn in January 1993 after a long criminal career in Russia. Ivankov is a short, compact man with thick brown hair and an elfin beard. He has eight-pointed stars tattooed on the front of either shoulder, which reflect his status as a *vory v zakone*. In 1980, he founded Moscow's Solontsevskaya gang, which specialized in posing as police officers and robbing the homes of wealthy Russians, according to authorities. Ivankov was convicted of one of those robberies in 1981 and sentenced to 14 years in a Soviet prison. But he allegedly bribed a judge and was released from Tulun prison in Siberia in 1991.[23] He fled the country two years later as Russian officials were seeking his arrest for a parole violation. Russia's Ministry of Internal Affairs immediately tipped off the FBI that he was headed for New York, and he could have been deported for lying about his criminal past on his visa application. But federal agents decided to let him stay and watch his movements.

Federal officials say Ivankov planned to use his reputation to tie together the nation's loosely organized Russian gangs into a criminal syndicate. "We believe that he has been sent here to take control of North America for a Russian crime group," said a high-ranking federal law enforcement official. FBI agents watched Ivankov meeting with other Russian mobsters in New York, Miami, Los Angeles, Boston and Toronto. He kept his base in Brighton Beach but also had an apartment in Denver. By early 1995, the FBI had intelligence that Ivankov's New York branch of the Solontsevskaya gang had about 100 members and was recognized on the street as the premier Russian crime group in Brooklyn. "Among the Russian organized crime groups in this country, his is the strongest," said Raymond Kerr, who heads the Russian organized crime squad in the New York FBI office.[24]

But his meteoric rise in the Russian rackets would not last. In

Vyacheslav Ivanov, reputedly the nation's top Russian crime boss, being led from the FBI office in New York City after his arrest on extortion charges in June 1995. (New York Daily News)

June 1995, Ivankov was charged with attempting to extort $3.5 million from two Russian-born owners of Summit International Corporation, a Manhattan investment firm. The Russian mobsters who carried out the extortion were recorded on wiretaps getting instructions from Ivankov on a cellular phone. In one conversation, the mobsters informed Ivankov that the father of one of the victims had been beaten to death on a Moscow subway platform. On May 25, 1995, the mobsters kidnapped the victims, Alexander Volkov and Vladimir Voloshin, from the lounge of the New York Hilton and brought them to the upstairs of the Troika Restaurant, described in court papers as a hangout for Russian gangsters in Fairview, New Jersey. There the two were forced to sign an agreement to come up with $3.5 million in a series of payments.[25] Federal authorities pulled in the net a month later, charging Ivankov and eight others in the extortion scheme. Little Japanese was arrested at his girlfriend's home in Brooklyn, where he cursed at federal agents. He was in no better a mood the next day. As he was led in handcuffs across Federal Plaza in Manhattan, he kicked and spat at several reporters and photographers.

12: Mob 2000

In the opening of his 1927 book, *The Gangs of New York*, underworld historian Herbert Asbury breathed a sigh of relief that the "gangster" had receded into the American past. "Happily, he has now passed from the metropolitan scene, and for nearly half a score of years has existed mainly in the lively imagination of industrious journalists, among whom the tradition of the gangster has more lives than the proverbial cat," Asbury wrote. "Hopeful reporters continue to resurrect him every time there is a mysterious killing in the slum districts or among the white lights of Broadway."[1] Asbury obviously had in mind gangs like the Five Pointers and the Eastmans, the veritable armies of young ruffians that once battled for the streets of Lower Manhattan, not the white-collar thugs that we regard as gangsters today. But given that he was writing in the middle of Prohibition, when the progeny of America's great brawling gangs were assembling into a national crime syndicate, his obituary for the American gangster still strikes something of an odd chord.

Asbury's mistake points up the hazards of trying to map the future of organized crime, but it has not prevented all manner of writers, academics and law-enforcement officials in the succeeding decades from predicting that the American gangster would shortly become an endangered species. This has been especially true of *La Cosa Nostra*. The Italian mob's reign has been so long, and its control of the underworld and many legitimate industries so well documented, that many observers perhaps find it hard to accept that such a medieval institution could continue to flourish in postmodern America. How else do we account for the misplaced optimism of so many in predicting the Mafia's demise?

Such speculation began cropping up in the mid-1970s, when black and Hispanic gangsters first flexed their muscles in the ghetto. As we have seen, Francis Ianni, Donald Goddard and a number of newspaper and magazine journalists speculated that not only were there new faces in the underworld—it's hard to argue with that proposition—but that the old faces were beginning to disappear.

The requiems for the Italian Mafia became louder in the 1980s, when the Reagan administration waged war on organized crime, toppling Mafia bosses around the country. With each major prosecution, FBI officials and prosecutors would sound a death knell for the Honored Society. After winning convictions in the famed Pizza Connection heroin case in 1987, Rudolph Giuliani, then the U.S. attorney in Manhattan, became perhaps the best-known proponent of the extinction theory. "Five or six years ago, nobody would have believed that we could convict the head of the Sicilian Mafia in New York," he said. "If we continue our efforts, there's not going to be a Mafia in five or ten years."[2] G. Robert Blakey, a University of Notre Dame professor and organized-crime expert, went even further in 1990: "They are dead or finished almost everywhere. Their strongholds in Boston, Philadelphia, Atlantic City, Cleveland, New Orleans, Chicago and New York or all gone or under siege."[3] Journalists have been just as quick to pick up on this theme. Selwyn Raab, the *New York Times'* well-sourced organized-crime reporter, seemed to write an article every couple of years about the Mafia's infirmity. His boldest report on the subject, published on October 22, 1990, began with this sentence: "Battered by aggressive investigators and weakened by incompetent leadership, most of America's traditional Mafia families appear to be fading out of existence. . . ."

Accompanying these rosy predictions about the Mafia's setting sun has been widespread speculation about what crime groups will take the place of the Italians at the forefront of organized crime. Over the years, the conventional wisdom about what crime group is "emerging" most quickly has been subject to wide variations. Ianni and the other pioneering ethnic-succession theorists seemed sure that blacks and Hispanics—the new kings of the ghetto—would be the new royalty in organized crime. By the early 1980s, James Moody was telling a Senate subcommittee that motorcycle gangs were the most potent of the new crime groups. Then the President's Commission on Organized Crime devoted an entire hearing to Asian organized crime in 1984, and the Chinese were tagged as the most threatening of the new groups. In the past two years, the Chinese have gone out of fashion. The attention of law enforcement and the media is now fixed on the Russian Mafia.

None of these shifts in public concern has been based entirely on reality. Motorcycle gangs are just as active in this country now as they were in the early 1980s, but one no longer hears them ballyhooed as a criminal threat. Chinese gangs were already well entrenched in extortion and gambling in the Asian community by 1970, and perhaps even then could have been seen as the mostly likely successors to the Mafia. But they had not yet been "discovered" by federal law enforcement and the media. Despite his insight into the changing face of the underworld, Ianni seems not to have even been aware of the Chinese mob. On top of all this, the author will argue below that the mid-1990s have shown that much of the speculation about the Mafia's decline has been wrong. When we add all these facts together, we see that, at least to some degree, the nation's focus on organized crime shifts more with the changing *Zeitgeist* than with the realities of the street.

What, then, is the real future of organized crime in this country? This author will not pretend to have any greater clairvoyance on that point than others who have tried to answer that question over the years. But a careful look at what is really occurring in the nation's underworld can help sweep aside some of our more glaring misconceptions.

When one surveys the new landscape of American organized crime, the Chinese clearly stand out. Chinese gangs, *tongs* and triads together are second only to the Italian Mafia among domestic crime groups in the sophistication and reach of their crimes. Like their Italian counterparts, Chinese gangsters are the progeny of a criminal conspiracy that is centuries old and whose traditions include an inviolate oath of secrecy that has changed little over hundreds of years.

This triad tradition gives Chinese crime groups in this country a strong international connection that not only helps them smuggle heroin across the globe but gives them a ready source of new recruits, especially since Asians continue to immigrate to this country in large numbers. That gang members are members of triads or *tongs* also gives them important alliances with similar groups in cities across the country. Indeed, none of the other emerging crime groups has the national scope of the Chinese. Dominicans may move drugs across the Northeast, but the trade is not governed by a central figure who shares in the proceeds of every crime that is committed. The Blood and Crip gangs that exist in cities across the country share at best a loose affiliation with the mother gangs in Los Angeles. With the Chinese crime groups, however, such affiliations are real and enduring. The Ghost Shadows chapters in New York, Boston, Chicago, New Orleans and other cities are all affiliated with the same national On Leong president. When the Wah Ching was at the height of its power, Vincent Jew was the boss of the Chinese rackets from Los Angeles to Portland, Oregon, and that fact was recognized in every *mah-jongg* parlor on the West Coast. Meetings between Chinese gang leaders from around North America have been well documented.

Chinese crime groups also have an exceptionally broad criminal base in their communities. Black gangs exist almost entirely to sell drugs. Without cocaine and heroin, Dominican organized crime would not exist. But in their own communities, Chinese crime groups control casino gambling, bookmaking, loan-sharking, extortion, the infiltration of legitimate businesses, credit-card fraud, video poker machines, alien smuggling, heroin smuggling, food-stamp fraud, and a wide array of other crimes. No other crime group save for the Mafia has such a diverse portfolio.

Chinese gangsters are also deeply wired into the civic life of American Chinatowns. Their sponsors are often the most powerful business interests in the Chinese community, an alliance that gives them a patina of respectability even in the eyes of Chinese who may not approve of their activities. When the Chinese merchant hands over an extortion payment to a gang member, he is not just doing so out of fear for his life. He is obeying a neighborhood code that has been in place since the first railroad workers established American Chinatowns in the 19th century.

Finally, Chinese crime groups in New York share another trait with the city's Mafia families—they are nearly indestructible. Just as the same five mob families have controlled New York's Italian crime since the 1930s, the criminal map of Chinatown has not changed since the early 1970s. The oldest three gangs—the Ghost Shadows, the Flying Dragons and the Tung On—have held down the same turf all these years despite the efforts of law enforcement to dislodge them. Authorities had proclaimed the Ghost Shadows finished after Nicky Louie and 24 others were locked up in the 1985 RICO prosecution. And yet federal authorities brought another racketeering case against the Shadows in 1994, which shows that the gang had little trouble rebuilding after its leaders were taken off the street. In the latest case, the Shadows' chief gambling-house operator, Moy Bong Shun, was charged with paying off a detective in the Police Department's public morals squad to warn him of police raids. To their credit, prosecutors were careful this time not to predict an end to the Ghost Shadows.

In these respects, the conventional wisdom about Chinese organized crime is correct—it is an insidious criminal virus that will afflict the country for years to come. But Chinese gangsters wield not even a fraction of the influence that the Italian Mafia has had in 20th century America, and it is doubtful that they ever will. Thirty years after they arrived on the American scene, Chinese gangs remain largely an immigrant phenomenon with little influence outside the Chinese community. To be sure, the heroin that Chinese import from the Golden Triangle affects a broad segment of society, but Chinese gangsters otherwise limit their crimes to their own people. The Italian Mafia has been about far more than just neighborhood rackets. Italian gangsters have controlled national labor unions and entire legitimate industries. They have been able to fix elections and hit every consumer in the pocket with the extra costs they have built into construction and trash hauling. It is highly unlikely that even two or three decades from now the Chinese will be able to achieve that kind of influence.

The Chinese are an Eastern people in a Western nation. Even second-generation Chinese criminals seem to lack interest in insinuating themselves into the non-Asian community. With a few exceptions, Chinese crooks have not shown an ability to make the kinds of friendships in the political clubhouses that gave the Mafia unfettered access to the halls of power. Part of the reason is that the old clubhouses themselves are not what they used to be. Machine politics, as practiced by the old Irish and Italian pols, is largely a thing of the past. The glare of television lights and decades of efforts by political reformers have seen to it that we will never again see bosses the likes of Big Tim Sullivan, Richard Daley of Chicago, James Michael Curley of Boston, or Frank Hague of Jersey City. We may not even see again the kind of clubhouse pols that existed in New York in the 1980s, like Queens Borough President Donald Manes and Brooklyn Democratic boss Meade Esposito, whose mob ties were legendary.

Chinese organized crime is likely to remain an immigrant's game. Chinese-Americans are an upwardly mobile people whose children are overrepresented in elite high schools and good colleges. Those Chinese who are Americanized enough to help the crime syndicates branch out beyond the Asian community are unlikely to do so in any great numbers. The Chinese emphasis on hard work and education is likely to undermine the spread of Asian organized crime more effectively than federal racketeering laws. Even people who spend their early 20s in gangs like the Ghost Shadows and the Flying Dragons often end up as legitimate restaurant owners by the time they are in their 30s. (By contrast, once you are in a Mafia family, you never quit.) And it is almost unheard of for the children of Chinese gangsters to end up in the rackets themselves. There don't seem to be any Michael Corleones or Junior Gottis in Chinatown. Chinese gangsters may well go the route of their Jewish rather than their Italian counterparts. If the mass immigration of Chinese should come to a halt, the Chinese gangster may disappear in a blaze of assimilation after a couple of decades.

Sadly, the same cannot be said of black gangsters. With more than half of the nation's African-Americans mired below the poverty line, the black ghetto seems destined to be an enduring feature of the inner city. And if the black underclass is not going to go away, neither is the problem of ghetto crime. For the near future, the drug trade will continue to be the only road to wealth for many inner-city youths whose backgrounds leave them ill prepared for college or the job market. Drugs will not go away. Guns will not go away. And neither will the problem of the black gangster. He is too much a creation of the pathology of the ghetto to disappear any time soon. Indeed, his kind are more likely to multiply. In a few short years, the children of mothers swept up in the crack epidemic of the 1980s will reach their teenage years. These are the children behind all those tales of drug-induced abuse and neglect, the children who stayed home alone in firetraps while their mothers went to the crack house, the children bounced from one foster home to another, unwanted, unloved and ill prepared for life. Come the dawn of the 21st Century, these children will be on the streets.

With the ghetto swarming with aspiring Al Capones, the Black Mafia dreamed of by Joe Gallo, Nicky Barnes, Aaron Jones and so many others cannot be counted as an impossibility. Certainly the black underworld as it currently exists, with millions of dollars in drugs changing hands on ghetto streets every day, will not get any kinder or gentler. The black gangsters will continue to fit prominently into the matrix of organized crime.

In the near future, drugs will no doubt remain the staple of black organized crime. The big question is whether black gangsters who retail drugs in New York and other cities will remain subservient to the Hispanic wholesale suppliers. The Colombian and Chinese suppliers have chosen to deal with Dominicans, Cubans and Mexicans, giving them a higher place in the pecking order of the underworld than black Americans. But Frank Matthews was one black kingpin who successfully rebelled against this criminal tutelage, and there is no reason others will not also try to bypass the middlemen and import their own drugs. In Detroit, a city with a minuscule Hispanic population, some black drug dealers have established connections directly with the Colombians. Blacks in other parts of the country are likely to tire of dealing with middlemen and forge their own links with Colombians, or Chinese, or whoever else is controlling the flow of drugs in the 21st Century.

The brash and violent drug gangsters of the ghetto may not be the Mafia successors that Ianni envisioned twenty years ago. They may never reach the level of organization that links them to the city-wide power structure and insinuates them into the legitimate economy—the true test of criminal supremacy. They may never free themselves entirely from dependence on wealthier and better-connected crime groups. But as long as there is an underclass, as long as there are American cities, American blacks will be a force in organized crime.

That Hispanic crime groups will also have a future in organized crime is a good bet. But their role is harder to predict. Cuban and Dominican gangs are the most organized of the Hispanic crime groups, but they have about them an aspect of impermanence. Cubans have seen rapid upward mobility in the last two decades. Many have abandoned the Cuban ghettos in Union City and West New York as more of them have saved enough money to move to suburban Bergen County, New Jersey. José Miguel Battle's chief source of income in the New York area is the illegal numbers game, an activity that is threatened in the long term by the proliferation of legal betting opportunities like the legalized state lottery, Indian reservation casinos and expanded Off Track Betting.

Cubans are no longer a big presence in the inner-city areas of New York and New Jersey. And except in Florida, they have never had much of a population concentration elsewhere in the country. Indeed, Cuban gangsters have managed to have a presence in the underworld of cities like Philadelphia and Detroit only by working with other Hispanic groups. Cubans will increasingly dominate organized crime in the Miami area, supplanting the Mafia groups from around the United States and Canada that used Florida as a playground in the past. But the future of Cuban organized crime elsewhere in the country hardly seems significant.

Dominicans, too, have an uncertain future in the rackets. Their spread in the American drug trade has been meteoric in the last 15 years, and they can be expected to continue playing a greater role in the movement of cocaine and heroin, especially in their new capacity as importers and major wholesalers. Young men from the poverty-ridden Dominican Republic will continue to make the journey to the streets of Washington Heights in search of fabulous wealth. But it is doubtful that Dominicans will take the next step and build well-structured, hierarchical crime groups with highly diverse criminal portfolios—that is, that they will begin to resemble the American Mafia. Most Dominican drug kingpins seem to have little interest in building a future in this country. They spend their lives as immigrants with one foot in the Dominican Republic, sustained by the dream that they will return to enjoy the good life in their native country when they have made enough money in New York. A good share of the millions of dollars made every week on the streets of Washington Heights is wired directly to the Dominican Republic. Those money-wiring houses lining every major thoroughfare of Harlem, Washington Heights and Inwood are there for a reason. That could leave the ultimate future of Hispanic organized crime to Puerto Ricans and Mexicans, whose rapidly proliferating gangs give them the same potential for growth in the criminal underworld as American black groups. But given their failure so far to organize stable, self-perpetuating crime groups, any criminal visionaries in the Puerto Rican and Mexican communities may not have an easy time building a Latin Mafia.

The future of the Russian Mafia is difficult to predict because it is so new in this country and relatively little is known of its operations. Russian immigrants are few in number compared to Asians and Hispanics. And since so many Russians coming into this country are well educated and upwardly mobile, it is likely that the Russian community will not remain long in the inner city. On the other hand, the fuel-tax evasion scam has shown how much damage can be done by a handful of Russian mobsters. And with organized crime so clearly on the rise in Eastern Europe, we could end up seeing a steady influx of Russian thugs for years to come. If many of them come here with the ambition of Vyacheslav Ivankov, a nationwide Russian crime syndicate could be the result—if it is not already secretly taking shape. And if the close working relationship that has developed between Russian and Italian mobsters continues, the Russian Mafia could end up as the natural heir to *La Cosa Nostra*. At the very least, the two groups could solidify their partnership and become a lasting combine. It was, after all, a Jewish-Italian combine that founded the first national crime syndicate.

In predicting tomorrow's dominant criminal ethnicity, one must also consider the possibility that new groups will arrive on the scene. For example, the Japanese *Yakuza* is a powerful criminal force that so far has been restricted to Asia, making only limited forays into the United States. There are also immigrant crime groups that operately quietly in parts of the country that are outside the media spotlight but have the potential to become a national problem. The best example of these is the Iraqi mob in Detroit.

We come finally to the question of how rapidly the Italian Mafia is likely to decline and whether it will ever follow the Irish and Jewish mobs by disappearing altogether. That the Mafia is no longer the power it was for the first three decades of the postwar period cannot be disputed. The Mafia has lost control of many of the national labor unions, including the Teamsters, that were perhaps its greatest source of influence. Gangsters no longer have undisputed control over the docks through the International Longshoremen's Association, although many of the ILA's locals are still influenced by the mob. What is more, the federal government has begun the process of weeding the Mafia out of legitimate industries ranging from seafood wholesaling and other food distribution companies to garbage hauling and concrete companies.

In some cities, the Mafia is hardly what it used to be. Cleveland's is perhaps the greatest success story of the FBI. In a city whose Mafia family was once violent and far-reaching, the mafiosi have virtually disappeared. Federal authorities have broken up major bookmaking rings in Cleveland in the mid-1990s without coming across a single Italian—the surest sign that the family that once ruled gambling with an iron fist is gone. "You just don't hear about mob guys being on the streets anymore," said Mark Rollenhagen, the federal-court reporter for the Cleveland *Plain Dealer*.

But even when they are listing their accomplishments, FBI bosses have to acknowledge that in no city other than Cleveland have they entirely eliminated a Mafia family. That leaves at least 23 regions where there are still active Italian criminal conspiracies that at the very least involve lucrative bookmaking activities. In some of these cities, the Mafia family is so obscure that the names of its leaders are rarely in the papers and mob rub-outs are a rarity. But people who are involved in the rackets know who the mafiosi are and make sure not to cross them.

Detroit is perhaps the best example of a city where the Mafia family is almost invisible but still exerts a major influence on the underworld. It is an extremely close-knit group that is run by the children of the same immigrants from Terrasina, Sicily, who helped found the family at the turn of the century. During Prohibition Detroit's underworld was a bloody free-for-all, with Sicilian, Neapolitan, and Jewish criminals killing each other over the booze trade and other rackets. But two Terrasina-born gangsters, Joseph Zerilli and William (Black Bill) Tocco, helped consolidate the feuding Italians into a strong crime family that took over the city's organized crime in the 1930s.[4]

The Mafia family reached the peak of its power in the 1950s and 1960s. It controlled every manner of racketeering not only in

Detroit but also across the river in Windsor, Ontario, and as far south as Toledo, Ohio. In testimony before the McClellan congressional committee in 1963, Detroit Police Commissioner George Edwards said the city's Mafia was "big business," with annual gross income of $150 million from criminal activities and $50 million from legitimate enterprises. Zerilli, Tocco, and three other "dons" formed a ruling council that oversaw illegal numbers, bookmaking, loan-sharking, and extortion and sank its money in legitimate businesses like bakeries, a juice company, a linen-supply business, real estate, and the Elias Brothers restaurant chain. Among the top lieutenants were Anthony Giacalone, the Detroit mob's gambling boss, and his brother Vito, a long-time loan shark. The Giacalones reached the height of their notoriety in 1975, when they were implicated in the disappearance of Teamster boss Jimmy Hoffa.

What is remarkable about the Detroit Mafia is not its heyday in the 1950s and 1960s, but rather how it has managed to stay a viable business even as the Italian criminal subculture in the Motor City has become extinct. It is a cautionary tale for those who think the Mafia will automatically disappear in other cities once there are no more poor Italians living in the inner city.

After Joseph Zerilli died in 1977, control of the family should have passed to his son, Anthony Zerilli. But the younger Zerilli was not boss material. He was a hothead who was careless enough to be personally charged with threatening Donald Robb, a man who owed $25,000 to mob loan shark Bernie Marchesani. Marchesani so terrified Robb by sending him two dead birds that the victim turned to the FBI and agreed to testify against Zerilli and others. Because of stunts like this, Zerilli had to accept the indignity of watching the leadership of the family pass to Jack Tocco, one of two sons of the late Black Bill Tocco.[5]

Jack Tocco is the figure behind the endurance of the Detroit Mafia. His cautious, low-key style has set the tone for the entire crime family. Tocco didn't take the usual route to the head of a crime family. Indeed, few of his friends and associates thought he would end up as a gangster. As a teenager, he had his own Christmas tree lot on Gratiot Avenue. After high school, he earned a business degree from the University of Detroit. His first job out of college was that of a salesman at Lafayette Motors, a dealership owned by his father and two other gangsters. "Jack was a good student," a longtime friend told *Monthly Detroit* magazine in 1981. "Even as a young man, he was always moving. He could have been chairman of General Motors had he gone into that business."[6]

Instead, he turned his brilliance toward building one of the nation's most impenetrable crime families. Other members of the family, including the Giacalone brothers, were angered at first by having to take orders from a man who had no experience in the rackets. But Tocco's low-key style prevailed, and the organization was better for it. For the last 20 years, the Detroit mafiosi have formed one of the wealthiest and most close-knit crime families in the country, one that settles disputes and maintains its influence with remarkably little bloodshed. By eschewing deep involvement in narcotics, the Detroit mob has avoided the messy turf wars and exposure to government informants that have made trouble for other crime families. Although the federal government locked up Mafia bosses around the country in the 1980s, they have yet to make a case against Tocco. Indeed, Detroit's top mobsters have been so successful in avoiding prosecution that most are virtually unknown to the public, leading quiet lives in the city's eastern suburbs that lend the impression that the local mob is extinct.

As of the early 1990s, the family had 23 "made"—or formally inducted—members known to the federal authorities, including several younger figures who could take over the family once its aging leadership retires. That is a little more than a third of the 63 members that Edwards was able to list at the McClellan committee hearings in 1963. But the family is still in control of the region's bookmaking and controls or gets a share of any high-stakes card games and loan-sharking operating in the Detroit metropolitan area. The key to its endurance with such small numbers is this: the actual Mafia members almost never dirty their hands with the direct operation of bookmaking and illegal gambling. Much of the low-level work is handled by Chaldeans and members of other ethnic groups. Federal authorities in May 1991 smashed a multimillion-dollar bookmaking operation in Detroit whose tentacles spread to Las Vegas, New York, Miami and Chicago. But the biggest fish taken down in Detroit was Henry Hilf, a longtime Jewish gambler. The only Mafia figure involved was Jack Vito Giacalone, a family soldier who is Vito's son. He was sentenced to three years, hardly enough to make anyone talk.

The Detroit Mafia presides over this empire of crime like a senior board of directors, making all the decisions, receiving all the tribute, but never involving its directors in the day-to-day operations of the business. Tocco, now in his late 60s, is especially removed from the day-to-day criminality. With this kind of arrangement, the Mafia hardly needs an inner-city Italian community to survive. It lets other ethnic groups do the dirty work and is able to keep them in line without violence. After all, the Detroit Mafia can offer other crime groups incentives to work for them. Without the mob's national bookmaking network, where else would independent Detroit bookies go if everyone was betting on the same team at once? The bookmaker can hardly risk being wiped out. He must have a larger pool where he can lay off his bets. The Detroit Mafia doesn't have to break kneecaps to maintain control of bookmaking. It stays at the top by adhering to the business principles that Jack Tocco no doubt learned in college—by offering the best service to its customers.

If a Mafia family can continue to flourish in a decidedly non-Italian city like Detroit, imagine how tough it will be for federal authorities to clean them out of places like New York and Chicago. If 23 Mafia members are able to control multimillion-dollar criminal rackets in Detroit, imagine what several hundred "made guys" can do in New York. The membership totals of New York's Mafia families are not getting any smaller. At the time of the McClellan committee hearings, authorities released a chart of the Genovese family structure that showed 114 known members. When the FBI made available a similar chart at Senate subcommittee hearings in 1988, there were 193 members. There were also hundreds of known members shown for the Bonanno, Lucchese, Gambino and Colombo families. These are daunting numbers, even allowing for the fact that 25 years of advancement in wiretapping technology has perhaps skewed the numbers upward by making it easier for agents to identify Mafia members.

While racketeering suits have managed to pry New York City's mobsters out of key labor unions like the Teamsters, the Carpenters and the Mason Tenders, they are still solidly in control of others. Authorities have been trying for 50 years to get the mob out of the union that runs the Fulton Fish Market, the largest wholesale seafood mart in the city. As of this writing, they were still trying. Just how deeply imbedded the mob remains in some quarters of New York City was amply demonstrated in August 1995, when federal authorities revealed that the Genovese family takes a cut from every vendor at Little Italy's San Gennaro Festival, the largest annual street fair in the city.

The Italian criminal subculture that feeds New York's Mafia families may have been weakened by the migration of whites to the suburbs and to more middle-class parts of the city, but it has hardly disappeared. It flourishes almost as effectively outside the cities. Mob families are using suburban companies to manufacture video poker machines for illegal betting in bars and other outlets in the city and suburbs alike, successors to the slot machines that once enriched an earlier generation of mobsters. In February 1995, Essex County, New Jersey, prosecutors smashed a bookmaking ring operating out of a high school in suburban Nutley. Several of the high-school students were acting as collectors for the betting and transporting the money to a mob figure. A year earlier, the Bergen County Prosecutor's Office took over the police department of South Hackensack, New Jersey after some of its members were tied to mob-sponsored gambling in the township's taverns.

Old-time mobsters complain that the Mafia is not what it used to be. They say "made guys" no longer have the loyalty that once made the Honored Society prosper. "Years ago, people had honor," said Anthony Accetturo, who was a Lucchese family captain in New Jersey before he became a government informant. "You sat down and gave a man your word. Honor, discipline—all these things are out the window." Accetturo said the lack of dis-cipline had deprived the Mafia of its greatest strength. "It's all over, in plain English. You're dealing with street gangs out there."[7] And yet other mobsters have told reporters that they think the Mafia's decline is vastly overestimated. The truth is somewhere in the middle. The Mafia is in a very gradual decline. It may fade away in Cleveland, St. Louis, Denver and other cities, but it will not be eliminated in Chicago and its eastern strong-holds for decades to come. And as long as it is powerful in New York, it will be a key player in the nation's organized-crime busi-ness. The difference is that it will not be the sole arbiter of big-time crime. It will increasingly become simply one among several powerful crime groups plundering the nation.

The view, then, is hardly optimistic for the nation. Tomorrow's chief racketeers will not be Italian, Chinese, black, Hispanic or Russian. They will be all of the above. Even more than today, or-ganized crime will be a diffuse threat that challenges law enforce-ment from a host of different nationalities, regions and activities. None will be as singularly powerful and impenetrable as the old Mafia groups, but there will be so many more of them that police will find themselves hankering for the old days of Mafia control.

More ominously, these crime groups are showing an increas-ingly propensity for joining forces. In New York's so-called Blue Thunder heroin case, Bonanno family mobsters were accused of buying heroin from Chinese suppliers and distributing it in part-nership with a Puerto Rican drug gang. Mafia figures sell Chinese the video poker machines that gangs like the Flying Dragons force on helpless merchants. Russian mobsters have been part-ners with the Mafia in fuel-tax scams. Italians have operated gambling joints with Albanians in the Bronx and Westchester County, and they have numerous partnerships with Cubans in the illegal numbers game. What is more, just about any crime group that sells cocaine—the Italians and the Russians in-cluded—gets it from the Colombians. The Italian and Irish mobs have been partners in South Boston bookmaking for a couple of decades. In January 1995, Boston's Mafia boss, Francis (Cadillac

Frank) Salemme and the city's Irish rackets boss, James (Whitey) Bulger, both went on the lam after they were charged together in a 37-count racketeering indictment.

Asian organized crime is destined to become an amalgam of Chinese, Vietnamese, and Koreans. Indeed, Korean gangs are rapidly becoming subsidiaries of larger Chinese syndicates in New York City, especially in Queens. While not as large or organized as Chinese crime groups, Korean gangs have become bolder and more deadly since they first appeared in New York and California in the early 1980s. In New York, gangs like the Korean Fuk Ching, the Korean Flying Dragons and the Korean Taiwanese Boys—all names borrowed from notorious Chinese gangs—have been tied to scores of extortions, home-invasion robberies, shootings, and the distribution of "ice," a smokeable form of methamphetamine. Korean Power, a gang with branches in California and New York, was shaking down dozens of restaurants in Manhattan's midtown Korean neighborhood before its leader, Young Sang Lee, and four other gang members were arrested in May 1993. Taking their cue from Chinese gangs, these Korean thugs would eat and drink in some of the restaurants and then write "KP"—the gang's initials—on the back of the checks and walk out. As they become more skilled in the rackets, some Koreans are recruited by Chinese gangs and inducted into the world of big-time racketeering. In the winter of 1994, for example, a Chinese Ghost Shadow named Gum Pi took to hanging around a Korean nightclub at Prince Street and Roosevelt Avenue in Flushing, Queens. Before long he was the *dai lo* for a Korean offshoot of the Ghost Shadows. Just about every major Chinese gang in New York now has some kind of Korean affiliate. "The Koreans so far are traditional street gangs, like the Jets and the Sharks, not the mob," said Sgt. William Nevins, head of the Asian gang unit in Queens. "But they're making their bones."[8]

Perhaps most frightening is that all these crime groups are forging much stronger international links. Major international criminal conspiracies like the Sicilian Mafia, the Colombian cartels, the Chinese triads and, more recently, the Russian Mafia, have begun to work together around the globe. The Sicilian Mafia has been especially active in forging links with the Colombian cartels to flood Western Europe and the United States with cocaine. In September 1994, three distinct Italian crime groups—the Sicilian Mafia, the Neapolitan Camorra, and the Calabrian 'Ndrangheta—joined forces in a massive scheme to import Colombian cocaine to the United States and Canada. Federal authorities arrested some 80 people here and in Europe and charged them with sending wholesale shipments of drugs out the door of a pizzeria in midtown Manhattan. "This case reveals the world-wide web of the illegal drug trafficking that plagues this country and countries abroad," Mary Jo White, the U.S. attorney in Manhattan, said in announcing the arrests. Remarkably, the three groups appeared to be operating independently of New York's Mafia families, suggesting that overseas Italian crime gangs could help fill the void left by the American mob's decline.

The Russian Mafia has migrated out of its own country and come to dominate organized crime in Germany, Poland and other Central European countries. The Russian mob steals cars from the streets of the United States and Germany and ships them to Eastern Europe. The Russians also have forged links with the Colombians to distribute cocaine in the United States and Europe.

By the same token, the Chinese triads guide heroin shipments around the world and use Hong Kong as the hub for the world-wide counterfeiting of credit cards. A clerk at a Hong Kong hotel will surreptitiously write down a series of credit card numbers and within a day or two counterfeit cards with the same account numbers are in the hands of Chinese gangs in Los Angeles and San Francisco, two cities that have become leaders in credit-card fraud—thanks to Asian organized crime and the two cities' links to crooks in the Pacific Rim. Chinese alien-smuggling rings are usually joint ventures of crime groups in southern China, Hong Kong and the United States.

The international criminal conspiracy is a nightmare for the entire world. We all pay the price of international organized crime in the form of more costly insurance premiums, higher credit-card fees and more dangerous streets. It took American law enforcement agencies decades to overcome the bureaucratic barriers between them and join forces to go after organized crime figures. We can only hope that such cooperation will not take so long to emerge on the international front. The early signs are that cooperation will happen. The FBI and DEA are in regular contact with law enforcement officials in Russia, West Germany, Italy, Hong Kong, Colombia, the Dominican Republic and elsewhere.

Indeed, the performance of law enforcement over the next few years to some degree will determine how big an impact the new diversity in organized crime will have on our lives. And the FBI and other agencies in the last half-decade have clearly begun overcoming the bureaucratic inertia that hampered their intial response to the changing face of the underworld. The biggest successes have grown out of the task forces that local and federal agencies have put together in the last few years. In New York, the task-force approach has achieved especially dramatic results. The New York City Police Department's major-case squad and the U.S. Bureau of Alcohol, Tobacco and Firearms have joined with the FBI in a series of hammer blows against Chinese organized crime. In 1994 and 1995, the task force brought major racketeering cases against the Ghost Shadows, the Flying Dragons, the Fuk Ching, the White Tigers, the Tung On gang, the Tung On *tong* and the On Leong *tong*'s leader. Of Chinatown's major groups linked to organized crime, only the Hip Sing *tong* and the Fukien American Association have escaped prosecution. Similar task forces have cracked down on the Ping On and Chinese Freemasons in Boston and the Wo Hop To triad and Hop Sing *tong* in San Francisco, as well as Vietnamese gangs in San Jose and Boston. Authorities have also used the task-force approach to target dozens of violent gangs around the country, including the Mexican Mafia in Los Angeles, the Latin Kings in New York, the El Rukns in Chicago, Best Friends in Detroit, the Abdullahs in Atlantic City, and the Junior Black Mafia in Philadelphia.

But law enforcement alone is hardly the solution to our nation's organized-crime problem. One of the things drawing the world's criminals to the United States is our incredibly rich market for narcotics. Drugs remain the single biggest factor driving

the underworld, and federal officials have rightly made the elimi-
nation of that illegal market a top priority. But they have gone
about it the wrong way. The drug war of the Reagan and Bush ad-
ministrations was an abject failure. It made the same wrong as-
sumption that the U.S. government made during Prohibition—
that you can somehow prevent gangsters from supplying
Americans with a commodity that they badly want. If the demand exists for drugs, all of the resources of the FBI, DEA, CIA
and U.S. military put together are not going to stop them from
being imported. The only real legacy of the drug war has been an
erosion of our civil liberties, as law enforcement officials gain
greater authority to search our homes and cars and legislatures
prescribe strict and inflexible drug penalties that cause relatively
blameless people to end up serving long terms in prison.

It may not be a popular notion in Newt Gingrich's America,
but law enforcement is not the solution to the nation's drug
problem. The remedy for that intractable national tragedy lies in
a major investment in the inner-city communities where drugs
and guns have reached epidemic levels. Bold new approaches are
needed. The legalization of cocaine and heroin may have many
pitfalls, the biggest danger being that it will greatly increase the
use of those drugs. But if legalization were given a five-year test
under tightly controlled circumstances in one major city, the results could be instructive. The homicide rate of a city like Detroit
would probably be cut in half if the violence of the drug trade
were eliminated. In that city alone, hundreds would be saved
from violent deaths every year.

Organized crime is a logical outgrowth of a society that was
founded on the violence of the frontier and that has made wor-
ship of the dollar its highest principle. As long as we are a society
that rests on greed, that neglects its poor and that promotes ma-
terialism in its media, organized crime in all of its aspects—no
matter what language it speaks—will continue to plunder our
nation.

Notes

1: The Criminal Mosaic

1. Author's interviews with Sgt. Dan Foley of the San Francisco Police Department gang task force, April 7 and April 13, 1993; *San Francisco Examiner*, Sept. 5–12, 1977; *San Francisco Chronicle*, Sept. 5–12, 1977.
2. *New York Times*, Oct. 14, 1988.
3. *New York Times*, June 4, 1989.
4. President's Commission on Organized Crime, *Organized Crime and Gambling*, Record of Hearing VII, June 24–26, 1985, pp. 101–26; author's article, New York *Daily News*, Sept. 17, 1993.
5. *Los Angeles Times*, Jan. 7, 1987; *Boston Globe*, Jan. 15, 1991; *Toronto Star*, Oct. 17–18, 1992.
6. Report on Detroit Mafia submitted by Floyd Clarke, assistant director of the FBI's criminal investigative division, to the Permanent Subcommittee on Investigations, U.S. Senate, Dec. 23, 1987.
7. Francis A. J. Ianni, *The Black Mafia: Ethnic Succession in Organized Crime* (New York: Simon & Schuster, 1974) p. 14.
8. Author's interview with William Gavin, Jan. 27, 1994.
9. Douglas Farah and Steve Coll, "The Cocaine Money Market," *Washington Post National Weekly Edition*, Nov. 8–14, 1993, p. 6.
10. Author's interview with James Killen, March 17, 1993.
11. *Detroit Free Press*, May 7, 1989.
12. Press release from U.S. Attorney's Office, Southern District of New York, Sept. 12, 1994.
13. Author's article, New York *Daily News*, June 4, 1994.
14. Ibid.
15. Ibid.
16. *Organized Crime: 25 Years After Valachi*, Hearings before the Perma-

nent Subcommittee on Investigations, U.S. Senate, April 11, 15, 21, 22, 29, 1988, p. 156.

17. Author's interview with the official, Dec. 7, 1993.
18. *Los Angeles Times*, July 9, 1987.
19. *Asian Organized Crime*, Hearing before the Permanent Subcommittee on Investigations, U.S. Senate, Oct. 3, Nov. 5–6, 1991, p. 24.
20. *San Francisco Examiner*, Dec. 5, 1991.
21. Arthur M. Schlesinger, Jr., *Robert Kennedy and His Times*, Volume I (Boston: Houghton Mifflin Co., 1978) p. 275.

2: "All that Is Loathsome Is Here"

1. Marjorie R. Fallows, *Irish Americans: Identity and Assimilation* (Englewood Cliffs, N.J.: Prentice-Hall, 1979) p. 23.
2. Thomas Sowell, *Ethnic America: A History* (New York: Basic Books, 1981) p. 26.
3. Herbert Asbury, *The Gangs of New York: An Informal History of the Underworld* (New York: Alfred A. Knopf, 1927) pp. 10–12.
4. Ibid., pp. 22–23.
5. *New York Times*, July 6, 1857.
6. Virgil W. Peterson, *The Mob: 200 Years of Organized Crime in New York* (Ottawa, Ill.: Green Hill, 1983) p. 39.
7. Asbury, *The Gangs of New York*, p. 228.
8. Peterson, *The Mob*, p. 96.
9. M. R. Werner, *Tammany Hall* (New York: Doubleday, Doran, 1928) pp. 438, 510.
10. Asbury, *The Gangs of New York*, pp. 258–259.
11. Ransom McCarthy, "A Murder Has Been Arranged: The Story of the Rosenthal-Becker Case," *Harper's*, Jan. 1935, pp. 175–189; *New York World*, July 16, 1912.
12. Jenna Weissman Joselit, *Our Gang: Jewish Crime and the New York Jewish Community, 1900–1940* (Bloomington, Ind.: Indiana University Press, 1983) pp. 56–57.
13. Cited by Robert Lacey, *Little Man: Meyer Lansky and the Gangster Life* (Boston: Little, Brown, 1991) p. 28.
14. Joselit, *Our Gang*, p. 1.
15. Howard M. Sachar, *A History of the Jews in America* (New York: Alfred A. Knopf, 1992) p. 142.
16. Ibid., p. 143.
17. Joselit, *Our Gang*, p. 37.
18. Sachar, *A History of the Jews in America*, p. 164.
19. Cited in Lacey, *Little Man*, p. 28.

20. Joselit, *Our Gang*, p. 24.
21. Asbury, *The Gangs of New York*, Introduction.
22. Joselit, *Our Gang*, p. 45.
23. Stephen Fox, *Blood and Power: Organized Crime in Twentieth Century America* (New York: William Morrow, 1989) p. 26.
24. Cited in ibid., p. 35.
25. Humbert S. Nelli, *From Immigrants to Ethnics: The Italian Americans* (New York: Oxford University, 1983) pp. 41–49.
26. Luciano J. Iorizzo and Salvatore Mondello, *The Italian Americans* (Boston: Twayne, 1980) p. 78.
27. Ibid., p. 103.
28. David Leon Chandler, *Brothers in Blood: The Rise of the Criminal Brotherhoods* (New York: E. P. Dutton, 1975) p. 75.
29. John Kobler, *Capone: The Life and World of Al Capone* (New York: G. P. Putnam's Sons, 1971) p. 48.
30. Ibid.
31. Iorizzo and Mondello, *The Italian Americans*, p. 189.
32. Ibid.
33. Chandler, *Brothers in Blood*, pp. 110–111.
34. Asbury, *The Gangs of New York*, pp. 290–292.
35. Herbert Asbury, *Gem of the Prairie: An Informal History of the Chicago Underworld* (New York: Alfred A. Knopf, 1940) p. 313.
36. Kobler, *Capone*, pp. 38–40.
37. Chandler, *Brothers in Blood*, p. 113.
38. Joseph Bonanno and Sergio Lalli, *A Man of Honor: The Autobiography of Joseph Bonanno* (New York, Simon & Schuster, 1983) p. 70.
39. Peter Maas, *The Valachi Papers* (New York: G. P. Putnam's Sons, 1968) pp. 104–105.
40. Ibid., p. 116.
41. Ibid., pp. 97–98; Ovid Demaris, *The Last Mafioso: The Treacherous World of Jimmy Fratianno* (New York: Bantam, 1981) pp. 2–3; *New York Times*, March 27, 1990; Chandler, *Brothers in Blood*, pp. 18–19.
42. John Kobler, *Ardent Spirits: The Rise and Fall of Prohibition* (New York: G. P. Putnam's Sons, 1973) pp. 260–266.
43. Fox, *Blood and Power*, pp. 33–34; Timothy Belknap, "Detroit's Purple Gang," *Detroit Free Press Magazine*, June 26, 1983, p. 6.
44. Kobler, *Ardent Spirits*, p. 241.
45. Kobler, *Capone*, p. 105.
46. Peterson, *The Mob*, p. 157.
47. Ibid., p. 158.
48. President's Commission on Organized Crime, *The Impact: Organized Crime Today*, April 1986, p. 447; President's Commission on Orga-

nized Crime, *Organized Crime and Gambling*, Record of Hearing VII, June 24–26, 1985, pp. 58–59.

49. Nicholas Gage, *Mafia, U.S.A.* (Chicago: Playboy Press, 1972) p. 324.
50. *Detroit Free Press*, Dec. 19–21, 1992.
51. New York *Daily News*, Dec. 13, 1993.
52. Fox, *Blood and Power*, p. 326.
53. Carl Sifakis, *The Mafia Encyclopedia* (New York: Facts on File, 1987) pp. 51–52.

3: Mr. Untouchable

1. Fred J. Cook, "Pari-mutuel handle, $3,119,073: The Black Mafia Moves Into the Numbers Racket," *New York Times Magazine*, April 4, 1971, p. 108.
2. Ibid.
3. Francis A. J. Ianni, *The Black Mafia: Ethnic Succession in Organized Crime* (New York: Simon & Schuster, 1974) p. 119.
4. Report on Detroit Mafia submitted by Floyd Clarke, assistant director of the FBI's criminal investigative division, to the Permanent Subcommittee on Investigations, U.S. Senate, Dec. 23, 1987; Fox, *Blood and Power*, p. 413.
5. New York *Daily News*, June 10, 1974.
6. New York *Daily News*, Jan. 12, 1973.
7. Donald Goddard, *Easy Money* (New York: Farrar, Straus and Giroux, 1978) pp. 107–108.
8. John Cummings and Ernest Volkman, *Goombata: The Improbable Rise and Fall of John Gotti and His Gang* (Boston: Little, Brown and Co., 1990) p. 79.
9. Goddard, *Easy Money*, p. 121.
10. New York *Daily News*, June 10, 1974; Fred Ferretti, "Mister Untouchable," *New York Times Magazine*, June 5, 1977, p. 106.
11. New York *Daily News*, June 10, 1974.
12. Ferretti, "Mister Untouchable," p. 15.
13. New York *Daily News*, June 10, 1974.
14. Ferretti, "Mister Untouchable," p. 17.
15. William Hoffman and Lake Headley, *Contract Killer* (New York, Thunder's Mouth Press, 1992) p. 198.
16. Ferretti, "Mister Untouchable," p. 16.
17. Ibid., p. 108.
18. *New York Times*, March 17, 1983.
19. *Time*, Nov. 13, 1972.
20. Ibid.

21. New Jersey State Commission of Investigation, *Afro-lineal Organized Crime*, March 1991, p. 3.
22. *Philadelphia Inquirer*, Sept. 23, 1953.
23. James Nicholson, "The Black Mafia," *TODAY/Philadelphia Inquirer*, Aug. 11, 1973.
24. Ibid.
25. Ibid; *Philadelphia Inquirer*, April 4 and 5, 1972.
26. *Philadelphia Inquirer*, July 27, 1975.
27. *Philadelphia Daily News*, July 28, 1978.

4: The Rainbow

1. *New York Times*, July 1, 1992
2. *Los Angeles Times*, April 5, 1987.
3. *Los Angeles Times*, April 6, 1987.
4. Newark *Star-Ledger*, Feb. 1, 1994.
5. Nicholas Pileggi, *Wiseguy: Life in a Mafia Family* (New York: Pocket Books, 1987) pp. 56–57.
6. *Organized Crime: 25 Years After Valachi*, Hearings before the Permanent Subcommittee on Investigations, U.S. Senate, April 11, 15, 21, 22, 29, 1988, p. 206.

5: A Myriad of Swords

1. Author was present when a colleague took the call.
2. *Asian Organized Crime*, Hearing before the Permanent Subcommittee on Investigations, U.S. Senate, Oct. 3, Nov. 5–6, 1991, p. 68.
3. Michael Daly, "The War For Chinatown," *New York*, Feb. 14, 1983, p. 33.
4. Author's interview with Nancy Ryan, assistant Manhattan district attorney, March 12, 1993.
5. *Asian Organized Crime*, U.S. Senate subcommittee hearing, pp. 30–33.
6. New York *Daily News*, Dec. 19, 1993.
7. *New York Times*, Dec. 24, 1982, and Feb. 21, 1983; *Boston Globe*, Jan. 13, 1991.
8. Interview with the author; the investigator asked that his name not be used in this book, but his identity is known to the New York Police Department's public information office, which approved the interview.
9. *Asian Organized Crime*, U.S. Senate subcommittee hearing, p. 102.
10. Prosecution documents in *U.S. v. Yin Poy Louie*, U.S. District Court, Southern District of New York, indictment No. 84 CR 1025.

11. Kevin Rafferty, *City on the Rocks: Hong Kong's Uncertain Future* (New York: Viking Penguin, 1990) p. 46.
12. Martin Booth, *The Triads: The Growing Global Threat from the Chinese Criminal Societies* (New York: St. Martin's Press, 1990) pp. 3–8.
13. Fenton Bresler, *The Chinese Mafia* (New York: Stein and Day, 1981) pp. 24–25.
14. Booth, *The Triads*, p. 15.
15. Gerald L. Posner, *Warlords of Crime: Chinese Secret Societies, The New Mafia* (New York: McGraw-Hill, 1988) p. 34.
16. Ibid., p. 41.
17. Betty Lee Sung, *The Story of the Chinese in America* (New York: Collier Books, 1976) pp. 34–35.
18. *San Francisco Examiner*, June 6, 1991.
19. Richard H. Dillon, *The Hatchet Men: San Francisco's Brotherhood of Blood* (Sausalito, Calif.: Comstock Editions, 1962) p. 23.
20. Ibid., pp. 31–32.
21. Ibid., p. 1.
22. Ibid., p. 236.
23. Herbert Asbury, *The Gangs of New York: An Informal History of the Underworld* (New York: Alfred A. Knopf, 1927) p. 302.
24. Ibid., pp. 308–309.
25. Ibid., pp. 305–306.
26. Sung, *The Story of the Chinese in America*, p. 144.
27. *New York Times*, Aug. 5, 1970; author's article, *Boston Phoenix*, Oct. 5, 1982.
28. Sung, *The Story of the Chinese in America*, pp. 137–138.
29. *New York Times*, April 14, 1991.
30. *New York Times*, Dec. 1, 1976.
31. Tom Wolfe, "The New Yellow Peril," *Esquire*, Dec. 1969, p. 194.
32. *Newsweek*, July 2, 1973.
33. *Newsweek*, Aug. 30, 1971.
34. Ibid.
35. *New York Times*, Aug. 6, 1970, and Jan. 23, 1972.
36. *New York Times*, July 10 and 18, 1972.
37. *New York Times*, Aug. 5, 1970.
38. Author's interview with Neil Mauriello, July 21, 1994.

6: Big Brothers

1. Author's interview with Nancy Ryan, Assistant Manhattan District Attorney, March 12, 1993; prosecution documents in *U.S. v. Yin Poy*

Louie, U.S. District Court, Southern District of New York, indictment No. 84 CR 1025.

2. Author's interview with John Feehan, Aug. 17, 1994.
3. Author's interview with Neil Mauriello, July 21, 1994.
4. Prosecution documents, *U.S. v. Yin Poy Louie*.
5. Feehan interview.
6. Prosecution documents, *U.S. v. Yin Poy Louie*.
7. *Village Voice*, Aug. 8, 1977.
8. Mauriello interview.
9. Prosecution documents, *U.S. v. Yin Poy Louie*.
10. *New York Times*, Aug. 24, 1976.
11. Prosecution documents, *U.S. v. Yin Poy Louie*.
12. Ibid.
13. Ryan interview.
14. Author's interview with James McVeety, senior rackets investigator with the Manhattan District Attorney's Office, March 15, 1993; prosecution documents, *U.S. v. Yin Poy Louie*.
15. Author's article, *Boston Phoenix*, Feb. 26, 1985.
16. Author's article, *Boston Phoenix*, Oct. 5, 1982.
17. Ibid.
18. Daniel Golden, "The Last King of Chinatown," *Boston Globe Magazine*, Nov. 3, 1991.
19. *Boston Phoenix*, Feb. 26, 1985.
20. Golden, "The Last King of Chinatown."
21. President's Commission on Organized Crime, *Organized Crime of Asian Origin*, record of Hearing III, Oct. 23–25, 1984, p. 52.; *Boston Globe*, March 24, 1986.
22. President's Commission, *Organized Crime of Asian Origin*, p. 55.
23. Author's interview with Dan Foley, April 7, 1993.
24. *San Francisco Examiner*, Oct. 29, 1990.
25. U.S. Department of Justice, *Report on Asian Organized Crime*, 1988, p. 49.
26. *San Francisco Examiner*, Oct. 29, 1990.
27. Feehan interview.
28. Ibid.
29. McVeety interview.
30. Feehan interview.
31. Mauriello interview.
32. Golden, "The Last King of Chinatown."
33. Feehan interview.
34. Hodding Carter IV, "King of the Jungle," M magazine, March 1991, p. 87.

35. *Chicago Tribune*, Sept. 9, 1988.
36. *Detroit Free Press*, Aug. 22, 1990.
37. *Asian Organized Crime: The New International Criminal*, Hearings before the Permanent Subcommittee on Investigations, U.S. Senate, June 18 and Aug. 4, 1992, p. 76.
38. Ibid.; *Wall Street Journal*, March 22, 1990; *New York Newsday*, March 15, 1988.
39. *New York Newsday*, March 15, 1988.
40. *New York Times*, March 7, 1993.

7: Four Seas, One Brother

1. Author's interview with Dan Foley, April 7, 1993.
2. *San Francisco Chronicle*, Feb. 15, 1992.
3. Foley interview.
4. Ibid.
5. Ibid.
6. Ibid.; FBI affidavits in support of applications for wiretaps in investigation of Wo Hop To, U.S. District Court, Northern District of California, No. CR 92 0034.
7. *San Francisco Chronicle*, Feb. 29, 1992.
8. Foley interview; *San Francisco Chronicle*, July 3, 1990.
9. Foley interview.
10. Author's interview with Harry Hu, April 8, 1993.
11. *San Francisco Chronicle*, Dec. 10, 1992.
12. Author's interview with Thomas Carlon, April 12, 1993.
13. *Boston Globe*, Aug. 19, 1990.
14. *Boston Globe*, June 6, 1992.
15. *San Francisco Examiner*, June 2, 1992.
16. Internal INS memorandum regarding antismuggling operation, Project Hester, March 20, 1986; New York *Daily News*, June 17, 1993.
17. *San Francisco Chronicle*, April 28, 1993.
18. New York *Daily News*, June 17, 1993.
19. *New York Newsday*, June 8, 1993.
20. Reuters, May 24, 1993.
21. Associated Press, May 25, 1993.
22. Author's interview with James McVeety, senior rackets investigator with the Manhattan District Attorney's Office, March 15, 1993.
23. Author's interview with Douglas Lee, June 16, 1993.
24. Lau has denied any involvement in illegal activities. New York *Daily News*, Sept. 13, 1993.

25. Arrest complaints in *U.S.* v. *Kwok Ling Kay*, U.S. District Court, Southern District of New York, Indictment No. 93 CR 783.

26. *New York Newsday*, Jan. 2, 1991.

27. Author's article, New York *Daily News*, June 9, 1993.

28. Arrest complaints in *U.S.* v. *Kwok Ling Kay*.

29. Ibid.

30. Bergen County *Record*, May 25, 1993.

31. Arrest complaints in *U.S.* v. *Kwok Ling Kay*.

32. *New York Times*, Sept. 20 and 21, 1995; New York *Daily News*, Sept. 21, 1995.

33. Author interviewed the store owner with New York *Daily News* reporter Vivian Huang, June 16, 1993.

8: Born to Kill

1. Author's interview with Linden Police Sgt. Vincent Klebaur, March 18, 1993; *New York Times*, July 29 and 30, 1990.

2. New York *Daily News*, from Knight-Ridder news wire, Aug. 7, 1990.

3. *Chicago Tribune*, April 15, 1991.

4. *Los Angeles Times*, Aug. 11, 1987.

5. President's Commission on Organized Crime, *Organized Crime of Asian Origin*, Record of Hearing III, Oct. 23–25, 1984, pp. 328–344.

6. *Washington Post*, Feb. 15, 1986; *New York Times*, Jan. 22, 1984.

7. Stanley Karnow, *Vietnam: A History* (New York: Viking Press, 1983) p. 386.

8. Alfred W. McCoy, *The Politics of Heroin in Southeast Asia* (New York: Harper & Row, 1972) pp. 166–174.

9. *New York Times*, Jan. 21, 1985.

10. San Jose *Mercury News*, from Knight-Ridder news wire, July 6, 1982.

11. Kwok B. Chan and David Loveridge, "Refugees 'in Transit': Vietnamese in a Refugee Camp in Hong Kong," *International Migration Review*, Volume XXI, No. 3, p. 749.

12. Reuters, Jan. 11, 1993.

13. Author's interview with Leland Yee, April 8, 1993.

14. *Los Angeles Times*, May 7 and Sept. 12, 1986.

15. Author's interview with Douglas Zwemke, April 9, 1993.

16. Ibid.

17. Ibid.

18. *Los Angeles Times*, Oct. 16, 1989.

19. Ibid.

20. San Jose *Mercury News*, via Knight-Ridder news wire, Jan. 6, 1994.

21. *New York Newsday*, Oct. 7, 1991.

22. Author's interview with Special Agents Daniel Kumor and Don Tisdale of the U.S. Treasury Department's Bureau of Alcohol, Tobacco and Firearms, March 18, 1993.
23. *New York Newsday*, Oct. 7, 1991.
24. Kumor and Tisdale interview.
25. *New York Newsday*, Oct. 7, 1991.
26. Author's interview with Peg Tyre, Aug. 17, 1994.
27. *Asian Organized Crime*, Hearing before the Permanent Subcommittee on Investigations, U.S. Senate, Oct. 3, Nov. 5–6, 1991, pp. 43–46.
28. *New York Newsday*, March 14, 1991.
29. Kumor and Tisdale interview.
30. Ibid.
31. Ibid.
32. *New York Newsday*, Oct. 7, 1991.
33. *Boston Globe*, Jan. 27, 1987.
34. Author's roommate found the body.
35. *Boston Globe*, Jan. 7, 1987.
36. *Boston Globe*, Dec. 18, 1986.
37. *Boston Globe*, March 24, 1986.
38. *Boston Globe*, Jan. 8, 1987.
39. Toronto *Globe and Mail*, Dec. 17, 1986.
40. Toronto *Globe and Mail*, Aug. 17, 1991.
41. *Toronto Star*, Sept. 21, 1983, and Oct. 17, 1992.
42. *Boston Globe*, Jan. 15, 1991.
43. *Toronto Star*, Oct. 17, 1992.
44. *Toronto Star*, March 4, 1991.
45. *Toronto Star*, Oct. 18, 1992.
46. Toronto *Globe and Mail*, Aug. 18, 1991; *Toronto Star*, Aug. 18, 1991.

9: "Get Down or Lay Down"

1. Author's interview with a Detroit homicide detective who chose to remain anonymous, Aug. 10, 1994; *Detroit Free Press*, Oct. 9 and 10, 1990.
2. Author's conversation with John Fonger, May 12, 1989.
3. Los Angeles County District Attorney's Office, *Gangs, Crime and Violence in Los Angeles*, May 1992, p. 121.
4. *Profile of Organized Crime: Great Lakes Region*, Hearings before the Permanent Subcommittee on Investigations, U.S. Senate, Jan. 26, 26 and 31, and Feb. 1, 1984, pp. 178–183.
5. Ibid.
6. Ibid.

7. *Detroit News*, Feb. 2, 1983.

8. *Detroit News*, Jan. 14 and 17, 1983.

9. *Detroit Free Press*, Sept. 23, 1988.

10. *Detroit Free Press*, March 6, 1988.

11. Author's interview with a law-enforcement official who asked not to be identified in this book but who is known to his superiors, March 30, 1993.

12. Pennsylvania Crime Commission, *Organized Crime in Pennsylvania: A Decade of Change*, 1990 Report, p. 229.

13. *Philadelphia Inquirer*, Jan. 10, 1991.

14. Pennsylvania Crime Commission, *Organized Crime in Pennsylvania: A Decade of Change*, 1990 Report, p. 229.

15. The interview with the law enforcement official on March 30, 1993.

16. Ibid.

17. *Philadelphia Inquirer*, Dec. 13, 1989.

18. *Philadelphia Inquirer*, Sept. 8, 1989.

19. *Philadelphia Inquirer*, June 26, 1989.

20. Interview with the law enforcement official, March 30, 1993.

21. *Philadelphia Inquirer*, April 10, 1991.

22. *Washington Post*, April 18, 1989.

23. *New York Times*, March 15 and 20, 1988.

24. *New York Times*, Oct. 19, 1987.

25. *New York Times*, March 7, 1988.

26. *Detroit Free Press*, May 7, 1991.

27. *Detroit Free Press*, Feb. 26, 1993.

28. Author's interview with Sgt. Wes McBride, a gang specialist with the Los Angeles County Sheriff's Department, April 16, 1993.

29. Los Angeles County District Attorney's Office, *Gangs, Crime and Violence in Los Angeles*, May 1992, p. 121.

30. McBride interview.

31. *Los Angeles Times*, Jan. 3, 1989; *Chicago Tribune*, March 20, 1988.

32. *New York Times*, Oct. 14, 1988.

33. Laurie Gurnst, "Johnny-Too-Bad and the Sufferers," *Nation*, Nov. 13, 1989, pp. 567–568; Faye V. Harrison, "The Politics of Social Outlawry in Urban Jamaica," *Urban Anthropology*, Vol. 17 (2–3), 1988, pp. 259–275.

34. Laurie Gurnst, "Johnny-Too-Bad and the Sufferers," p. 567.

35. Author's interview with Chris Marzuk, June 29, 1993.

36. *Miami Herald*, Feb. 24, 1992.

37. Author's interview with Alex Minor, Jan. 28, 1994.

38. Associated Press, Nov. 17, 1993.

39. *Chicago Tribune*, from Knight-Ridder news wire, Dec. 30, 1992.

40. James Alan McPherson, "Almighty Black P Stone: And What Does That Mean," *Atlantic Monthly*, May 1969, pp. 74–84.
41. Ibid.
42. Ibid.
43. *Newsweek*, Jan. 12, 1981.
44. McBride interview.

10: The Corporation

1. President's Commission on Organized Crime, *Organized Crime and Gambling*, Record of Hearing VII, June 24–26, 1985, pp. 101–127.
2. *Organized Crime: 25 Years After Valachi*, Hearings before the Permanent Subcommittee on Investigations, U.S. Senate, April 11, 15, 21, 22, 29, 1988; pp. 1017–18.
3. *Miami Herald*, Aug. 26, 1985.
4. Author's article, New York *Daily News*, Sept. 17, 1993.
5. Robert Lacey, *Little Man: Meyer Lansky and the Gangster Life* (Boston: Little, Brown and Co., 1991) p. 227.
6. New York *Daily News*, Jan. 30 and 31, 1978.
7. Donald Goddard, *Easy Money* (New York: Farrar, Straus and Giroux, 1978) p. 19.
8. New York *Daily News*, Jan. 30 and 31, 1978.
9. *Detroit Free Press*, Oct. 15, 1992.
10. Author's article, New York *Daily News*, Sept. 17, 1993; President's Commission on Organized Crime, Record of Hearing VII, pp. 101–127.
11. New York *Daily News*, Jan. 30 and 31, 1978.
12. President's Commission on Organized Crime, Record of Hearing VII, pp. 101–127.
13. Ibid.
14. New York *Daily News*, Jan. 30 and 31, 1978; *Miami Herald*, Aug. 26, 1985.
15. Ibid.
16. New York *Daily News*, Oct. 8, 1985.
17. Presentment of the Special Hudson County Grand Jury into government corruption in Union City, N.J., 1987.
18. Author's interview with Hialeah Police Chief Rolando Bolanos, Sept. 14, 1993.
19. Author's interview with David Green, Sept. 15, 1993.
20. President's Commission on Organized Crime, Record of Hearing VII, pp. 101–127.
21. Author's article, New York *Daily News*, Sept. 17, 1993.

22. *New York Newsday*, Sept. 11, 1986.

23. New York *Daily News*, May 3, 1993.

24. Author's interview with Sgt. Frank Perez of the New York Police Department's Public Morals Division, Oct. 26, 1994.

25. Author's article, New York *Daily News*, Aug. 1, 1993.

26. Author's article, New York *Daily News*, Dec. 5, 1993.

27. U.S. Drug Enforcement Administration, *Country Profile: Dominican Republic*, February 1991.

28. Associated Press, Dec. 27, 1993.

29. Author's interview with William Mockler, assistant special agent in charge of the New York DEA office, June 30, 1993; *New York Times*, July 31, 1987.

30. Edward Conlon, "The Pols, the Police and the Gerry Curls," *American Spectator*, Nov. 1994, pp. 36–47; *New York Times*, Oct. 24, 1991.

31. New York *Daily News*, Oct. 24, 1991.

32. Edward Conlon, "The Pols, the Police and the Gerry Curls"; *New York Times*, Oct. 24, 1991.

33. Press release accompanying indictment in *State of New York* v. *Lenin Sepulveda*, N.Y. State Supreme Court, Sept. 15, 1993.

34. *New York Times*, April 4, 1994.

35. New York *Daily News*, Feb. 14, 1993.

36. Author's interview with Harry Brady, June 30, 1993.

37. Author's article in the New York *Daily News*, Aug. 1, 1993.

38. Ibid.

39. Author's interview with Joseph Occhipinti, July 2, 1993.

11: The Organizatsiya

1. Author's interview with Joel Campanella, U.S. Customs Service agent, March 19, 1993; Robert I. Friedman, "Brighton Beach Goodfellas," *Vanity Fair*, Jan. 1993, p. 26; *Washington Post*, June 24, 1990.

2. Daniel Burstein, "The Russian Mafia: A New Crime Menace Grows in Brooklyn," *New York*, Nov. 24, 1986, p. 40.

3. Campanella interview.

4. Friedman, "Brighton Beach Goodfellas," p. 36.

5. Author's interview with Robert Shepherd, June 22, 1995.

6. Author's interview with Robert Buccino, June 21, 1995.

7. *International Organized Crime and Its Impact on the United States*, witness list and prepared statements for hearing on May 25, 1994, before the Permanent Subcommittee on Investigations, U.S. Senate, Louis Freeh's prepared statement, p. 7.

8. Rita J. Simon, "Refugee Families' Adjustment and Aspirations: A

Comparison of Soviet Jewish and Vietnamese Immigrants," *Ethnic and Racial Studies*, October 1983, pp. 492–504.

9. Mike Mallowe, "From Russia With Guns," *Philadelphia*, May 1983, p. 143.

10. Campanella interview; *New York Times*, June 4, 1989.

11. Mallowe, "From Russia With Guns," p. 142.

12. Campanella interview.

13. Friedman, "Brighton Beach Goodfellas," p. 32.

14. Campanella interview.

15. Ibid.

16. Ibid.

17. *New York Times*, July 8, 1994.

18. *International Organized Crime and Its Impact on the United States*, witness list and prepared statements, Louis Freeh's prepared statement, p. 1.

19. Author's interview with James Moody, head of the FBI's organized crime division in Washington, Jan. 18, 1995.

20. Louis Freeh's prepared statement, p. 6.

21. *New York Times*, April 11, 1992.

22. Moody interview.

23. Arrest complaint in *U.S.* v. *Vyacheslav Ivankov*, Complaint No. 95-0899M, U.S. District Court, Eastern District of New York.

24. Author's interview with Raymond Kerr, June 20, 1995.

25. Arrest complaint in *U.S.* v. *Vyacheslav Ivankov*.

12: Mob 2000

1. Herbert Asbury, *The Gangs of New York: An Informal History of the Underworld* (New York: Alfred A. Knopf, 1927), Introduction.

2. *New York Times*, March 3, 1987.

3. *New York Times*, Feb. 18, 1990.

4. Edward P. Whelan, "Jack Tocco: Mob Boss or Model Citizen?" *Monthly Detroit*, Sept. 1981, p. 55; Fox, *Blood and Power*, pp. 52–60.

5. Whelan, "Jack Tocco: Mob Boss or Model Citizen?" p. 52–60.

6. Ibid., p. 57.

7. Newark *Star-Ledger*, March 3, 1994.

8. Author's interview with William Nevins, Jan. 27, 1994.

Index